McGRAW-HILL EDUCATION

CONQUERING THE SAT WRITING AND LANGUAGE TEST AND ESSAY

McGRAW-HILL EDUCATION

CONQUERING THE SAT WRITING AND LANGUAGE TEST AND ESSAY

Third Edition

Christopher Black

Director, College Hill Coaching, Greenwich, CT

New York Chicago San Francisco Athens London Madrid
Mexico City Milan New Delhi Singapore Sydney Toronto

1 2 3 4 5 6 7 8 9   LHS   25 24 23 22 21 20

ISBN   978-1-260-46263-0
MHID   1-260-46263-3

e-ISBN   978-1-260-46264-7
e-MHID   1-260-46264-1

McGraw Hill books are available at special quantity discounts to use as premiums and sales promotions, or for use in corporate training programs. To contact a representative, please visit the Contact Us pages at www.mhprofessional.com.

*SAT is a registered trademark of the College Entrance Examination Board, which is not involved in the production of, and does not endorse, this product.

College Hill Coaching™ is a registered trademark under the control of Christopher F. Black.

CONTENTS

**SECTION 5
THREE PRACTICE SAT ESSAYS / 245**

SECTION 1
INTRODUCTION

CHAPTER 1

HOW TO USE THIS BOOK

Using This Book as a Coach

This book will help you master every skill you need to ace the SAT Writing and Language Test and Essay, even if you've had little or no formal instruction in grammar or academic writing. Although my goal is to get you a top score on the SAT, the skills this book teaches— analytical reading and writing—are also at the heart of success in college, especially in the liberal arts. Knowing how to extract the essential information from your reading, how to summarize it, and how to write about it are all essential skills of lifelong learners.

In this book, I will explain all of these key skills and concepts and provide the practice you need to master them yourself. I'll tell you how frequently each concept or skill is tested on actual SATs so that you can home in on the most relevant topics and optimize your preparation time. I will focus primarily on the "must-know" SAT skills and concepts, but will also explain all of those that are tested less frequently.

At College Hill Coaching, we get the most from our SAT students by training them much as elite running coaches would train their athletes to run a marathon: with *skills workouts* for technique, *strength* workouts for power, *race-pace workouts* for timing, and *tempo workouts* for efficiency.

Skills Workouts

Consistent skills workouts are the key to mastery and SAT score improvement. The skills workouts are provided in **Chapters 3–15** of this book, which show you how to parse sentences and to analyze word choice, sentence structure, and paragraph structure to spot and correct common errors, as well as how to read and analyze a rhetorical essay and write a well-structured analytical essay about it. Every week, **4–5 of your 6–7 daily workouts should be skills workouts.**

Strength Workouts

Strength workouts are provided in **Section 4 and 5** of this book. Section 4 includes three "heavyweight" SAT Writing and Language practice tests, and Section 5 includes three SAT essay samples. The Writing and Language Tests are "heavyweight" because they include slightly higher-level reading passages and more of the "challenge" grammar questions than a typical SAT does. Do these strength workouts on the alternate weeks from your race-pace workouts. Every week, **1–2 out of your 6–7 daily workouts should be cross-training workouts.**

Race-Pace Workouts

Race-pace workouts test your performance on *official* SATs under *real* test conditions. For SAT prep, this means taking all or part (perhaps just the Writing and Language Test) of an **official SAT practice test** under strictly timed and realistic testing conditions. You can download these practice SATs for free at CollegeBoard.com, and score them with a free smartphone app that you can download from the same site. Use the official answer sheet and take the test in one sitting (or according to any officially approved testing accommodations you may have). Your performance on these tests is the real measure of your progress. **Take 4–8 full-scale SAT practice tests over the course of your 12-week prep program, but no more than one per week.**

Tempo Workouts

Tempo workouts are "speed" workouts to train for efficiency. Take a sample SAT Writing and Language Test, official or "heavyweight," and try to score as many points as you can in 25 or 30 minutes instead of 35 minutes. **Do no more than two tempo workouts per week.**

CHAPTER 2
FAQS ABOUT THE SAT

WHAT DOES THE SAT REALLY TEST?

The SAT tests a wide range of reasoning skills that are at the core of college success. Although it doesn't test your knowledge in specific subjects like history, chemistry, or foreign languages, or even important personal skills like diligence and creativity, it does test the broader skills of analytical reading, analytical writing, and mathematical problem solving that are at the heart of success in the liberal arts and sciences. Here is a slightly more comprehensive list of SAT skills, broken down by test:

SAT Reading

- Interpreting, analyzing, comparing, and drawing inferences from college-level texts across the liberal arts and sciences such as arguments, narratives, and expository essays
- Interpreting and drawing inferences from data in the form of graphs, tables, and diagrams that accompany reading passages

SAT Writing and Language

- Analyzing sentences and paragraphs in terms of their adherence to the standards of grammar, usage, clarity, and stylistic coherence
- Interpreting data from graphs or figures and logically incorporating that information into a passage

SAT Math

- Solving algebraic problems involving equations, inequalities, systems, formulas, and functions
- Solving data-analysis problems involving concepts such as ratios, proportions, percentages, units, and numerical relationships
- Solving problems in advanced mathematics involving concepts such as quadratics, polynomials, angles, polygons, areas, volumes, exponentials, complex numbers, and trigonometry

5

SAT Essay (Optional)

- Analyzing a rhetorical essay in terms of its developmental structure, persuasive elements, style, and effectiveness
- Writing a well-organize essay that analyzes the persuasive and stylistic elements of the given rhetorical passage

HOW IS THE SAT FORMATTED?

The SAT is a 3-hour test (3 hours 50 minutes with essay) consisting of four Sections and an optional essay. You will get two breaks during the test: a 10-minute break after Section 1 (Reading), and a 5-minute break after Section 3 (Math, No calculator).

Section 1. Reading	52 questions
	65 minutes
Section 2. Writing and Language	44 questions
	35 minutes
Section 3. Mathematics Test (No calculator)	20 questions
	25 minutes
Section 4. Mathematics Test (Calculator)	38 questions
	55 minutes
Section 5. Essay (optional)	1 question
	50 minutes

WHAT WILL COLLEGES DO WITH MY SAT SCORES?

Your SAT scores show colleges how ready you are to do college-level work. Students with high SAT scores are more likely to succeed in college courses that emphasize problem-solving skills, writing, and analytical reading—in other words, liberal arts, humanities, and STEM courses.

SAT scores also correlate strongly with post-college success, particularly in professions like medicine, law, the humanities, the sciences, and engineering. Students with high SAT scores are also more likely to graduate from college and to have successful careers after college.

But let's face it: one reason colleges want you to send them SAT scores is that high scores make them look good. The higher the average SAT score of a college's applicants, the better its rankings and prestige. This is why most colleges cherry-pick your top sub-scores if you submit multiple SAT results. (Ironically, it's also why some colleges have adopted "SAT-optional" policies: since only the high-scoring students are likely to submit them, the college's average scores increase, thereby improving its national rankings.) In addition to your SAT scores, most colleges are interested in your course profile, your grades in those courses, recommendations, leadership skills, extracurricular activities, and essays.

Although many colleges are expanding the testing options for their students, standardized testing is becoming more important as colleges across the spectrum become more selective. High SAT scores always provide you with an admission advantage, even if the college does not require them. Some large or technical schools will weigh test scores heavily, and many use SAT scores to determine who qualifies for honors programs. If you have any questions about how a college uses your SAT scores, or whether they use them for honors placements, call the admissions office and ask.

When looking at your SAT scores, most colleges use your "superscore," picking your top individual RW and M scores from all the SATs you submit. For instance, if you submit your March SAT scores of 520RW 610M (1130 composite) and your June SAT scores of 550RW 580M (1130 composite), the college will consider your SAT score to be 550RW 610M (1160 composite). Nice of them, huh?

WHAT CONTROL DO I HAVE OVER MY SAT SCORES?

Colleges can't see your SAT or Subject Test scores until you submit them, so don't panic if your first SAT scores aren't great. Even better, many colleges let you select which SAT and SAT Subject Test scores to submit. (The College Board calls this "Score Choice.") Check your colleges admission websites, or ask the admissions representatives, to see which colleges allow Score Choice.

Some colleges, however, request that you submit all of the scores for all of the SATs you've taken. Don't let this intimidate you: colleges do this to give you the maximum possible "superscore," as explained in the previous answer.

Regardless of a college's Score Choice policy, don't be concerned about taking the SAT two, three, or even four times if you need to. Having a bad SAT score or two on your profile probably won't hurt you at all because of Score Choice and/or superscoring. But don't go overboard. Taking the SAT more than four times can come across as a bit obsessive, at least if you don't have an extenuating circumstance.

WHEN SHOULD I TAKE THE SATS AND SUBJECT TESTS?

Most competitive colleges require either SAT or ACT scores from all of their applicants, although some schools are "test-optional," allowing you to choose whether or not to submit your standardized test scores with your application. Many competitive colleges also require or recommend two or three Subject Test scores. The Subject Tests are hour-long tests in specific subjects like mathematics, physics, chemistry, foreign languages, U.S. history, world history, and literature.

If you are considering applying to any highly competitive colleges, plan to take the SAT at least twice and to take at least two SAT Subject Tests by the end of spring semester of junior year. If necessary, you can retake any of those tests in the fall of your senior year. This way, you will have a full testing profile by the summer after your junior year, giving you a much clearer picture of where you stand before you start your college applications.

Even if your favorite colleges don't require standardized tests, you may be able to submit them anyway, if they're good, to boost your application. The Subject Tests, specifically, can provide a strong counterbalance to any weaknesses in your grades. For instance, a strong chemistry Subject Test score can offset a poor grade in chemistry class.

Take your Subject Test when the subject material is fresh in your mind. For most students, this is in June, just as they are preparing to take their final exams. However, if you are taking AP exams in May, consider taking the SAT Subject Tests in May also. Learn which SAT Subject Tests your colleges require, and try to complete them by June of your junior year. You can take up to three SAT Subject Tests on any test date.

WHAT'S THE BEST WAY TO PREPARE FOR THE SAT?

"Start where you are. Use what you have. Do what you can."

—Arthur Ashe

Step 1: Start 3 months ahead

Everyone is different, but most students need between 12–15 weeks to do the kind of diagnostics, review, and practice they need to optimize their SAT scores. Sit down with your guidance counselor early in your junior year and work out a full testing schedule for the year, taking into account the SAT, SAT Subject Tests, AP tests, and possibly the ACT. Once you have decided on your schedule, commit yourself to starting your SAT preparation at least 3 months prior to your first SAT.

Step 2: Create a study plan and stick with it

Chapter 1 describes the different kinds of daily workouts that will give you the best results. Make a study plan that sets aside 30–40 minutes a day, 5–6 days per week, to complete a daily workout, perhaps supplementing the exercises in this book with materials from the College Board, Khan Academy, or other books like McGraw-Hill's *SAT* or *SAT Elite*. Also, make sure your plan includes time to take between 3 and 8 practice tests, as discussed in Step 5.

Step 3: Take a full diagnostic SAT

Start your SAT preparation by downloading and self-administering Practice SAT #1 from collegeboard.com. It requires 3 hours (or 3 hours and

50 minutes if you include the essay). Take it on a Saturday morning, if possible, at roughly the time you will start the real SAT (around 8:00 a.m.), and make sure that you have a quiet place, a stopwatch, a calculator, and a few #2 pencils. Use the official answer sheet, which is included with the test, and follow the instructions carefully. (Remember that on the real SAT you should get a 10-minute break after Section 1, and a 5-minute break after Section 3.) This will give you a good idea of what taking the SAT is really like. When you've finished, score it with the College Board's "Daily Practice for the SAT" phone app or by hand with the printable answer key and conversion table.

Step 4: Review weak skills areas daily

The tests in this book and from the College Board will give you plenty of feedback about the topics that you may need to review. Once you've identified those topics, find the corresponding lessons in this book. If you set aside about 30 minutes per night to work through those lessons and complete the exercises, you can make substantial progress and see big SAT score improvements in just a few weeks.

Step 5: Take practice tests regularly and diagnose your performance

Practice is the key to success. This book includes three "heavyweight" practice SAT Writing and Language tests in Section 4 and three practice SAT Essays in Section 5. Take one every week or two to assess your progress as you work through the specific skills review in Chapters 3–15. In addition, every week or two, download and take an SAT from the College Board website to assess your progress on "official" tests.

Step 6: Read often and deeply

Strengthening your analytical reading skills is key to success in college and on the SAT, especially on the Reading Test, Writing and Language Test, and Essay. The best way to improve your reading skills is to practice by reading great books and engaging great ideas. Make a point of working your way through these books and checking these periodicals regularly.

Online/Periodical

The New York Times (Op-Ed, Science Times, Front Page)

BBC News (Views, Analysis, Background)

The Atlantic (Feature Articles)

Slate (Voices, Innovation)

Scientific American (Feature Articles)

The Economist (Debate, Science & Technology)

TED Talks (Innovation, Culture, Politics, Inspiration)

The New Yorker (Talk of the Town, Feature Articles)

ProPublica (Feature Articles)

Edge (Essays)

Radiolab (Weekly Podcast)

Books

To Kill a Mockingbird, Harper Lee

Macbeth, William Shakespeare

Frankenstein, Mary Shelley

The Color Purple, Alice Walker

Pride and Prejudice, Jane Austen

Jane Eyre, Charlotte Bronte

Heart of Darkness, Joseph Conrad

Narrative of the Life of Frederick Douglass, Frederick Douglass

The Great Gatsby, F. Scott Fitzgerald

Walden, Henry David Thoreau

The American Language, H. L. Mencken

Notes of a Native Son, James Baldwin

The Stranger, Albert Camus

Night, Elie Wiesel

Animal Farm, George Orwell

Things Fall Apart, Chinua Achebe

The Language Instinct, Steven Pinker

The Mismeasure of Man, Stephen J. Gould

The Republic, Plato

A People's History of the United States, Howard Zinn

Guns, Germs, and Steel, Jared Diamond

A Short History of Nearly Everything, Bill Bryson

The Righteous Mind, Jonathan Heidt

Sapiens, Yuval Noah Hariri

Meditations, Marcus Aurelius

The Coddling of the American Mind, Jonathan Heidt

Manufacturing Consent, Noam Chomsky

How the Mind Works, Steven Pinker

The Man Who Mistook His Wife for a Hat, Oliver Sacks

WHAT'S A GOOD SAT WRITING AND LANGUAGE SCORE?

To know how "good" any SAT test score is, you need to ask two questions: what is the *percentile score*, and what is the *reference group*? The percentile score tells you what percent of the people in the reference group you outscored.

For instance, your SAT score report might say your *National* percentile is 46th, but your *SAT User* percentile is 43rd. This means that you *would have* scored better than 46% if every 11th or 12th grade student in the country had taken the SAT on that date, and that you scored better than 43% of the students who *actually* took the test on that date.

If you want to set your SAT Writing and Language score goal based on the national percentiles, here's a handy guide:

Percentile Score	Scaled Writing and Language Score
50%ile	~26
55%ile	~27
60%ile	~28
65%ile	~29
70%ile	~30
75%ile	~31
80%ile	~32
85%ile	~34
90%ile	~35
95%ile	~36
98%ile	~37
99%ile	~39

HOW DO I GET THE MOST OUT OF MY DAILY SAT STUDY SESSIONS?

1. Use Your Study Log.   Create a log or notebook dedicated to your SAT work. Write down a plan for each week, specifying which type of daily workout to do—**skills**, **strength**, **race-pace**, or **tempo**, as discussed in Chapter 1— and commit to it like you would to a daily class. Also, write down a summary of each study session, including key strategies, rules, vocabulary words, and strategic advice for your next test.

2. Stick to Focused 30 to 40-Minute Sessions.   For skills workouts, set a very clear agenda for each study session, such as "Master dangling participles and complete one exercise set." Then find your study spot, shut out all distractions, and set to work. Try not to go beyond 40 minutes for each session: stay focused and engaged, and keep it manageable.

3. Make Your Study Space Work.   Do your studying at a well-lit desk with a straight-back chair. Make sure you have plenty of pencils, a timer for practice tests, flashcards, your study log, and even a stash of brain-healthy snacks.

4. *Eliminate Distractions.* Turn off all alerts on your phone or laptop, and tell everyone in the house that this is your study time. Make sure everyone is in on the plan. Don't even let your pets distract you.

5. *Learn It Like You Have to Teach It.* When you've finished your session, imagine you have to teach a class of eighth graders everything you just learned. How would you communicate these ideas clearly? What examples would you use to illustrate them? What tough questions might the students ask, and how would you answer them? How can you explain the concepts and strategies in different ways? How can you help the students to manage with potential difficulties they might have in a testing environment?

6. *Sleep on It.* Good sleep habits are essential to a good study program. Try to get at least eight hours of sleep per night. To make your sleep as effective as possible, try to fall asleep while thinking about a challenging problem or strategy you're trying to perfect. As you sleep, your brain will continue to work on the problem by a process called "consolidation." When you awake, you'll have a better grasp on the problem or skill whether you realize it or not. If you struggle to get to sleep because of worry or stress, try some simple yoga exercises to get your mind ready for rest.

7. *Think Positively.* Constantly ask yourself, what do I need to do to perform better on my next test? Do I need to focus more on relaxation? Should I try to improve my reading speed? Should I ask different questions as I read? Should I refresh myself on my trigonometry? Having a clear set of positive goals that you reinforce with inner dialogue helps you to succeed. Banish the negative self-talk. Don't sabotage your work by saying, "This is impossible," or "I stink at this."

8. *Make a Plan to Work Through Your Problem Areas.* Before each practice test, have a clear agenda. Remind yourself of the key ideas and strategies for the week. But remember that there will always be challenges. Just meet them head on and don't let them get you down.

WHAT SHOULD I DO THE WEEK BEFORE MY SAT?

1. *Get Plenty of Sleep.* Don't underestimate the power of a good night's sleep. During sleep, not only do you restore balance and energy to your body, but you also consolidate what you've learned that day, and even become more efficient at tasks you've been practicing.

2. *Eat Healthy.* Don't skip meals because you're studying. Eat regular, well-balanced meals. A well-fed brain thinks better.

3. *Exercise.* Stick to your regular exercise program the weeks before the SAT. A strong body helps make a strong mind.

4. *Visualize Success and Talk Success.* In the days before your SAT, envision yourself in the test room, relaxed and confident, working through even the toughest parts of the test without stress or panic. Talk positively to yourself: remind yourself that you are ready to tackle the SAT with all of its challenges.

5. *Stay Sharp, But Don't Cram.* In the days before the SAT, resist the urge to cram. Your best results will come if you focus on getting plenty of sleep and staying positive and relaxed. If you're feeling anxious, take out your notes for a few minutes at a time, or review your old tests just to remind yourself of basic strategies, but don't cram.

6. *Keep Perspective.* Remember that you can take the SAT multiple times, and that colleges will almost certainly "superscore" the results, so don't get down about any single set of test results. Also, keep in mind that colleges don't base their acceptance decisions on SAT scores alone.

7. *Lay Everything Out.* The night before your SAT, lay out your admission ticket, your photo ID, your #2 pencils, your calculator (with fresh batteries), your snack, and directions to the test site (if necessary). Having these all ready will let you sleep better.

WHAT SHOULD I DO ON TEST DAY?

1. *Wake Up Early and Do Some Cardio.* A brisk but easy 20-minute cardiovascular workout before the test can get your blood flowing, wake up your brain, and release stress so you can do your best. If you have a regular exercise routine that has been cleared by your doctor, use your favorite cardio workout. But be smart about it: don't do anything that you haven't tried in a while, or that is too stressful. Your goal is simply to get your blood flowing, wake up your brain, and burn off some of that excess nervous pre-test energy.

2. *Eat a Good Breakfast.* Don't skip breakfast! This is critical: your brain needs fuel for the 3 to 4-hour mental marathon you are about to run. Complex carbohydrates and proteins like those found in oatmeal are ideal brain food. Try to avoid super-sugary cereals that might give you a quick energy boost but lead to a "sugar crash," perhaps just as you are starting your test!

3. *Bring a Snack and Beverage.* You'll have a couple of short breaks during the SAT during which you can have a quick snack. Bring a granola bar or some other quick burst of energy. Studies show that reviving your blood sugar after a few hours of fasting can sharpen your mental skills and even brighten your mood.

4. *Take Slow, Deep Breaths—Often.* Test nerves are normal. If you feel yourself getting anxious during the SAT, just take three long, deep, relaxed breaths. Tell yourself that nerves are a normal physiological response to important tasks, and they demonstrate that your brain is ready to take this task seriously. Remind yourself that you are prepared, and that you will perform better if you are relaxed rather than tense.

5. *Dress in Layers.* Since you don't know whether your test room will be too hot, too cold, or just right, dress in layers so you'll be ready for anything. You won't be shivering if you're too cold, and you can peel off layers if you're too warm.

6. *Don't Worry About What Anyone Else Is Doing.* Some SAT takers get nervous when they hear the first person in the room turn the first page of the test. They think: "She's already on question 6 and I haven't even answered question 2!" If you've been practicing as I recommend in this book, you will have a good sense of your own pacing and game plan. Trust it. Be confident in your skills and preparation and resist any temptation to take your cues from what anyone around you is doing.

7. *Don't Panic When Things Get Tough.* Don't psych yourself out when you get to a hard question or section. Don't let any one question bog you down, and remember that you can get a top score even if you miss a few questions. Expect a few roadblocks, and don't think of each one as the end of the road. Just take a few deep breaths and press on.

SECTION 2

HOW TO CONQUER THE SAT WRITING AND LANGUAGE TEST

CHAPTER 3

THE FIVE QUESTION TYPES AND HOW TO ATTACK THEM

In baseball, the best hitters can instantly recognize every kind of pitch: fastball, curveball, slider, cutter, sinker, knuckleball and so on, so they can adjust their swings accordingly. Similarly, to conquer the SAT Writing, you need to recognize every type of question it can throw at you—**grammar and usage, coherence and logical development, diction and clarity, style and tone,** and **infographics**—so you can attack it with confidence.

On the next few pages we will discuss the five major question types you will see on the SAT Writing and Language test.

A. GRAMMAR AND USAGE QUESTIONS

About 50–60% of SAT Writing and Language Test questions are **grammar and usage** questions. On any given test, you can expect about 21–27 questions of this type.

Grammar and usage questions ask whether a word or phrase obeys the rules of Standard American English. They require you to understand the rules of verb and pronoun agreement, punctuation, modifier use, mood, voice, syntax, coordination, and idiom.

If that sounds mysterious or scary—or if you haven't received much instruction in these rules—don't worry. We will cover all of them in the lessons to follow.

As the American population grows, ages, and gains better access to affordable health care insurance, the demand for primary medical services are expected to skyrocket.

1

A) NO CHANGE
B) is
C) has been
D) would be

When a question has just a word or phrase underlined with no other instructions, as here, it is either a **grammar and usage** question or a **diction and clarity** question. This happens to be a grammar and usage question, so the question to ask is, "Does this follow the rules of standard American English?"

In the original phrasing, the verb *are* does not **agree in number** (Chapter 5, Lesson 1) with the singular subject *demand*. (The subject cannot be *services* because that is the object of a prepositional phrase—see Chapter 4, Lesson 1: Parsing Sentences and Clauses.) All of the other choices correspond to a singular subject, but only choice B works in this context. Choice C is incorrect because the **present consequential** (Chapter 5, Lesson 11) form, *has been*, implies that a previous event extends a consequence to the present, but the sentence is about an *ongoing and future* state of affairs. Choice D is incorrect because the **subjunctive mood** (Chapter 5, Lesson 15), *would be*, implies a hypothetical or non-factual statement, which is illogical because this sentence is making a factual claim.

Physician assistants and nurse practitioners can talk with patients about treatment options, prescribe medications, and even **14** perform technical procedures like bone marrow aspirations.

14

A) NO CHANGE
B) performing technical procedures
C) technical procedures
D) to perform technical procedures

This sentence contains a list, and therefore must follow the **law of parallelism** (Chapter 5, Lesson 3), which says that words or phrases in a list should have the same grammatical form.

This sentence is listing the things that physician assistants and nurse practitioners can do. The first two items in the list are present tense verbs and their objects: *talk with patients . . . prescribe medications. . . .* Therefore, the third item in the list should also be a present tense verb and its object: *perform technical procedures,* as in choice A. Choice B is incorrect because *performing* is a **gerund** (Chapter 5, Lesson 3), not a present tense verb. Choice C is incorrect because it contains no verb, and choice D is incorrect because *to perform* is an **infinitive** (Chapter 5, Lesson 3), not a present tense verb.

B. COHERENCE AND LOGICAL DEVELOPMENT QUESTIONS

About 35–45% of SAT Writing and Language Test questions are **coherence and logical development** questions. On any given test, you can expect about 13–20 questions of this type.

Coherence and logical development questions ask you to pay attention to the logical flow of ideas in the passage from phrase to phrase, sentence to sentence, and paragraph to paragraph, as well as how the secondary ideas in a passage relate to the main idea.

Pay attention when the sentences or paragraphs in a passage are **numbered**. This numbering means you will be asked about the logical flow and coherence of the passage, for example whether the sentences in a paragraph should be **re-arranged**, where a given sentence should be **inserted**, or whether a given sentence should be **deleted**.

---

18 Montessori dedicated herself to travelling the world and preaching the benefits of child-centered education. In the 25 years after their founding, Montessori schools were regarded as a remedy to the educational problems associated with rapid urban population growth throughout Europe. However, as fascism began to proliferate in the 1930s throughout Spain, Italy, and Germany, child-centered education came to be seen as a threat to the power of the state. In 1933, the totalitarian regimes in Italy and Germany closed all Montessori schools and declared them subversive.

18

Which choice provides the most effective introduction to the paragraph?

A) NO CHANGE
B) Montessori's first school enrolled 50 students from poor working class families.
C) Montessori did not have a particularly nurturing relationship with her own son, Mario, who was raised by another family.
D) As the Montessori method was gaining a foothold, Europe was undergoing dramatic social and political change.

Choice A is a poor introduction because it indicates a fact that is not developed in the rest of the paragraph. The only appropriate option is choice D, since the paragraph is about how the growth of fascism in Europe and affected Montessori schools. Choice B is incorrect because the paragraph is not about the first Montessori school. Choice C is incorrect because the paragraph is not about Montessori's personal family relationships.

Plato believed that the sphere is an example of an "ideal form," inaccessible to our physical senses yet comprehensible through pure reason. He also argued that, since our senses can be fooled, logic alone provides the most reliable path to the truth. Therefore, Platonists believe that abstract forms such as ideal spheres are even more "real," in a way, than sensory experience. **29**

29

At this point, the author is considering adding the following sentence:

> The sphere is just one of many ideal forms, like lines and tetrahedrons, that are studied in geometry.

Should the writer make this addition here?

A) Yes, because it indicates a particular fact about ideal forms.
B) Yes, because explains a claim made in the previous sentence.
C) No, because it detracts from the paragraph's discussion of philosophy.
D) No, because it undermines Plato's claim bout sensory experience.

The central idea in this paragraph is that Plato and his followers believed that "ideal forms" are more real than sensory experiences. Although the new sentence gives examples of ideal forms, it does not address, develop, or explain this question about what is "real." Therefore, it detracts from the paragraph's discussion of philosophy, and the correct answer is C. Don't be tempted by choice A: although this sentence does *indicate a particular fact about ideal forms*, this does not make it appropriate for a paragraph about the difference between sensory experience and ideal forms.

C. DICTION AND CLARITY QUESTIONS

About 5–10% of SAT Writing and Language Test questions are **diction and clarity** questions. On any given test, you can expect about 2–5 questions of this type.

Clarity questions ask whether a phrasing conveys an idea clearly and precisely. You must use your reading skills and language sense to understand what the writer is trying to say—even if the phrasing is awkward and unclear—and to clarify that idea when necessary.

In fact, nothing that we observe in our physical world—not the moon, not a beach ball, not even a water droplet— 24 complies perfectly with the mathematical definition of a sphere.

24

A) NO CHANGE
B) overlaps perfectly with
C) corresponds perfectly to
D) concurs perfectly with

This sentence is trying to express the relationship between the real world and the abstract world of mathematical definitions, but *complies* doesn't quite fit because it means *acts in accordance with a wish, command, or regulation*, and a mathematical definition is none of those. Also, *overlaps* doesn't work, because it means *extends over so as to cover partly*, but this idea does not apply to the relationship between the real world and an abstraction. Finally, *concurs* doesn't work because it means *is of the same opinion*, but mathematical definitions don't have opinions. The best choice is C because it makes sense to say that a situation does or does not *correspond to* a definition.

Anyone thinking about pursuing a physician assistant or nurse practitioner degree should keep in mind that these programs aren't cheap, either, and that most states impose strict limits on the kinds of treatment 11 they can provide.

11

A) NO CHANGE
B) he or she
C) these professions
D) these professionals

Although there is a grammatical issue here—pronouns like *they* must agree with their **antecedents** (the nouns they stand for)—the real question is about **clarity**: "What does *they* logically refer to?" To answer this, we have to think about what idea the sentence is trying to convey.

The pronoun *they* is the subject of a dependent clause: *they can provide treatment*. In the context of this sentence, what can logically *provide treatment*? In context, the only reasonable answer is a *physician assistant* or a *nurse practitioner*. Since these are both *professionals*, and not *professions* (a *profession* is not a person), the best answer is D, *these professionals*. Choice A is incorrect because *they* is not specific enough: it lacks a clear **antecedent** (Chapter 5, Lesson 8). It might refer to any plural noun in the sentence, such as *programs* or *states*, but neither of these is a logical antecedent. Choice B is incorrect because *he or she* does not have a logical antecedent in the sentence: the phrase *physician assistant or nurse practitioner* is not used as a **noun phrase**, but rather as an **adjective phrase** describing *degree*.

In one **37** <u>experiment, subjects</u> performed a word association task, scientists measured the activity in the region of the brain called the right hemisphere anterior superior temporal gyrus (RH aSTG).

37

A) NO CHANGE
B) experiment by which subjects
C) experiment where subjects
D) experiment in which subjects

This sentence sounds pretty good, at least until we reach the comma: *In one experiment, subjects performed a word association task*. Nothing wrong here, right? Wrong.

This question shows how important it is to **read the whole sentence**. The phrase following the comma is an **independent clause** (Chapter 5, Lesson 1): it can stand alone as a sentence. But this means that the sentence would have a **comma splice** (Chapter 5, Lesson 2) if we keep it as it is. (Two independent clauses may not be joined with only a comma.) The best choice to fix this problem is choice D, which turns the first phrase into a modifier. Choice B is incorrect because it does not use proper **idiom** (Chapter 5, Lesson 13), and choice C is incorrect because the pronoun *where* is illogical: an experiment is not a place.

▮ D. STYLE AND TONE QUESTIONS

About 0–7% of SAT Writing and Language Test questions are **style and tone** questions. On any given test, you can expect about 0–3 questions of this type.

Style and tone questions ask whether a word, phrase, or sentence is consistent in style and tone with other elements of the passage. To tackle these questions, we need to pay attention to elements like **formality**, **pattern**, and **attitude**.

Don't be surprised when you don't hit your goal on the first try. You need to fail to succeed. And although you should ask for help when you need it, don't whine about your failures and setbacks. **22** <u>If one cannot learn to process failure with dignity, any ultimate victory is less honorable.</u>

22

Which choice best maintains the stylistic pattern of the previous sentences?

A) NO CHANGE
B) You can't have a pity party and a victory party at the same time.
C) Self-pity is not conducive to success in either the short or long term.
D) The honor of one's victory is measured by the dignity with which it is met.

Since the question asks only about the *stylistic pattern* of the paragraph, we need to focus more on the **style** of this paragraph than on its content. The style of the first three sentences is **informal**, **imperative** (giving direct commands), and **aphoristic** (characterized by pithy sayings).

The style of choice A, however, is **indirect**, **formal**, and **abstract**. It uses the formal third person pronoun *one*, which breaks from the use of the informal *you* in the rest of the paragraph. Choice C breaks the pattern of addressing the reader directly, and uses the formal word *conducive*. Likewise, choice D uses abstract terms like *honor* and *dignity* and formal syntax in the phrase *the dignity with which it is met*. The best choice is therefore B, which maintains the tone and style of a snappy dictum with a second-person subject.

My palate had wildly different reactions to the dishes Kyra made for us, from empanadillas (yummy) to nopales **16** <u>(an odd cactus dish)</u>.

16

Which choice best fits the content and stylistic pattern of the sentence?

A) NO CHANGE
B) (weird)
C) (which I found a bit strange)
D) (presented in a floral ceramic bowl)

Note that this question asks us to pay attention to *both* the content *and* the stylistic pattern. (Remember: the wording of the questions is *always* important.) What is the content of the underlined phrase? It is a **parenthetical noun phrase**.

However, it isn't **parallel** (Chapter 5, Lesson 3) with the first parentheses in the sentence which, like this one, follows the name of a food. The first parentheses contains an **adjective** that describes one of the writer's reactions to the food.

To fit the pattern, choice B is best, because it matches the first parentheses in **tone** (personal), **part of speech** (adjective), **length** (single word), and **function** (describing the writer's opinion of the food). Note, also, that choice B also supports the main idea of the sentence better than choices A and D, which is that the writer had *wildly different reactions* to the food.

E. INFOGRAPHICS QUESTIONS

About 1–7% of SAT Writing and Language Test questions are **infographics** questions. On any given test, you can expect about 1–3 questions of this type.

Infographics questions ask you to look at a graph, table, or diagram and incorporate its informaiton into the passage.

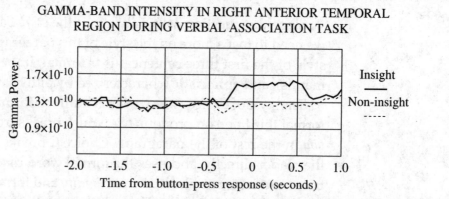

GAMMA-BAND INTENSITY IN RIGHT ANTERIOR TEMPORAL REGION DURING VERBAL ASSOCIATION TASK

adapted from Beeman, Bowden et. al., *Neural Activity When People Solve Problems with Insight*, PLOS, 2004

Interestingly, experimenters found that the insight solutions were accompanied by an elevated level of "gamma-band" activity in the right anterior temporal region (rATR), supporting the theory that the feeling corresponds to a cognitive process rather than a purely emotional one. **42** The gamma power in rATR for the insight solution is more than double that for the non-insight solution.

42

Which choice provides accurate and relevant information from the graph?

A) NO CHANGE
B) This increase in activity seems to begin about 0.3 second prior to the button-press response.
C) The gamma activity for the insight solution appears to be roughly the same as that for the non-insight solution until the instant the button is pressed.
D) This increase in activity seems to last just under 0.5 second.

Most of the graphs you'll see on the SAT won't be as technical and complicated as this one. However, this question is useful for showing the basic techniques of graphical interpretation.

To interpret a graph or table, carefully read the **title and** the **axis or row/column labels** (including the **units**), and make sure that you notice any labels that distinguish **multiple data sets**.

First, read the graph title: "Gamma-band intensity in right anterior temporal region during verbal association task." **Don't worry about what all these technical terms mean.** The important thing is that the graph is measuring something called *gamma-band intensity* in a part of the brain called the *right anterior temporal region*, which the paragraph abbreviates to *rATR*. The horizontal axis is labeled *Time from button-press response (seconds)*, so 0 on this axis must represent the time that the button-press response occurred.

Now look at the two lines on the graph: one is labeled *Insight* and the other *Non-insight* (whatever that means). What is interesting about the graph? The *insight* line seems to jump starting around −0.3 second (that is, 0.3 second before the button-press response), but returns to normal by about 0.6 second. Choice A is incorrect because the jump from about 1.3×10^{-6} to about 1.6×10^{-6} power units is not a doubling. Choice C is incorrect because the jump starts before the button is pressed. Choice D is incorrect because the jump appears to last about 0.9 second, from −0.3 to about 0.6 second. Therefore, the correct answer is B.

CHAPTER 4

BASIC SENTENCE DIAGNOSTICS

If you're a good reader, you can probably identify most common grammar and diction errors "by ear." When a sentence "sounds wrong," your ear tells you what kind of word or phrase "sounds better," even if you can't say exactly why.

However, to spot and fix the trickier grammatical problems you have to master the skills of **parsing** and **trimming** sentences.

LESSON 1: PARSING SENTENCES AND CLAUSES

What Is Parsing?

Parsing means taking a sentence apart into its essential components—clauses, verbs, subjects, objects, punctuation, conjunctions, and modifiers—and seeing how they all work together. You need to know how to parse if you want to ace the SAT Writing Test.

Clauses

A **clause** is any phrase, such as *stress can cause insomnia*, that conveys a complete idea. Every clause must contain a **subject** (*stress*), a **verb** (*can cause*), and any necessary **verb complements** (*insomnia*, the verb object). It may also include modifiers and modifying phrases, which we will discuss in detail later.

Independent Clauses and Dependent Clauses

A clause can be **dependent** or **independent**. Independent clauses are phrases that can stand on their own as sentences. **Dependent clauses** are clauses that can't stand alone because they include words, such as *because, but*, or *although*—that link to other clauses. To fit a dependent clause into a sentence, we need to link it to an independent clause.

Consider the sentence

Although we were tired, we kept going.

The first clause, *although we were tired*, is a **dependent clause** because it includes *although*, which links it to the next clause, but the second clause, *we kept going*, is **independent**, because it would make a perfectly good sentence if we just capitalized the first word.

Parsing Sentences

Here's one of my favorite Groucho Marx jokes:

Time flies like an arrow, fruit flies like a banana.

Do you get it? If so, you've passed the first test in parsing. If not, read it again. Why is this sentence funny, instead of just strange?

Let's start with the first clause:

Time	*flies*	*like an arrow*
subject	verb	adverb phrase

Simple enough. It's a simile. It makes a point about how time moves quickly, right? The subject is *time*, the verb is *flies*, and the phrase *like an arrow* answers a question about the verb (*how does it fly?*), so it is an **adverbial phrase** (Chapter 5, Lesson 6).

Now, when we get to the second clause, we might want to parse it the same way:

fruit	*flies*	*like a banana*
subject	verb	adverb phrase

Okay . . . so I guess fruit can fly because you can throw it, But isn't it weird to compare the way fruit *in general* flies through the air to the way that one *particular* fruit flies through the air? That's not insightful at all. It's just a little strange.

Until you realize that it can be parsed in a much more sensible way:

fruit flies	*like*	*a banana*
subject	verb	object

Oh, okay! This clause is about *fruit flies*! Of course they like bananas! Groucho was trying to be cute.

Simple Sentences

Every sentence consists of one or more clauses. Let's look at two sentences—one simple, one complex—and parse them into their clauses.

Go!

This is the simplest sentence in the English language, so parsing it is pretty simple.

You	*go!*
subject	verb

It contains the bare minimum that a sentence requires (a verb and a subject). Since this sentence is in the **imperative mood** (Chapter 5, Lesson 15), which means that it gives a direct command, the subject is implied to be the second person *you*, and so it doesn't need to be explicitly stated.

Complex Sentences

Now for a slightly more complex sentence.

Generally regarded as the most daunting course in the undergraduate science curriculum, Introduction to Organic Chemistry not only provides a necessary foundation in the principles of physical chemistry, but also introduces students to important experimental methods at the heart of modern medical research.

This sentence conveys two **main ideas** and a **secondary idea**. Let's look at how their pieces work together.

Main Idea #1

Introduction to Organic Chemistry	subject
provides	verb
a necessary foundation	direct object
in the principles	prepositional phrase (adjectival)
of physical chemistry	prepositional phrase (adjectival)

The main idea is always conveyed in an independent clause. In addition to a subject and verb, this clause also contains a **direct object** (*a necessary foundation*) and a pair of prepositional phrases (Chapter 4, Lesson 2) that modify two nouns in the sentence (and so they are **adjectival**). A prepositional phrase is a preposition followed by a noun or noun phrase. The first prepositional phrase (*in the principles*) modifies the noun *foundation*, and the second prepositional phrase (*of physical chemistry*) modifies the noun *principles*.

Main idea #2

Introduction to Organic Chemistry	subject
introduces	verb
students	direct object
to important experimental methods	prepositional phrase (adverbial)
at the heart	prepositional phrase (adjectival)
of modern medical research	prepositional phrase (adjectival)

This clause also has a subject, verb, and direct object. It also contains three **prepositional phrases** that modify a verb and two nouns. The first prepositional phrase (*to important experimental methods*) modifies the verb *introduces*, the second prepositional phrase (*at the heart*) modifies the noun *methods*, and the third (*of medical research*) modifies the noun *heart*.

Secondary Idea

Introduction to Organic Chemistry	subject
(is) generally regarded	participial phrase (implied verb phrase)
as the most daunting course	prepositional phrase (adverbial)
in the undergraduate science curriculum	prepositional phrase (adjectival)

The secondary idea is conveyed in a **participial phrase**. As we will discuss in Chapter 5, Lesson 4, participial phrases are basically clauses without a subject, because the subject is "borrowed" from the main clause. This phrase also contains two prepositional phrases. The first prepositional phrase (*as the most daunting course*) modifies the verb participle *regarded*, and the second prepositional phrase (*in the undergraduate curriculum*) modifies the noun *course*.

Coordination of the Main Ideas

> . . . *not only (predicate of main clause #1), but also (predicate of main clause #2)*

The two main clauses are coordinated with a **standard parallel construction** (Chapter 5, Lesson 3) *not only . . . but also. . . .* This phrase shows that the second main idea extends the first idea by describing an additional benefit of the chemistry course. This construction includes the **predicates** of the two clauses, that is, the clauses without the subjects.

LESSON 2: TRIMMING SENTENCES

The Law of Trimming

Every sentence must convey a clear and coherent idea even after it has been "trimmed."

How to Trim

Trimming means eliminating modifiers and modifying phrases from a sentence to see its **core** —the **subject**, **verb**, and any necessary **verb complements** of each clause. It involves three steps:

1. Eliminate any non-essential **prepositional phrases**.
2. Eliminate introductory, interrupting, or concluding **modifying phrases**.
3. Eliminate any remaining **non-essential modifiers** like adjectives and adverbs.

Prepositions

A **preposition** is any word—such as *up, to, around, from, into, by, on, for, of, as,* or *with*— that can be used to complete sentences such as these:

> *The squirrel ran _____ the tree.*
>
> *Democracy is government _____ the people.*
>
> *I went to the party _____ a brain surgeon.*

Prepositional Phrases

A **prepositional phrase** consists of a preposition plus the **noun phrase** that follows it, such as:

> . . . *from* sea to shining sea . . .
>
> . . . in the beginning . . .
>
> . . . for the *money* . . .

Modifying Phrases

Modifying phrases, which include **prepositional phrases** but also include **participial phrases** (Chapter 5, Lesson 4), **appositive phrases** (Chapter 5, Lesson 5), **adjectival phrases** (Chapter 5, Lesson 6), and **adverbial phrases** (Chapter 5, Lesson 6), are often (but not always) separated from the main clause by commas or dashes.

> *As luck would have it*, we were saved at the last minute.
>
> We were saved—*as luck would have it*—at the last minute.
>
> We were saved at the last minute, *as luck would have it*.

Non-Essential Modifiers

Non-essential modifiers are **adjectives** or **adverbs** that are not essential to conveying the central idea of the clause.

> I have a *terrible* headache.
>
> She ran *quickly* from the house.

Essential Modifiers

Essential modifiers—modifiers that are essential to conveying the core idea—should **not** be trimmed. One type of *essential* modifier is the **predicate adjective.**

> The sky is *blue*.

The subject is tied to the subject by the **linking verb** *is*.
   Sometimes prepositional phrases can also act as predicate adjectives.

> The cake is *in the oven*.

Why Trim?

Trimming sentences helps you to eliminate clutter so you can better analyze the essential parts of the sentence and check them for clarity, logic, and grammatical errors.

Untrimmed:	*In one experiment in which subjects performed a word association task, scientists measured the activity in the region of the brain called the aSTG.*
Trimmed:	*Scientists measured the activity*

▨ EXERCISE SET 1: TRIMMING

Write the "trimmed" version of each sentence in the column on the right and <u>underline</u> the verb in each clause. Remember that a sentence may contain more than one clause.

[1] Born in 1870 in Chiaravalle, Italy, Maria Montessori showed a strong, independent will, even as a child. [2] As a teenager, she told her parents that she wanted to study engineering, despite its reputation for being unladylike. [3] By the age of 20, she had changed her mind and decided to pursue an even less traditional path: medicine. [4] Despite suffering ridicule and isolation, Montessori completed her medical studies at the University of Rome and became one of the first female physicians in Italy.

[5] Although Montessori's practice focused on psychiatry, her interests gravitated toward education. [6] In 1900, she was appointed co-director of the Scuola Magistrale Ortofrenica, a training institute for special education teachers.

1. _____
   _____
   _____

2. _____
   _____
   _____

3. _____
   _____
   _____

4. _____
   _____
   _____

5. _____
   _____
   _____

6. _____
   _____
   _____

[7] Montessori believed that, in order for so-called "deficient" children to thrive, they need respect and stimulation rather than the regimentation they were receiving in institutions.

[8] In 1907, Maria opened the Casa dei Bambini, or "Children's House," a daycare center for impoverished children in which she could test her theory that each child learns according to his or her own schedule. [9] She personalized a curriculum for each child rather than providing a standardized course of study. [10] While learning important academic and life skills, many formerly aggressive and unmanageable children became more emotionally balanced and self-directed. [11] Word of her success with the Casa dei Bambini soon began to spread internationally, and her methods for child-centered education became widely adopted across Europe.

7. _____

8. _____

9. _____

10. _____

11. _____

EXERCISE SET 2: PARSING

1. The team of advisors, arriving slightly ahead of schedule, <u>were</u> met at the airport by the Deputy Prime Minister.
   - A) NO CHANGE
   - B) were being
   - C) was
   - D) being

2. Today, juggling the demands of family and work often <u>seem</u> too difficult for many young professionals.
   - A) NO CHANGE
   - B) seems
   - C) will seem
   - D) would seem

3. The fact that even well-intentioned institutions can so easily become dysfunctional <u>have forced</u> many observers to become cynical about social change.
   - A) NO CHANGE
   - B) would force
   - C) has forced
   - D) are forcing

4. The Immigrant Defense Project, based in New York City, <u>provide</u> expert legal advice and advocacy for immigrants and their loved ones.
   - A) NO CHANGE
   - B) have provided
   - C) provides
   - D) have been providing

5. The intensity of these workouts, which include both agility circuits and weight training, <u>are a problem</u> for many who are not already in good shape.
   - A) NO CHANGE
   - B) are problems
   - C) are problematic
   - D) is a problem

6. The anthology focuses on the works of modern poets, <u>but includes</u> some older works as well.
   A) NO CHANGE
   B) includes
   C) but include
   D) include

7. The theory of quantum electrodynamics, although maddeningly counterintuitive, <u>makes</u> astonishingly accurate predictions about the behavior of subatomic particles.
   A) NO CHANGE
   B) making
   C) would make
   D) make

8. Surprisingly absent from the game <u>were the crowds</u> traditional routine of taunting the opposing players.
   A) NO CHANGE
   B) was the crowds
   C) were the crowd's
   D) was the crowd's

9. An education at an inexpensive public university can be <u>as good, if not better, than</u> an elite private college.
   A) NO CHANGE
   B) as good as, if not better than, one at
   C) as good as, if not better than,
   D) as good, if not better, than one at

---

10. **Challenge Question**

Buffalo buffalo Buffalo buffalo buffalo buffalo Buffalo buffalo Buffalo buffalo buffalo.

Believe it or not, the sentence above is perfectly sensible and grammatical, and no punctuation has been omitted. Can you parse the sentence to make sense of it? Specifically, can you underline the main verb?

ANSWER KEY

Exercise Set 1: Trimming

1. Maria Montessori (subject) <u>showed</u> (verb) a strong will (object).
2. She (subject) <u>told</u> (verb) her parents (indirect object) that she wanted to study engineering (direct object).
3. She (subject) <u>had changed</u> (verb) her mind (object) and <u>decided</u> (verb) to pursue medicine (direct object).
4. Montessori (subject) <u>completed</u> (verb) her medical studies (direct object) and <u>became</u> (verb) one of the first female physicians (predicate nominative).
5. Her interests (subject) <u>gravitated</u> (verb) toward education (essential prepositional phrase).
6. She (subject) <u>was appointed</u> (verb) co-director (object).
7. Montessori (subject) <u>believed</u> (verb) that children need respect and stimulation (object).
8. Maria (subject) <u>opened</u> (verb) the Casa dei Bambini (object).
9. She (subject) <u>personalized</u> (verb) a curriculum (object).
10. Many children (subject) <u>became</u> (verb) more balanced and self-directed (predicate adjective).
11. Word (subject) <u>began to spread</u> (verb), and her methods (subject) <u>became adopted</u> (verb).

Exercise Set 2: Parsing

1. C

After trimming, the core is *The team were met.* But since *team* is a singular collective noun, it does not agree with the plural verb *were.* (Notice that *advisors* cannot be the subject because it is part of a prepositional phrase.) The only choice that provides us with a singular verb is C. (This may sound strange if you were raised in the UK or a Commonwealth country, since, in the Queen's English, *team* and other such collective nouns are regarded as plurals. But the SAT is an American test, so here we must treat them as singulars.)

2. B

The subject of this sentence is *juggling* (a **gerund**, Chapter 5, Lesson 3) which is singular, so it disagrees in number with the plural verb *seem.* (Notice that *demands* cannot be the subject because it is part of a prepositional phrase.) Choice B corrects the agreement problem. Choice C is incorrect because the sentence specifies a fact about *today*, which requires the present tense, not the future tense. Choice D is incorrect because *would* indicates the **subjunctive mood** (Chapter 5, Lesson 15), and so incorrectly implies that the statement is hypothetical or counterfactual.

3. C

The singular subject of this sentence, *fact*, disagrees with the plural verb *have forced*. (Notice that *institutions* cannot be the subject of this clause because it is the subject of a separate clause, *institutions . . . become dysfunctional*.) Choice C fixes this problem because *has* can take a singular subject. Choice B is incorrect because it uses the subjunctive mood, contradicting the **indicative** (Chapter 5, Lesson 15) nature of the sentence. Choice D is incorrect because *are* disagrees with the singular subject.

4. C

The singular subject *Project* disagrees with the plural verb *provide*. Choice C provides the correct singular conjugation. Choices B and D are incorrect because both are conjugated for plural subjects.

5. D

The singular subject *intensity* disagrees in number with the verb *are*. (Notice that *workouts* cannot be the subject because it is part of a prepositional phrase.) Choice D corrects this problem. Choices B and C are incorrect because they also disagree in number with the subject.

6. A

The original phrasing is clear and logical. The singular subject *anthology* agrees with the verb *includes*. (Notice that *works* cannot be the subject because it is part of a prepositional phrase.) Choice B is incorrect because the two **parallel predicates** require a conjunction between them. Choices C and D are incorrect because *include* does not agree with the singular subject.

7. A

The original phrasing is clear and logical. The singular subject *theory* agrees with the verb *makes*. Choice B is incorrect because the participle *making* cannot stand alone as a verb. Choice C is incorrect because the subjunctive mood should not be used when conveying facts. Choice D is incorrect because *make* does not agree with the singular subject.

8. D

This sentence has an inverted syntax (Chapter 5, Lesson 1). The "uninverted" version is *The crowds traditional routine of taunting the opposing players were surprisingly absent from the game*. This sentence has two problems: *crowds* should be changed to the possessive *crowd's* because it is modifying the noun *routine*, and the verb *were* does not agree with the singular subject *routine*. Only choice D corrects both problems.

9. B

In each choice, the phrase between the commas is an interrupting phrase. According to the Law of Trimming, the sentence must remain clear and coherent even after it has been removed. Choices A and D are incorrect because *as good than* is not **idiomatic** (Chapter 5, Lesson 13). Choice C is incorrect because it makes an **illogical** comparison (Chapter 5, Lesson 7). One type of education can only be compared with another type of education, so the logic and phrasing in choice B is correct.

10.   **(Challenge Question)**

The verb of this sentence is the sixth word. To understand this sentence, we need to see that *B/buffalo* has at three different meanings here. First, *buffalo* (n, pl) are large wild oxen. Second, *Buffalo* (n) is a city is western New York. Therefore, we can say that oxen from a city in western New York are *Buffalo buffalo*. Third, *buffalo* (v) means *to intimidate*. If oxen from western New York tend to intimidate their peers, we could say *Buffalo buffalo* <u>*buffalo*</u> *Buffalo buffalo*. Now, if the oxen from Buffalo that *are intimidated* by other oxen from Buffalo also intimidate their peers, we would say *[The] Buffalo buffalo [that] Buffalo buffalo buffalo* <u>*buffalo*</u> *[the] Buffalo buffalo [that] Buffalo buffalo buffalo.*

CHAPTER 5

ADVANCED SENTENCE DIAGNOSTICS

Identifying the parts of a sentence is just the first step in diagnosing grammar problems. The next step is to see if any of the basic grammar rules are being violated, and correct them if so. Don't let this part intimidate you. There are only a couple dozen basic rules to know, so let's dig into each one.

LESSON 1: VERB AGREEMENT

Subject-Verb Agreement

After you've trimmed a sentence, ask: **does every verb agree with its subject?** Consider this sentence.

> *My favorite team are losing.*

Here, the verb *are* disagrees with its subject in **number**: since *team* is a singular subject, *are* should be changed to *is*. Subject-verb agreement problems often show up when sentences have **tricky subjects** or **inverted syntax**.

Tricky Subjects

> The phenomena studied by climate scientists ▧32 is of interest to the entire planet.
>
> ▧32
>
> A) NO CHANGE
> B) has been
> C) are
> D) being

The correct answer is C because the subject, *phenomena*, is the plural of *phenomenon*. Some Latin-derived words have tricky plurals, for instance *bacterium/bacteria, continuum/continua, criterion/criteria, curriculum/curricula, datum/data,* and *medium/media*.

> Neither of the books **15** <u>are</u> appropriate for a fourth-grade class.
>
> **15**
>
> A) NO CHANGE
> B) is
> C) have been
> D) being

The correct answer is B because the subject is not *books*, but *neither*, which is singular. Notice that the phrase *of the books* is a prepositional phrase, so it can be trimmed.

Inverted Syntax

Some sentences have an **inverted** syntax: the subject comes *after* the verb, making it a bit tricky to see whether they agree. It often helps to "un-invert" these sentences by **removing any "dummy subjects" and rearranging the remaining phrases**.

> Behind every Portiello sculpture **12** <u>lies</u> countless hours of planning and work.
>
> **12**
>
> A) NO CHANGE
> B) lie
> C) laid
> D) lain

The correct answer is B, because the subject of the sentence is *hours*, which is plural. This one is hard to catch because the sentence is inverted. You can "un-invert" the sentence by just swapping the phrases on either side of the verb: *Countless hours of planning and work <u>lie</u> behind every Portiello sculpture.* Notice that *sculpture* cannot be the subject of the verb because it is the **object** of the prepositional phrase *behind every Portiello sculpture*.

> Last year, there **19** <u>was</u> nearly fifty applications submitted for every seat in the first-year class.
>
> **19.**
>
> A) NO CHANGE
> B) would be
> C) were
> D) has been

The correct answer is C, because the subject of the sentence is the plural *applications*. Again, this sentence is inverted, and the "un-inverted" version is *Last year, nearly fifty applications <u>were</u> submitted for every seat in the first-year class*. Notice that every word in the original sentence is accounted for, except for *there*, which is a **dummy subject**.

EXERCISE SET 3: VERB AGREEMENT

1. Just as dusk was settling on the pond, the flock of geese <u>scattered</u> by a shotgun blast.
   A) NO CHANGE
   B) were scattered
   C) was scattered
   D) was scattering

2. In every teaspoon of topsoil <u>is</u> over two million microorganisms, forming a highly complex ecosystem.
   A) NO CHANGE
   B) was
   C) are
   D) being

3. How important <u>should</u> strength conditioning to a marathon training regimen?
   A) NO CHANGE
   B) are
   C) is
   D) would

4. This technology, <u>developed</u> by the American military for field communications, has become essential to many private industries as well.
   A) NO CHANGE
   B) was developed
   C) was being developed
   D) having developed

5. The committee agreed that the new principal should both inspire students and <u>should maintain</u> a rigorous academic culture.
   A) NO CHANGE
   B) should also maintain
   C) also maintain
   D) maintain

6. The labor coalition, which consists of representatives from all of the skilled worker unions, <u>have expressed concern in</u> the new hiring policies.
   A) NO CHANGE
   B) has expressed concern about
   C) have expressed concern with
   D) has expressed concern with

7. The explosiveness of political revelations in the book <u>explain why it is selling at such a feverish pace</u>.
   A) NO CHANGE
   B) explains why it is selling at such a feverish pace
   C) explain the feverish pace of it's sales
   D) explains why its selling at such a feverish pace

8. <u>S. J. Perelman's absurdist and florid writing style</u> is regarded as one of America's greatest humorists.
   A) NO CHANGE
   B) S. J. Perelman's absurdist and florid writing style
   C) S. J. Perelman, whose writing is characterized by an absurdist and florid style,
   D) S. J. Perelman and his absurdist and florid writing style

9. Grizzlies rarely attack humans, but they will protect their territory from anyone they <u>would have regarded</u> as a threat.
   A) NO CHANGE
   B) regarded
   C) had regarded
   D) regard

10. **Challenge Question**

   Just when those who were observing the heart surgery assumed the worst, the surgeons <u>themselves were</u> most confident in its success.

   A) NO CHANGE
   B) they were
   C) themselves are
   D) are, themselves,

LESSON 2: COORDINATING IDEAS

Paragraph Cohesiveness

Many SAT Writing and Language questions ask you to address problems with **cohesiveness**. Every good paragraph must be **focused**, **logical**, and **consistent**. It should focus on a single main idea, develop any necessary aspects of that idea, and avoid irrelevancies.

One natural gas extraction technique, hydraulic fracturing or "fracking," continues to spark debate. Opponents suggest that the high-pressure fluid used to fracture deep rock formations may release carcinogens such as radon into groundwater supplies, and that fracking can induce earthquakes. Supporters, on the other hand, counter that this activity is taking place well below even the deepest aquifers and is sealed off from public water supplies. **30** <u>Earthquakes, also known as seismic tremors, are notoriously difficult to predict.</u>

30

Which choice best develops the main idea of the paragraph?

A) NO CHANGE
B) Seismologists have been studying such human-induced seismic activity for may years.
C) Most of these supporters have financial ties to the industry.
D) Further, any seismic activity fracking induces is miniscule, since the rock fractures it creates are tiny.

The correct answer is D. The first sentence of the paragraph establishes that the central idea is the debate sparked by fracking. The second sentence specifies two objections to fracking made by its opponents. The third sentence specifies a counterpoint to this first objection, but not to the second one. If the paragraph is to continue developing its main idea, therefore, it should specify a counterpoint to the second objection, as in choice D. The other choices are incorrect because they depart from the central purpose of the paragraph, which is to describe the substantive points on both sides of the fracking debate.

Coordinating Style

Pay attention to the **consistency of style** within and between paragraphs. Although individual sentences should vary in content, length, and structure as needed, they should nevertheless maintain a consistent style unless a shift in style serves a clear purpose.

Whenever you make a decision, you can never be fully aware of the millions of little chemical and electrical reactions in your brain that have nudged you toward that choice. But even if you could be, you could never say that you *chose* any of those reactions. They are beyond your control. **18** So how can we ever really say that we "make" our own decisions? What you call your free will may not be so free after all.

18

Which change to this sentence best maintains the stylistic cohesiveness of the paragraph?

A) Change "So" to "But."
B) Omit "really."
C) Change "we" to "you" and "our" to "your."
D) Omit "that."

This question asks you to focus on **style** rather than logic. (Of course, the logic has to work too.) Choice C is best because the rest of the paragraph is written in the **second person** (*you* and *your*). Using first person plural pronouns (*we* and *our*) in this sentence doesn't violate any rule of grammar or logic, but it does disrupt the style of the paragraph as a whole.

Coordinating Ideas Within Sentences

A sentence with multiple ideas must use proper phrasing to indicate the **importance** and **logical relationship** of those ideas. The main idea should be expressed in the **main independent clause**, and secondary ideas are usually conveyed with **dependent clauses** or with **modifiers** or **modifying phrases**. The logical relationships among ideas are usually conveyed with **logical conjunctions or adverbs** such as *because*, *therefore*, or *however*.

28 We are not the customers; we are the product in this transaction, even when we subscribe to a newspaper or website. We are an audience being sold to advertisers, and our attention must be maintained and manipulated regardless of our needs and wants.

28

A) NO CHANGE
B) In this transaction, we are the product and not the customers, even when we subscribe to a newspaper or website.
C) We are the product in this transaction, even when we subscribe to a newspaper or website, not the customers.
D) Even when we subscribe to a newspaper or website, we are not the customers in this transaction, but the product.

In choices A, B, and C, the reference to *this transaction* is not clear, because in each case this phrase precedes the referent clause, *we subscribe to a newspaper or website.* (The *transaction* is the act of subscribing, a fact that is only clear if the reference to subscribing comes before the reference to the transaction.) Only choice D arranges the clauses to make this reference clear. Also, the sequencing of the clauses in choice D emphasizes the ironic relationship between them: it should surprise us to know that we are not the customers *even when* we are paying for a service. Lastly, the concluding phrase in choice D, *but the product,* sets up the following sentence, which explains how we are *the product.*

Coordinating with Punctuation

When coordinating ideas within a sentence, you often have to decide whether and how to use **commas**, **semi-colons**, and **colons**. Here are three rules to remember:

- When combining independent clauses with a **comma**, you must also use a **logical conjunction**. Leaving out this conjunction is a mistake called a **comma splice.** For instance, you can't write *We had a great time, Matt played his guitar,* but you can write *We had a great time, <u>but</u> Matt played his guitar.* (We had a great time *despite* Matt.)
- You may join two independent clauses with a **semi-colon**, but only if the clauses support each another. For instance: *We were having a great time; Matt played his guitar.* (Matt didn't hurt the mood.)
- You may join two independent clauses with a **colon**, but only if the second clause **explains** the first. For instance: *We had a great time: Matt played his guitar.* (We had a great time *because of* Matt.)

---

31 <u>Despite being a best-selling author, Brian Greene is a professor of physics, he is also a co-founder of the World Science Festival in New York City, an event that</u> draws nearly half a million people each year.

31

A) NO CHANGE
B) As a physics professor and best-selling author, Brian Greene is the co-founder of the World Science Festival in New York City, which
C) The World Science Festival in New York City, being co-founded by physics professor and best-selling author Brian Greene,
D) Co-founded by best-selling author and physics professor Brian Greene, the World Science Festival in New York City

---

This sentence coordinates four separate but related ideas. Choice A has two main problems: it contains a comma splice, and it is logically incoherent because it implies that being an author contrasts with being a physics professor. Choice B is incorrect because the introductory modifier, *As a physics professor and best-selling author*, does not logically modify the main clause. Choice C is incorrect because the interrupting modifier, which is phrased as an explanation, doesn't logically modify the main clause. The only choice that logically coordinates all three ideas is choice D.

Transitions

When starting a new sentence, pay attention to its logical relationship to the previous sentence, and make sure you include any necessary language to clarify any logical relationship with an appropriate **transition**. Transitions serve as guideposts to help readers follow your train of thought.

- **To extend an idea:** *indeed, further, furthermore, also, moreover, in fact, additionally*
- **To illustrate or clarify an idea:** *for instance, for example, such as, especially, in particular, to illustrate, namely, specifically, in other words, that is, actually*
- **To show a contrast:** *however, although, despite, nevertheless, but, on the other hand*
- **To make a comparison:** *similarly, likewise, alternatively, also, too*
- **To show consequence:** *as a result, so, thus, subsequently, therefore, hence, accordingly, for this reason*
- **To show explanation or reason:** *because, since, how, why, as, thus*

This study and others like it have profound implications for the classroom. Several experiments have demonstrated that "pay-to-read" programs, where students are given money or gift credits to read books, have surprisingly negative effects on literacy. Such programs do get students to "read" more books, but the kind of reading they do is not ideal. Students tend to read superficially and only to get the reward. In follow-up studies, these students show not only lower reading skills but also less desire to read. **10** Nevertheless, the reward system turns reading from a fun activity into drudgery. Students think, if reading is such a rewarding experience, why do they need to pay us to do it?

10

A) NO CHANGE
B) Evidently,
C) However,
D) Therefore,

This paragraph discusses studies that have shown *that "pay-to-read" programs . . . have surprisingly negative effects on literacy*. The sentence before this transition says that students who are paid to read *show not only lower reading skills but also less desire to read*. The main clause in the new sentence, *the reward system turns reading from a fun activity into drudgery*, <u>explains</u> the results of the studies summarized in the previous sentence, and therefore choice B, *Evidently*, provides the most logical transition. Choices A and C are incorrect because the new sentence does not provide a contrast. Choice D is incorrect because the new sentence does not indicate a necessary consequence to the previous idea.

References

When a sentence uses a **pronoun**—such as *this*, *such*, or *that*—to refer to an idea or event from a previous clause or sentence, make sure that this reference is **clear and precise**. If it is not, you may need to replace the pronoun with a more precise **noun or noun phrase** in order to clarify the idea.

The opponents of fracking are correct to ask questions about the safety and sustainability of this practice. Could it poison the local water supply with carcinogens? Can we spare the vast amount of injection water it requires, especially in times of drought? Could it be causing potentially dangerous seismic activity? **13** But <u>this</u> is not enough—it must also be followed by careful, scientific, and impartial investigation, not just more fear-peddling.

13

A) NO CHANGE
B) this questioning
C) these practices
D) such a concept

In the original phrasing, the pronoun *this* is ambiguous. What does *this* refer to? *seismic activity*? *drought*? *fracking*? No, the developmental pattern of the paragraph as a whole indicates that the *questioning* is what must be followed by careful investigation. Therefore, the only logical choice is B.

Anyone thinking about pursuing a PA (physician assistant) or NP (nurse practitioner) degree should keep in mind that these programs aren't cheap, and that most states impose strict limits on the kinds of treatment **11** they can provide.

11

A) NO CHANGE
B) he or she
C) these professions
D) these professionals

The phrases *physician assistant* and *nurse practitioner* cannot serve as the antecedents of the pronoun *they*, because, first, they are parenthetical, and second, they are not actually nouns: they are adjectives modifying the noun *degree.* Therefore, the pronoun reference must be specified. Choice B is incorrect because *he or she* is no more specific than the original. To choose between C and D, we should ask, are physician assistants and nurse practitioners examples of *professions* or *professionals*? They are individual caregivers, so they are *professionals*. The *professions* they represent are *medicine* or *nursing.* The correct answer is D.

EXERCISE SET 4: COORDINATING IDEAS

1. <u>Director H. K. Schaffer's third movie has received widespread critical acclaim. This movie is entitled *The Return*, and she is the daughter of legendary playwright George Schaffer.</u>

   A) NO CHANGE
   B) *The Return*, the third movie directed by H. K. Schaffer, daughter of legendary playwright George Schaffer, has received widespread critical acclaim.
   C) The daughter of legendary playwright George Schaffer, director H. K. Schaffer's third movie, *The Return*, has received widespread critical acclaim.
   D) H. K. Schaffer's third movie is *The Return*: as the daughter of legendary playwright George Schaffer, her movie has received widespread critical acclaim.

2. Neuroscientists <u>have made an important discovery concerning the pre-frontal cortex of the brain. They discovered that this governs impulse control in humans. This discovery can help us to</u> understand the causes of criminal behavior.

   A) NO CHANGE
   B) have discovered that impulse control in humans is governed by the prefrontal cortex of the brain, which can help us
   C) have discovered that the prefrontal cortex of the brain governs impulse control in humans, which in turn can help us
   D) have discovered that impulse control in humans is governed by the prefrontal cortex of the brain. This finding can help us

3. Electric cars may not be as environmentally friendly as we think, because the electricity they use is often produced in coal-burning power plants, <u>this</u> can produce large quantities of greenhouse gas.

   A) NO CHANGE
   B) the burning of which
   C) which
   D) which, when it burns,

4. Regular exercise not only strengthens your <u>muscles, it also strengthens your brain by keeping it well-oxygenated</u>.

   A) NO CHANGE
   B) muscles; by keeping it well-oxygenated it also strengthens your brain
   C) muscles, but also it oxygenates your brain to make it strong
   D) muscles, but also strengthens your brain by keeping it well-oxygenated

5. Widely regarded as one of the most influential economic treatises of the 20th-century, <u>John Maynard Keynes' *The General Theory of Employment, Interest, and Money*</u> forever changed the way social scientists view recessions.

   A) NO CHANGE
   B) John Maynard Keynes, with his book *The General Theory of Employment, Interest, and Money,*
   C) *The General Theory of Employment, Interest, and Money* was written by John Maynard Keynes, which
   D) John Maynard Keynes, through his book *The General Theory of Employment, Interest, and Money,* which

6. **Challenge Question**

Our <u>principles can change, but these are often what motivate us: our experiences affect our priorities and</u> deepest values.

A) NO CHANGE

B) experiences affect our priorities: our principles often motivate us and can change our

C) principles can change, and they are often what motivate us: our experiences affect our priorities and

D) principles are often what motivate us, but they can change: our experiences affect our priorities and

EXERCISE SET 5: TRANSITIONS AND REFERENCES

1. Even though the ancient Greeks were likely to see themselves as victims of fate, they were also inclined to regard humans as a privileged species. <u>Coincidentally,</u> in Sophocles' *Antigone*, the chorus proclaims that "many wonders there be, but naught more wondrous than man."

   A) NO CHANGE
   B) For example,
   C) Furthermore,
   D) Nevertheless,

2. As satisfying as it may be to punish wrongdoers, the real impetus behind tough sentencing laws is the belief that long prison terms deter crime. <u>Even worse,</u> the loss of autonomy and dignity that many prisoners experience often exacerbates any psychological issues that made them susceptible to crime in the first place.

   A) NO CHANGE
   B) However,
   C) In other words,
   D) As a result,

3. As societies become more complex and diverse, many people become more fearful and anxious, and thus are inclined to become more reactionary in their political views. <u>Consequently,</u> extremists in the media—talk radio hosts, cable news pundits, and radical bloggers—have access to a deep pool of resentment that they can exploit for financial gain.

   A) NO CHANGE
   B) Nevertheless,
   C) Likewise,
   D) For instance,

4. Challenge Question

For decades, biologists have been trying to explore the genetic relationship between ancient humans and Neanderthals. However, they have lacked the technology to prevent the contamination of ancient DNA during the extraction process. <u>Fittingly,</u> the "clean room" at the Max Planck Institute has solved this problem, allowing scientists to examine minute bits of genetic material from 400,000 year-old hominid bones.

A) NO CHANGE
B) Fortunately,
C) In turn,
D) Accordingly,

LESSON 3: PARALLELISM

The Law of Parallelism

When a sentence contains a **list**, **contrast**, or **comparison**, the items being listed, contrasted, or compared should have the **same grammatical form**.

In the 70s and 80s, American high school math teachers taught almost exclusively by lecture; today, **25** <u>interactive and cooperative methods are more likely to be used.</u>

25

A) NO CHANGE
B) interactive and cooperative methods are more likely to be used by those teachers
C) they are more likely to use interactive and cooperative methods
D) they would be more likely to use interactive and cooperative methods

The two clauses share a common topic, but they are not in the same grammatical form. The first is in the **active voice** (Chapter 5, Lesson 14) but the second is in the **passive voice**. The Law of Parallelism demands that we phrase the second clause in the active voice as well, as in choice C. Choice D is incorrect because, although it is phrased in the active voice, it uses the **subjunctive mood** (Chapter 5, Lesson 15), *would be*, which violates both the parallelism and the logic of the sentence.

Ms. Kelly always tries to provide **23** clear instructions that show respect and are fair to all of her students.

23

A) NO CHANGE
B) clear instructions, showing respect and being
C) clear instructions that also are respectful and are
D) instructions that are clear, respectful, and

Choice D provides the most concise and parallel list: *clear, respectful,* and *fair* are all simple adjectives. Also, all of these adjectives work **idiomatically** (Chapter 5, Lesson 13) with the prepositional phrase *to all of her students.*

Standard Parallel Constructions

In Standard American English, many contrasts or comparisons are made with **standard parallel constructions**. When using any of these constructions, you must follow two rules:

- Use the standard phrasing **precisely**.
- Make sure the words or phrases in the *A* and *B* slots are **parallel**.

Standard Parallel Constructions

. . . rather A than B . . .	*. . . neither A nor B . . .*
. . . prefer A to B . . .	*. . . both A and B . . .*
. . . less A than B . . .	*. . . not A but B . . .*
. . . A more than B . . .	*. . . A is like B . . .*
. . . either A or B . . .	*. . . not so much A as B . . .*
. . . the more A, the more B . . .	

It often seems that politicians would rather give snappy soundbites **13** instead of working to solve our problems.

13

A) NO CHANGE
B) than work
C) rather than working
D) but not work

Although this sentence sounds okay to most people, it doesn't conform to Standard American English. It uses the standard parallel construction *rather A than B,* but neither choice A nor choice D uses the correct phrasing, since they both omit the word *than.* Only choice B plays by the rules of idiom and parallelism: *rather (give snappy soundbites) than (work to solve our problems).*

Analyzing Parallel Constructions

Sometimes tackling parallelism problems can be tough. Here's a step-by-step approach to make it easier:

1. **Underline** any phrase that shows a list, contrast, or comparison.
2. **Put parentheses** around each item being listed, contrasted, or compared.
3. Make sure that anything **outside** the parentheses uses **standard idiomatic phrasing**.
4. Make sure the items **inside** the parentheses have **parallel form**.

The film festival was not so much a celebration of independent `27` <u>artists; instead it was garish, not to mention a</u> series of commercials for overproduced blockbusters.

`27`

A) NO CHANGE
B) artists but rather a garish
C) artists as a garish
D) artists, instead it was a garish

The phrase *not so much* indicates a contrast between two things: someone's expectations of a film festival and the reality. Let's isolate this portion that makes the contrast and put parentheses around the items being contrasted:

not so much (a celebration of independent artists); instead it was (garish, not to mention a series of commercials for overproduced blockbusters)

Does the part *outside* the parentheses use standard idiomatic phrasing? No. On the previous page, we saw that the proper phrasing is *not so much A as B*. Let's fix that:

not so much (a celebration of independent artists) as (garish, not to mention a series of commercials for overproduced blockbusters)

Now, are the items parallel? No. The first item is a noun phrase starting with a **determiner** (a word such as *the, a, an, some, any,* or *many*), but the second item starts with an adjective. Let's fix that:

not so much (a celebration of independent artists) as (a garish series of commercials for overproduced blockbusters)

Therefore, the correct answer is C.

Gerunds vs Infinitives

An **infinitive**—the basic *to*– form a verb like *to eat, to think,* or *to be*—is usually used as a noun. For instance, infinitives serve as both the subject and the predicate nominative of this sentence:

> *To know her is to love her.*

A **gerund**—a noun formed by adding *-ing* to a verb such as *eating, thinking,* and *being*—can also work like any other noun:

> *Being healthy is more important than being thin.*

When constructing a list, contrast, or comparison, you can often choose between an **infinitive form** (for example, *I like to hunt, swim, and fish*) and a **gerund form** (for example, *I like hunting, swimming, and fishing*). Often, the two forms are interchangeable, but sometimes one is clearly preferable to the other.

When using an **infinitive** or **gerund** in a sentence, always ask: **would the alternate form sound better?** There are few clear-cut rules for choosing between infinitives and gerunds, and most are based on convention or idiom, so once you've taken care of all grammatical considerations, trust your ear.

The real purpose of this meeting is **27** <u>for brainstorming</u> ideas about opening new markets for our European product line.

27

A) NO CHANGE
B) to brainstorm
C) the brainstorming of
D) brainstorm

The core of this sentence is *the purpose is—,* so what follows this phrase must be a noun phrase that defines the *purpose.* The prepositional phrase *for brainstorming* cannot serve as a noun phrase, because prepositional phrases are modifiers, not nouns. The only two choices that could serve as noun phrases are B and C. However, choice C is not **idiomatic** (Chapter 5, Lesson 13), and therefore the correct answer is B. As a rule of thumb, **infinitives** serve concisely to express **purpose**, as in *I went to the store <u>to buy</u> milk.*

EXERCISE SET 6: PARALLEL STRUCTURE

1. The new party platform focuses on <u>tax code reform</u>, improving the schools, and repairing relations with the labor unions.

   A) NO CHANGE
   B) reformation of the tax code
   C) reforming the tax code
   D) tax code reformation

2. Good study habits are not so much about working <u>hard, but rather about how wisely you use your time</u>.

   A) NO CHANGE
   B) hard, but using your time wisely
   C) hard as how wisely you use your time
   D) hard as about using your time wisely

3. The food here is not only very fresh, but <u>the price is also very reasonable</u>.

   A) NO CHANGE
   B) also very reasonably priced
   C) it is also very reasonably priced
   D) also very reasonable as well

4. The financial crisis was exacerbated by two important factors: the skittishness of investors and <u>the fecklessness of regulators</u>.

   A) NO CHANGE
   B) the feckless regulators
   C) how feckless the regulators were
   D) the regulators' fecklessness

5. I can't decide whether <u>I should give Maria the tickets or</u> Caitlyn.

   A) NO CHANGE
   B) to give Maria the tickets or
   C) Maria should get the tickets or
   D) to give the tickets to Maria or to

6. I prefer Liszt's technical <u>virtuosity, as opposed to</u> Chopin's romantic beauty.

   A) NO CHANGE
   B) virtuosity, rather than
   C) virtuosity to
   D) virtuosity, to

7. The festival draws tourists from all over who come not so much for the music <u>but rather because of</u> the free-wheeling, Bohemian atmosphere.

    A) NO CHANGE
    B) as for
    C) but for
    D) as because of

---

8. **Challenge Question**

Perhaps the most disappointing thing about the meeting was <u>our agenda item was never even discussed</u>.

A) NO CHANGE
B) they never even discussed our agenda item
C) that they would never even discuss our agenda item
D) that our agenda item was not even discussed

LESSON 4: DANGLING PARTICIPLES

Dangling Participles

If a **participial phrase** starts a sentence, the subject of the main clause must match the subject of the participle. If it doesn't, it's called a **dangling participle**.

- **Participles** are words, such as *broken* and *thinking*, that derive from verbs but cannot, by themselves, serve as verbs in a sentence.
- **Present participles** are words that end in *–ing*, such as *swimming*, that serve either as **components of verb phrases** or as **adjectives**:

I <u>am swimming</u>.	(verb phrase)
The pool teemed with <u>swimming</u> children.	(adjective)

NOTE: Although present **participles** and **gerunds** look identical, don't confuse them. Gerunds are *–ing* words that serve as **nouns**, as in *I love swimming*.

- **Past participles** are words, such as *toasted* or *broken*, that either end in *–ed* or take an irregular past participle form, and that also serve either as **components of verb phrases** or as **adjectives**:

I <u>have toasted</u> the bagels.	(verb phrase)
The glass <u>has broken</u>.	(verb phrase)
I love <u>toasted</u> bagels.	(adjective)
Be careful of the <u>broken</u> glass.	(adjective)

- **Consequential (or "perfect") participles** combine *having* with a past participle:

> *Having broken* the curse, Fiona finally became her true self.

Consequential participles indicate that some previous action or status **extends a consequence** to the subject of the participial phrase. In this case, the breaking of the curse affects what Fiona can do.

- A *participial phrase* is a modifying phrase that includes a participle:

> Having finished our project, we celebrated with a nice dinner.
>
> Widely considered one of the most challenging pieces for piano, Franz Liszt stretched the boundaries of musical technique with his *Etude no. 5.*
>
> **7**
>
> A) NO CHANGE
> B) the boundaries of musical technique were stretched by Franz Liszt's *Etude no. 5*
> C) Franz Liszt's *Etude no. 5* stretched the boundaries of musical technique
> D) the boundaries of musical technique were stretch by Franz Liszt with his *Etude no. 5*

The sentence begins with a participial phrase based on the past participle *considered.* What is its subject? That is, what is *widely considered one of the most challenging pieces for piano?* Clearly it is *Etude no. 5.* Since the subject of the main clause must match the subject of the participial phrase, the correct answer is C.

> Pondering this this question as so many ancient Greek philosophers did, **20** the argument Plato made was that the sphere is an "ideal form," inaccessible to our physical senses.
>
> **20**
>
> A) NO CHANGE
> B) it was Plato who argued
> C) Plato argues
> D) Plato argued

The sentence begins with a participial phrase based on the present participle *pondering.* What is its subject? That is, who was *pondering this question as so many ancient Greek philosophers did?* Clearly it is *Plato.* The subject of the main clause must therefore also be *Plato*. This eliminates A and B. Since this sentence is stating a historical fact about a long-dead philosopher, it must use the past tense, so the correct answer is D.

LESSON 5: MISPLACED MODIFIERS

Misplaced Modifiers

Modifying phrases must obey the **Law of Proximity: Every modifying phrase should be placed as close as possible to the word it modifies without disrupting the sentence.**

---

31 In an emergency, I am amazed by how composed Marco can be.

31

A) NO CHANGE
B) I am amazed, in an emergency, by how composed Marco can be.
C) I am amazed by how composed Marco can be in an emergency.
D) I am, in an emergency, amazed by how composed Marco can be.

All of these sentences are identical except for the placement of the prepositional phrase *in an emergency*. Where should it go? The Law of Proximity says it should be as close as possible to the word that it modifies. So what word does it modify? A good way to answer that is to ask: What *question* does it answer? It answers the question, *When is Marco composed?* Therefore, it is an adverbial phrase modifying the adjective *composed*, and so choice C is best, because it places the prepositional phrase after *composed*. Notice that choices A, B, and D suggest that *in an emergency* modifies the main verb of the sentence, which implies that *I am amazed* in an emergency, not that *Marco is composed* in an emergency.

---

40 A splendid example of synthetic cubism, Picasso painted *Three Musicians* in the summer of 1924.

40

A) NO CHANGE
B) Picasso painted *Three Musicians*, a splendid example of synthetic cubism,
C) Picasso, who painted *Three Musicians*, a splendid example of synthetic cubism
D) Picasso painted *Three Musicians*, a splendid example of synthetic cubism, it was

---

This sentence starts with a modifying phrase known as an **appositive**. An **appositive** is a **noun or noun phrase that acts like an adjective** and modifies the noun or noun phrase that it is adjacent to. For instance, in the phrase *baseball game*, the word *baseball* is an appositive, modifying the noun *game*. Even though *baseball* is a noun, it is acting like an adjective. Appositives are always adjacent to the nouns they modify. Since the appositive phrase *a splendid example of synthetic cubism* describes the painting, and not Picasso himself, choice A is incorrect. Choice C is incorrect because it does not contain an independent clause, and choice D is incorrect because it commits a comma splice (Chapter 5, Lesson 2), and so the correct answer is B.

EXERCISE SET 7: COORDINATION OF MODIFIERS

1. Although emotionally drained, <u>Martha's creative instinct compelled her</u> to keep writing.
   A) NO CHANGE
   B) it was her creative instinct that compelled Martha
   C) Martha was compelled by her creative instinct
   D) her creative instinct compelled Martha

2. <u>Even with a sprained ankle, the coach forced Adam</u> to go back into the game.
   A) NO CHANGE
   B) Even though Adam had a sprained angle, the coach forced him
   C) The coach, even with a sprained ankle, forced Adam
   D) Adam was forced by the coach, even with a sprained ankle,

3. Lacking any real sailing skills, <u>David's primary concern was</u> keeping the boat upright.
   A) NO CHANGE
   B) David had the primary concern of
   C) it was David's primary concern to
   D) David was primarily concerned with

4. <u>We found the long-lost manuscript searching through a box of old letters in the attic.</u>
   A) NO CHANGE
   B) Searching through a box of old letters in the attic, we found the long-lost manuscript.
   C) We found the long-lost manuscript in the attic searching through a box of old letters.
   D) In the attic, we found the long-lost manuscript searching through a box of old letters.

5. <u>To get a good jump out of the blocks, sprinters say that proper hip positioning is essential</u>.

 A) NO CHANGE

 B) For getting a good jump out of the blocks, sprinters say that proper hip positioning is essential.

 C) Sprinters say it is essential for getting a good jump out of the blocks for hip positioning to be proper.

 D) Sprinters say that proper hip positioning is essential for getting a good jump out of the blocks.

6. Although unhappy with the angry tone of the debate, <u>the senator's plan was</u> to remain calm and rational and to stick to her central policy issues.

 A) NO CHANGE

 B) the senator planned

 C) it was the senator's plan

 D) the plan was for the senator

7. After searching for months for the perfect rug, <u>we finally found one</u> at a garage sale.

 A) NO CHANGE

 B) then we finally found one

 C) one finally appeared

 D) one was finally found by us

---

8. **Challenge Question**

Although <u>famous for its visual and performing arts scene, Portland's</u> musical culture is also a source of local pride.

A) NO CHANGE

B) famous for Portland's visual and performing arts scene, its

C) Portland, being famous for its visual and performing arts scene, its

D) Portland is famous for its visual and performing arts scene, its

---

LESSON 6: MISUSED MODIFIERS

Illogical Modifiers

The modifiers in a sentence must never convey **contradictory** or **redundant** ideas.

---

21 Whenever I use Grand Central Station, my train usually never comes on time.

21

A) NO CHANGE
B) My train usually never comes on time whenever I use Grand Central Station.
C) My train usually always doesn't come on time whenever I use Grand Central Station.
D) When I use Grand Central Station, my train rarely comes on time.

The original sentence contains three words that modify the main verb: the conjunction *whenever* and the adverbs *usually* and *never*. But they are contradictory. Is my train late *whenever* I use Grand Central Station? Is it *usually* late? Is it *never* on time? Choice B just swaps the location of the modifying phrase, so it doesn't solve the problem. In choice C, *usually* contradicts both *always* and *whenever*. Choice D is best because it contains no contradictory modifiers.

Although the twins were reared by different adoptive parents in different countries, many of their idiosyncrasies **27** and peculiarities are absolutely identical.

27

A) NO CHANGE
B) are absolutely identical
C) and peculiarities are identical
D) are identical

Choices A and C are redundant because *idiosyncrasies* and *peculiarities* are synonyms. Choice B is incorrect because *identical* is an **absolute modifier**, which means that it is redundant to modify it further with adverbs such as *so, very, more, most, extremely,* or *absolutely*. (One pair of things cannot be *more identical* than another pair.) Therefore, the correct answer is D.

Adjectives vs Adverbs

Never use an **adjective** to do the job of an **adverb**.

- **Adverbs** (such as *quickly* and *gently*) modify **verbs, adjectives,** or **other adverbs**, and **usually end in -*ly*.** Some common adverbs that don't end in -*ly* are *always, away, ever, never, there, here, so, too, yet,* and *very*.
- **Adjectives** (such as *fast* and *gentle*) modify **nouns**, and usually **don't** end in -*ly*, but some do, such as *lovely, lonely, motherly, fatherly, neighborly, friendly, costly, sickly, beastly, lively, womanly, likely,* and *scholarly*.

I was impressed by how poised Ricardo was and **36** how cogent his argument was presented.

36

A) NO CHANGE
B) how cogently he presented his argument
C) his argument was presented cogently
D) he presented his argument cogently

The Law of Parallelism (Chapter 5, Lesson 3) requires that the underlined phrase begins with *how* or a similar **interrogative pronoun** (Chapter 5, Lesson 8). However, we can't use the adjective *cogent* to modify the verb *was presented*; we must use the adverb *cogently*. The only parallel option that doesn't misuse a modifier is choice B.

The movers carried the dishes **16** gentler than they did the lamp, which they had broken by accident.

16

A) NO CHANGE
B) gentler than
C) more gently than they did
D) more gently than

The underlined modifier describes the verb *carried*, so it must be a comparative adverb *more gently* rather than the comparative adjective *gentler*. Choice D is incorrect because the phrase *than the lamp* makes an **illogical comparison** (Chapter 5, Lesson 7) between a verb and a noun. The correct answer, therefore, is C.

Ambiguous Modifiers

Some words can serve as **either** adjectives or adverbs, depending on the context.

Adjective	Adverb
I drove that <u>very</u> car.	It is <u>very</u> hot.
The cat is not <u>well</u>.	She performed <u>well</u>.
She is a <u>fast</u> reader.	Don't go so <u>fast</u>.
It was a <u>straight</u> shot.	I can't shoot <u>straight</u>.
It was a <u>just</u> decision.	She <u>just</u> arrived.
We had a <u>late</u> lunch.	She arrived <u>late</u>.
You have set a <u>low</u> bar.	Don't sink so <u>low</u>.
I have <u>high</u> standards.	I can't jump very <u>high</u>.
That test was <u>hard</u>.	Don't push so <u>hard</u>.

You are not expected to come into the office if you are ▓21▓ <u>feeling sickly;</u> <u>please stay home until you are well</u>.

21

A) NO CHANGE
B) feeling sick; please stay home until you are good
C) feeling sickly; please stay home until you are good
D) feeling sick; please stay home until you are well

The word *sickly*, although it may look like an adverb because it ends in -*ly*, is an adjective meaning *feeble and often sick*. It is not appropriate to use *sickly* to describe someone who just isn't feeling well. Since the sentence is clearly referring to a temporary illness, the correct phrase is *feeling sick*. Also, the opposite of *sick* is *well*, not *good*. Therefore, the correct answer is D.

Binary and Non-binary Comparisons

Comparative adjectives (such as *faster, more beautiful, cheaper,* or *more interesting*) are used to make **binary** comparisons, that is, comparisons between only two things. **Superlative** adjectives (such as *fastest, most beautiful, cheapest,* or *most interesting*) are only used to compare **more than two things**.

I don't know which is **33** <u>most troubling:</u> his apathy or his incompetence.

33

A) NO CHANGE
B) most troubling;
C) more troubling:
D) more troubling;

The sentence mentions only two qualities, *apathy* and his *incompetence*, so the comparison requires the comparative adjective, *more troubling*. Choice D is incorrect because the phrase following the **semi-colon** (Chapter 5, Lesson 16) is not an independent clause. Choice C is correct because a **colon** (Chapter 5, Lesson 16) can indicate a **specifier**.

Comparative Forms

Comparative adjectives that are **participial** always take *more*:

> *more grueling, more tired, more shocked*

and those with **more than two syllables** usually take *more*:

> *more beautiful, more painstaking, more confrontational*

but adjectives with **one or two syllables** usually take the *-er* suffix:

> *faster, kinder, gentler.*

Incorporating the business turned out to be **11** <u>much more simple</u> than our lawyers thought it would be.

11

A) NO CHANGE
B) much more simply
C) much simpler
D) simpler by much

Since the adjective *simple* is not participial and doesn't have more than two syllables, its standard comparative form is *simpler*. Also, since it modifies the gerundive noun *incorporating,* it must take must be the comparative adjective form, *simpler,* rather than the comparative adverb form, *more simply.* Therefore, the correct answer is C.

▰▰ EXERCISE SET 8: USING MODIFIERS LOGICALLY

1. In the second debate, she was able to emphasize <u>her points much stronger</u> than she did in the first one.

   A) NO CHANGE
   B) her much stronger points
   C) her points much more strongly
   D) much more her strong points

2. Although we love to hike as a family, we <u>never usually</u> get to spend extended time in the wilderness.

   A) NO CHANGE
   B) almost never
   C) usually never
   D) hardly never

3. Once the storm winds subsided and their vehicles could be dispatched, the response teams coordinated their efforts <u>much more effective than they had after</u> the previous hurricane.

   A) NO CHANGE
   B) much more effectively than
   C) much more effectively than they had after
   D) much more effective than

4. The joy on the children's faces proved that the party was <u>an unqualified success</u>.

   A) NO CHANGE
   B) successfully unqualified
   C) a disqualified success
   D) unqualified in its success

5. Good trainers know that, although challenge is a key to success, pushing athletes <u>harder doesn't always</u> lead to better outcomes.

   A) NO CHANGE
   B) more hardly doesn't always
   C) more hard always doesn't
   D) harder always doesn't

6. Our chemistry teacher <u>never told</u> us about the test until three minutes before she gave it.

   A) NO CHANGE
   B) didn't tell
   C) never had told
   D) hardly ever told

7. Even the drastic spending cutbacks <u>won't hardly</u> address the growing budget deficit.

   A) NO CHANGE
   B) hardly wouldn't
   C) wouldn't hardly
   D) will hardly

---

8. **Challenge Question**

The works of absurdist playwrights such as Ionesco and Beckett exemplify the idea that plays <u>need not</u> rely on plot as a unifying element.

A) NO CHANGE
B) need not have to
C) don't have the need to
D) have not to

LESSON 7: LOGICAL COMPARISONS

Logical Comparisons

All comparisons must be **logical** in two ways: they must compare **only things in the same category**, and they must **not be self-contradictory**.

Anna has earned the respect of her fellow teammates by working **14** <u>harder than anyone</u> on the team.

14

A) NO CHANGE
B) more hardly than anyone
C) more hardly than anyone else
D) harder than anyone else

Recall from Chapter 5, Lesson 6 that *hard* can serve as either an adjective or an adverb, depending on the context. Here, *harder* works as a comparative adverb, modifying the verb *work*. However, the comparison is **illogical** because Anna herself is on the team, and she cannot work *harder* than she herself can. Therefore, she must be excluded from the comparison, and the correct answer is D.

The turnout for this year's art festival was even better than it was for
14 last year's.

14

A) NO CHANGE
B) last year
C) that of last year's festival
D) last year's festival's turnout

This sentence contrasts two things: *the turnout for last year's festival* and *the turnout for this year's festival*. The correct answer is A, because this phrasing makes a clear and logical contrast even though the noun phrase *art festival* is omitted. This is okay because it is implied by **parallel inference**: *The turnout for this year's art festival was even better than it was for last year's (art festival)*. Choice B makes an illogical comparison (a *turnout* cannot be compared to a *year*), and choices C and D are redundant because they both repeat the reference to the *turnout*, which is already accomplished by the pronoun *it*.

Quantitative Comparisons

Use *less*, *much*, and *amount* to refer to **continuous or uncountable quantities**, as in:

> *less traffic, much more money,* and *a large amount of food.*

Use *fewer*, *many*, and *number* to refer to **countable quantities**, as in:

> *fewer cars, many more dollars,* and *a large number of pizzas.*

If you want to refer to a quantity that is both **countable *and* continuous**, you can go either way, depending on which aspect of the quantity you want to emphasize. For instance, units like *miles* are countable yet can take continuous values, so it is not technically incorrect to say either *This car gets fewer miles per gallon* or *This car gets less miles per gallon*. But both phrases are awkward. You can avoid this awkwardness altogether by saying something like *This car is less fuel-efficient*.

> In an attempt to decrease the **41** amount of violent incidents at the festival, authorities will be selling less licenses to vendors of alcoholic beverages.
>
> **41**
>
> A) NO CHANGE
> B) amount of violence at the festival, authorities will be selling fewer
> C) number of violent incidents at the festival, authorities will be selling less
> D) amount of violent incidents at the festival, authorities will be selling fewer

Choice A is incorrect because *amount* should not be used with a countable and non-continuous quantity such as *incidents*, and *less* should not be used with a countable and non-continuous quantity such as *licenses*. Choice B corrects both problems because *violence* is uncountable but *licenses* are countable, so *amount of violence* and *fewer licenses* are both logical phrases. Choice C is incorrect because *less licenses* is illogical, and choice D is incorrect because *amount* should not be used to refer to countable quantities.

EXERCISE SET 9: LOGICAL COMPARISONS

1. Ignoring online trolls, especially the persistent ones, is often more difficult than <u>attacking them outright</u>.

   A) NO CHANGE
   B) to outright attack them
   C) to attack them outright
   D) it is attacking them outright

2. Many critics agree that Kyrchek's latest film is better than <u>anything she has done</u>.

   A) NO CHANGE
   B) everything she has done
   C) anything else she has done
   D) any of the work she did

3. The motors of all-electric cars are much quieter than <u>combustion engine cars</u>.

   A) NO CHANGE
   B) combustion engines
   C) cars with combustion engines
   D) those of combustion engines

4. The Surrealists were as <u>inscrutable, if not more so, than</u> the Dadaists.

   A) NO CHANGE
   B) inscrutable as, if not more inscrutable than,
   C) inscrutable as, if not more so, than
   D) inscrutable, if not more inscrutable, than

5. Mathematics lessons given by the Japanese teachers, unlike <u>teachers in American classrooms</u>, were focused on solving a single complex problem rather than many simpler but similar problems.

   A) NO CHANGE
   B) American teachers
   C) those given by American teachers
   D) American classrooms

6. To contemporary readers, Modernist poetry is much less accessible than even <u>Victorian or Elizabethan poetry</u>.

   A) NO CHANGE
   B) Victorian or Elizabethan poets
   C) those of Victorian or Elizabethan poets
   D) that of Victorian or Elizabethan poetry

7. As transparency in banking increases, <u>less customers will</u> voluntarily pay unreasonable account fees.

   A) NO CHANGE
   B) fewer customers would
   C) fewer customer will
   D) less customers would

---

8. **Challenge Question**

At high altitudes, even more taxing than climbing without supplemental oxygen was <u>we had to watch</u> for avalanches.

A) NO CHANGE
B) we needed to watch
C) needing to have watched
D) having to watch

LESSON 8: PRONOUN AGREEMENT

Pronoun-Antecedent Agreement

Every **definite pronoun**, such as *it*, *him*, *herself*, and *their*, must **agree in number with its antecedent**.

Our team of financial advisors safeguards the identity and confidentiality **10** of their clients.

10

A) NO CHANGE
B) of each and every client of theirs
C) of its clients
D) of every one of their clients

The pronoun *their* disagrees in number with its antecedent, *team*. (In the U.K., collective nouns like *team* are treated as plurals, but in American English they are singular.) The only choice with a singular pronoun is C.

Interrogative Pronouns

Interrogative pronouns are the pronouns we use to ask questions: *who? what? where? when? why?* and *how?* When used as **definite pronouns**, they must agree in **category** with their antecedents:

---

who = person	*when* = time
what = thing, action, or concept	*why* = reason
where = place	*how* = explanation

The filibuster is a strategy **18** <u>where</u> senators can extend debate in order to delay or prevent a vote.

18

A) NO CHANGE
B) when
C) that
D) whereby

A *strategy* is not a place, so *where* disagrees with its antecedent. It is also not a time, so B is wrong. Choice C creates an illogical sentence fragment. The correct answer is D because *whereby* means *by which*. (Unlike *where*, *whereby* does not necessarily refer to a place.)

Closest Antecedents

When an interrogative pronoun is used as a **definite pronoun**, it takes the **closest preceding noun** as its antecedent.

---

19 The game lasted until nightfall, <u>which</u> ended with a dramatic walk-off home run.

19

A) NO CHANGE
B) and
C) that
D) it

The original phrasing is incorrect because *nightfall* is the closest preceding noun to the pronoun *which*, but cannot be the logical antecedent of *which*. Choices C and D are incorrect because the both create comma splices (Chapter 5, Lesson 2). Therefore, the correct answer is B.

Shifting Pronouns

Once you choose a pronoun to refer to a particular antecedent, **stick with it**.

My wife and I enjoy going to all of our alumni events because **19** <u>you meet so many interesting people there</u>.

19

A) NO CHANGE
B) the many people that you meet there are so interesting
C) we meet so many interesting people there
D) of meeting so many interesting people there

Choices A and B contain **pronoun shifts**: the first person plural pronouns (*my wife and I, our*) shift to the second person (*you*), even though these pronouns refer to the same antecedent. Choice D is unclear and awkward because the gerund *meeting* is not linked to the subject.

EXERCISE SET 10: PRONOUN AGREEMENT

1. There are many times during a match <u>where you can lose points</u> if you fail to focus on the fundamentals.

   A) NO CHANGE
   B) where one's points can be lost
   C) when you can lose points
   D) when one's points can be lost

2. Although <u>one should never</u> read so quickly that you can't absorb the material, increasing your reading speed slightly can actually help to increase your focus and retention.

   A) NO CHANGE
   B) you should never
   C) one could never
   D) you shouldn't even

3. Learning new vocabulary words requires much more than memorizing <u>their definitions</u>.

   A) NO CHANGE
   B) it's definition
   C) they're definitions
   D) its definition

4. The mission of the Arts Council is to encourage young students to appreciate the fine and performing arts. <u>Their</u> programs have been adopted by schools citywide.

   A) NO CHANGE
   B) It's
   C) Its
   D) They're

5. Our study shows that the new training program has helped players to avoid injuries, and to recover more quickly <u>when they do</u>.

   A) NO CHANGE
   B) if they do
   C) when their injured
   D) if they do get injured

6. The bonobo, *Pan paniscus*, may be the most peaceful primate species, but <u>it is</u> not beyond occasional outbreaks of violence.

   A) NO CHANGE
   B) its
   C) they are
   D) their

7. The nitrogen cycle is the process <u>when</u> nitrogen becomes converted into different chemical forms as it is processed by marine and terrestrial eco-systems.

   A) NO CHANGE
   B) where
   C) by which
   D) so that

---

8. **Challenge Question**

The call for new hearings postponed the judge's confirmation vote, <u>that</u> fueled resentment among her supporters.

A) NO CHANGE
B) which
C) and this delay
D) this

LESSON 9: PRONOUN CASE

The Subjective and Objective Cases

A pronoun must take the **subjective** case—*I, he, she, we,* or *they*—when it acts as or is being equated with **the subject of a verb**. A pronoun must take the **objective case**—*me, him, her, us,* or *them*—when it is acting as **the object of a verb or a prepositional phrase**.

As the waiter was talking to [12] <u>Jenna and me, we</u> could see the enormous tattoo on his neck.

[12]

A) NO CHANGE
B) Jenna and I, we
C) Jenna and I, both of us
D) Jenna and me both

To determine the proper case of a pronoun, you must ask, *Is it the **subject** of a verb, or the **object** of a verb or prepositional phrase?* Since the phrase *Jenna and me* is the object of the prepositional phrase *to Jenna and me*, this pronoun is correctly in the objective case. Since the pronoun *we* serves as the subject of the verb *could see*, it is correctly in the subjective case. Therefore, the correct answer is A.

I am honored that the team has selected **7** <u>Alex and myself as</u> captains.

7

A) NO CHANGE
B) Alex and I as
C) Alex and myself for
D) Alex and me as

The original sentence uses a **reflexive** pronoun where an **objective** pronoun is required. Since the phrase *Alex and myself* is the object of the verb *has selected*, it should take the objective form, *Alex and me*, as in choice D.

But wait—isn't the reflexive *myself* required because the subject of the sentence is *I*? No, because *I* is the subject of the *first* clause, *I am honored*, but the underlined phrase is part of the *second* clause, *the team has selected Alex and me*. Since the subject and object are not one and the same in the second clause, the reflexive case is incorrect.

The Reflexive Case

A **reflexive** pronoun, such as *myself, himself, herself, oneself, ourselves*, or *themselves*, can be used as the **object of a verb or preposition when it is identical to the subject**:

> *I did it all by <u>myself</u>. She cut <u>herself</u>.*

or as an **emphatic adjective**:

> *Joan had dinner with Oprah <u>herself</u>.*
> *I <u>myself</u> would never have been invited.*

After Ronaldo's written request was rebuffed by the board, **22** <u>he took his case to Elena</u>.

22

Which choice best emphasizes the fact that Elena has a special status?

A) NO CHANGE
B) he himself took his case to Elena
C) he took his case by himself to Elena
D) he took his case to Elena herself

The only choice that *emphasizes Elena's status*, as the question requires, is D. In choice B, the reflexive pronoun emphasizes Ronaldo's *initiative*. In choice C, it emphasizes Ronaldo's *solitude*.

The Possessive Case

The possessive pronouns *your, whose, their,* and *its* **do not use apostrophes**. Their homophones with apostrophes—*you're, who's, they're, it's*—are **contractions**.

---

29 Its hard to know when you're dog is becoming dehydrated unless you check it regularly.

29

A) NO CHANGE
B) It's hard to know when your
C) Its hard to know when your
D) It's hard to know when you're

The correct answer is B. Only the contractions should get the apostrophes. Notice that the only contraction in the underlined phrase is *It's = It is*.

EXERCISE SET 11: PRONOUN CASE

1. The challenge problems were much easier for Alexa and Jill than they were for Julian and I.

    A) NO CHANGE
    B) myself and Julian
    C) Julian and me
    D) mine and Julian's

2. Since our flight leaves on Saturday, it might be difficult for him and me to stay for the entire conference.

    A) NO CHANGE
    B) him and I
    C) he and I
    D) he and myself

3. There really is no point in us delaying this decision any longer.

    A) NO CHANGE
    B) ourselves
    C) we
    D) our

4. If we are going to resolve this matter, <u>you and me</u> are going to have to make some compromises.

    A) NO CHANGE
    B) you and myself
    C) you and I
    D) I and yourself

5. Although we haven't seen each other in years, Justine and <u>myself</u> have always been closest friends.

    A) NO CHANGE
    B) me
    C) I
    D) mine

6. <u>Us Giants fans</u> have suffered through our share of disappointing defeats.

    A) NO CHANGE
    B) Us Giant's fans
    C) We Giants fan's
    D) We Giants fans

7. The owner of the restaurant offered my wife and <u>me</u> a complimentary bottle of wine.

    A) NO CHANGE
    B) myself
    C) I
    D) mine

---

8. **Challenge Question**

Gina will be spending the night at <u>a friend of her's</u> house.

A) NO CHANGE
B) her friends
C) her friend's
D) a friend of her

LESSON 10: VERB TENSE

Coordinating Tenses

The **tense** of any verb must coordinate logically with that of **any other verbs in the sentence**, as well as with the **developmental pattern of the passage as a whole**. Multiple verbs in the same sentence **do not always have to have the same tense**, but they do have to **work together to convey a clear and logical set of ideas**.

Although Frances Perkins was not the first government official to advocate for workplace safety, she **12** <u>has been the first who implemented</u> substantial labor reform through legislation such as the Fair Labor Standards Act of 1938.

12

A) NO CHANGE
B) is the first to have implemented
C) was the first having implemented
D) was the first to implement

Since both clauses refer to events that happened many decades ago, they should both use past tense verbs. Choices A and B are incorrect because they both use present tense verbs. Choice D is best because it uses the correct tense and the infinitive *to implement* is parallel to the infinitive *to advocate* in the first clause.

When Marie Curie shared the 1903 Nobel Prize in Physics with two other scientists—her husband Pierre Curie and Henri Becquerel—she **40** <u>has been</u> the first woman to win the prize.

40

A) NO CHANGE
B) would be
C) was
D) is

The two clauses in this sentence are linked by the conjunction *when*, indicating that they are indicating simultaneous events or states of being. Since the first verb, *shared*, is in the past tense, the second one should be as well. Therefore, the correct answer is C.

Historical vs Timeless Facts

In standard English, **historical** facts take the **past tense**, but **timeless** facts or beliefs take the **present tense**.

The ancient Greek philosopher Zeno **19** taught that change is an illusion.

19

A) NO CHANGE
B) teaches that change is an illusion
C) teaches that change was an illusion
D) taught that change would be an illusion

The fact that Zeno was a teacher is a *historical* fact and so *taught* should take the past tense, but the belief that *"change is an illusion"* may or may not be tied to a previous era. If you want to imply that this belief is no longer accepted, you may put it in the past tense: *The ancient Greek philosopher Zeno taught that change was an illusion.* But if you want to imply that it is still widely believed, you may use the present tense: *The ancient Greek philosopher Zeno taught that change is an illusion.* The only grammatically correct option, then, is choice A.

Currency

Facts about the content of currently available works of art or literature—even if they were created long ago—have **currency**, and therefore take the **present tense**.

In Act V of *King Lear*, Cordelia and Lear **10** were captured by Edmund, who had promised to show them no mercy.

10

A) NO CHANGE
B) were captured by Edmund, who has
C) are captured by Edmund, who had
D) are captured by Edmund, who has

Since *King Lear* is a widely available work of literature, its action is conventionally described in the present tense. Only choice D places both verbs correctly in the present tense.

LESSON 11: VERB ASPECT

Verb Aspects

The **aspect** of a verb indicates **how its action or status applies to the subject or situation**. For example, several different aspects can be applied to the present tense verb *to eat*.

I eat.	= I am in the habit of eating. (**habitual** aspect)
I am eating.	= I am in the process of eating. (**progressive** aspect)
I have to eat.	= I feel compelled to eat. (**compulsive** aspect)
I have eaten.	= My present status is a consequence of previous eating. (**consequential** aspect)
I have been eating.	= My present status is a consequence of previous eating, and I am still eating. (**consequential** and **progressive** aspects)

Ever since it reached its peak in 1991, violent crime **10** declined precipitously, not just in the United States but around the globe.

10

A) NO CHANGE
B) have declined
C) has declined
D) would decline

This sentence indicates that a current status is a **consequence** of a previous situation, and therefore the present consequential form in choice C, *has declined*, is correct. Choice A is incorrect because the phrase *ever since* indicates that the decline is not an isolated event in the past. Choice B is incorrect because the verb does not agree in number with the subject, *crime*. Choice D is incorrect because this statement is not counterfactual or hypothetical, and therefore the **subjunctive mood** (Chapter 5, Lesson 15) is inappropriate.

The Consequential Aspect

The **consequential aspect** in verbs such as *have eaten*, *had eaten*, and *will have eaten* indicates **status-as-consequence**.

> *I have lost my keys.*

The consequential aspect in this sentence indicates that my **current status is a consequence** of some previous act of losing. In other words, I don't currently have my keys. Notice that the simple past tense does not do this:

> *I lost my keys yesterday, but found them this morning.*

This does not imply that the act of losing extends any consequence to my current state, because I *do* in fact have my keys now.

Unlike its competitors, which have enjoyed a long period of profitability, PinkCorp **31** <u>had</u> its share of financial troubles.

31

A) NO CHANGE
B) has had
C) would have
D) would have had

Since the first verb, *have enjoyed*, is in the present tense, this sentence is comparing the *current* fortunes of PinkCorp with the *current* fortunes of its competitors. Therefore, the main verb should also be in the present tense. Choice A is incorrect because it is in the past tense. Choices C and D are incorrect because the sentence is indicating facts, not hypothetical or counterfactual situations, and therefore the **subjunctive mood** (Chapter 5, Lesson 15) is incorrect. Choice B is correct because it uses the **present consequential** form to show that PinkCorp's previous troubles affect its current status.

Irregular Verb Forms

Verbs in the **consequential aspect** always use the **past participle** (Chapter 5, Lesson 4) form of the verb, as in *had taken*, *has taken*, and *will have taken*. Some of these past participles take **irregular forms**.

Verb	Past tense	Past participle
to arise	arose	arisen
to beat	beat	beaten
to begin	began	begun
to blow	blew	blown
to break	broke	broken
to come	came	come
to do	did	done
to draw	drew	drawn
to drink	drank	drunk*
to drive	drove	driven
to fly	flew	flown
to go	went	gone
to know	knew	known
to lay (put)	laid	laid
to lie (down)	lay	lain
to ride	rode	ridden
to run	ran	run
to shrink	shrank	shrunk*
to sink	sank	sunk*
to speak	spoke	spoken
to spring	sprang	sprung
to swim	swam	swum
to take	took	taken
to tear	tore	torn
to write	wrote	written

*When these participles are used as **adjectives**, they can also take the -en suffix, as in *drunken sailor, shrunken heads*, and *sunken ship*. However, these alternate forms are **not** used in verb phrases. For instance, we would never say *baby Leonard has drunken his milk*. Instead, we would say *baby Leonard has drunk his milk*.

Douglas was not offered the CEO position, even though he `10` has ran one of the largest divisions within the company for nearly ten years.

`10`

A) NO CHANGE
B) runs
C) is running
D) has run

Choice A is incorrect because the present consequential form requires the past participle, but *ran* is the past tense form of *to run*, not the past participle.

Choices B and C are incorrect because neither the simple present tense *runs* nor the present progressive *is running* works logically with the modifier *for nearly ten years*.

Present vs Consequential Participles

A **present participle phrase** indicates that the participial verb and the main verb have the **same tense**. If you want to indicate that the participial verb **precedes and extends a consequence to** the main verb, use the **consequential participle**. The consequential participle combines *having* with the past participle, as in *having spoken*.

---

36 Taking the honors-level introductory physics course, Jess felt prepared to begin AP physics level 2.

36

A) NO CHANGE
B) Having took
C) Having taken
D) She took

The present participle *taking* implies that Jess took introductory physics and AP physics at the **same time**. Of course, this is illogical: she felt good about taking AP physics because she had *already taken* introductory physics. Therefore, the consequential participle *having taken* is required, as in choice C. Choice B is incorrect because *took* is the past tense form, not the past participle form. Choice D is incorrect because it creates a comma splice and does not indicate any logical relationship between the clauses.

▮▮ EXERCISE SET 12: VERB TENSE AND ASPECT

1. <u>Developing the first hydrogen cell engine, the team should hope</u> to reveal it at the technology expo this December.
   A) NO CHANGE
   B) Having developed the first hydrogen cell engine, the team would hope
   C) Developing the first hydrogen cell engine, the team hopes
   D) Having developed the first hydrogen cell engine, the team hopes

2. Without <u>spending so much as an hour on research, Dale already wrote</u> the first draft of her term paper.
   A) NO CHANGE
   B) having spent so much as an hour on research, Dale has already written
   C) spending so much as an hour on research, Dale has written
   D) having spent so much as an hour on research, Dale has already wrote

3. As soon as Hannah <u>arrived home from vacation, she had</u> immediately started to plan her next trip.

    A) NO CHANGE
    B) had arrived home from vacation, she
    C) had arrived home from vacation, she had
    D) arrived home from vacation, she

4. <u>Having taken the wrong path, the hikers feared</u> that they might not be able to reach base camp by nightfall.

    A) NO CHANGE
    B) Taking the wrong path, the hikers feared
    C) Having taken the wrong path, the hikers had feared
    D) Taking the wrong path, the hikers had feared

5. Although *Pinocchio* may seem like a quaint children's story, its characters <u>would represent</u> some of the central archetypes from Greek, Roman, Judeo-Christian, and even Babylonian mythological traditions.

    A) NO CHANGE
    B) represented
    C) represent
    D) had represented

6. Elayna is well-qualified for this position because she <u>has performed</u> very well as a team leader on many similar projects.

    A) NO CHANGE
    B) had performed
    C) would perform
    D) was performing

7. Hundreds of recreational divers come each year to explore the site where the galleon <u>had sank </u>over three hundred years ago.

    A) NO CHANGE
    B) sank
    C) has sunk
    D) has sank

8. At his death in 2010, J.D. Salinger was regarded as one of the premier writers of the 20th-century, <u>he had only published</u> one full-length novel, *The Catcher in the Rye*.

    A) NO CHANGE
    B) although he would have published only
    C) despite having published only
    D) although he would publish only

Elite Challenge Question

9. In *Twenty Thousand Leagues Under the Sea*, Jules Verne predicted the electric submarine, a device that <u>would not be invented</u> for another 90 years.

A) NO CHANGE
B) had not been invented
C) would not have been invented
D) will not be invented

LESSON 12: DICTION AND REDUNDANCY

Redundancy

The Law of Parsimony states that, all else being equal, **shorter is better**.

When considering whether to add a word or phrase to a sentence, always ask: does this actually **add relevant meaning** to the sentence? If not, leave it out.

Michael stole the ball and 31 <u>sped quickly down the court with only seconds remaining left to go</u> in the game.

31

A) NO CHANGE
B) sped quickly down the court with only seconds remaining
C) sped down the court with only seconds left
D) sped down the court with only seconds remaining to go

The original sentence is triply redundant. The verb *to speed* means *to run quickly*, so the phrase *sped quickly* is redundant. Also, the phrase *remaining left to go* is doubly redundant, since the phrases *seconds remaining in the game*, *seconds left in the game*, and *seconds to go in the game* all mean the same thing. The only option without redundancy is C.

In 1922, the totalitarian governments of Italy and Germany closed all Montessori schools and declared 20 <u>them subversive in that they might undermine the regimes</u>.

20

A) NO CHANGE
B) that they were subversive in undermining the regimes
C) them subversive in undermining the regimes
D) them subversive

The adjective *subversive* means *seeking to undermine the established power structure*. Therefore, the phrases in choices A, B, and C are redundant, so the best choice is D.

Clarity of Expression

Clarity of expression questions ask you to choose the word or phrase that best conveys a particular idea. When tackling these questions, read the entire sentence, note the phrase in which the word or phrase is embedded, and make sure that it **clearly and logically conveys the idea** that the sentence intends.

Word of Montessori's success with the Casa dei Bambini soon began to **17** distribute internationally, and her methods for child-centered education became widely adopted across Europe.

17

A) NO CHANGE
B) increase
C) spread
D) exhibit

The subject of the verb *distribute* is *Word of Montessori's success*, which is a type of information. But information cannot logically *distribute* anything, so choice A is incorrect. Choice B is incorrect because information cannot *increase*. Choice D is incorrect because information cannot *exhibit*. The only choice that conveys a clear and logical idea is choice C, *spread*, which helps convey the fact that news of Montessori's success became widely known.

Common Mix-Ups

Some diction errors are **"sound-alike"** errors, in which words are confused with similar-sounding words. Below is a list of common mix-ups. Make flashcards for the pairs that confuse you.

accept (v) = to agree to take
I accept the offer.
except (prep) = not including
I like all except that one.

adapt (v) = to make suitable to a purpose
I adapted the motor to fit the boat.
adopt (v) = to choose as one's own
They adopted a child.
adept (adj) = highly skilled
She's an adept speaker.

affect (v) = to influence
It affected me deeply.
effect (n) = result or consequence
It had a good effect.

allude (v) = to make an indirect reference
He alluded to their secret.
elude (v) = to escape from; to avoid
They eluded capture.

allusion (n) = an indirect reference
Her speech included an allusion to Othello.
illusion (n) = misconception or misperception
I love optical illusions.

ambivalent (adj) = having conflicting feelings
I feel ambivalent about going the party.
ambiguous (adj) = having more than one meaning
That phrase is ambiguous.

cite (v) = to credit as a source of information
The author cited many sources.
cite (v) = to commend for meritorious action
She was cited for bravery.
site (n) = location of a particular activity or structure
That is the site of the battle of Antietam.
sight (v) = to see at a specific location
She was sighted in the crowd.

compliment (n) = a praising personal comment
Compliments are always appreciated.
complement (n) = something that makes a whole
Brie is a fine complement to this wine.

council (n) = an advisory committee
I'm a member of the executive council.
counsel (v) = to give advice
She counseled me wisely.

discrete (adj) = distinct
The machine has hundreds of discrete parts.
discreet (adj) = prudently secretive
Please be discreet about our meeting.

elicit (v) = to bring out or to call forth
The joke elicited uncomfortable laughter.
illicit (adj) = unlawful
Don't engage in illicit activities.

eminent (adj) = prominent and distinguished
She is an eminent historian.

imminent (adj) = about to happen
I sense imminent laughter.

flaunt (v) = to show (something) off
If you've got it, flaunt it.

flout (v) = to show disregard for
Don't flout the rules.

gambit (n) = a risky opening move
He made a bold strategic gambit.

gamut (n) = the complete range
Her emotions ran the gamut.

imply (v) = to suggest or hint at
A handshake implies an agreement.

infer (v) = to draw a conclusion from evidence
Please don't infer hostile intent.

phase (n) = stage in a process
This is the third phase of the project.

faze (n) = to disturb (someone's) composure
She was not fazed by the interruption.

precede (v) = to come before
Thunder is always preceded by lightning.

proceed (v) = to go on, usually after a pause
Please proceed with the task.

principal (n) = head of a school
Our principal spoke at the assembly.

principal (n) = the initial investment in an account
Many investments risk a loss of principal.

principle (n) = guiding rule or value
I reject that proposal on principle.

reticent (adj) = reserved or reluctant to talk freely
He has been reticent in our therapy sessions.

reluctant (adj) = disinclined to do something
I'm reluctant to reveal personal information.

EXERCISE SET 13: DICTION AND REDUNDANCY

1. Even the strongest pesticides could not <u>abolish</u> the beetles.
    A) NO CHANGE
    B) delete
    C) retract
    D) eradicate

2. Although statistics cannot prove theories, <u>but they can invalidate</u> them by ruling out the correlations they imply.
    A) NO CHANGE
    B) they can refute
    C) but they can debunk
    D) they can smear

3. Well-trained wine experts can <u>separate out</u> the tastes of dozens of different grapes, regions, and vintages.
    A) NO CHANGE
    B) certify
    C) acknowledge
    D) discern

4. It's almost impossible to achieve <u>a consensus of unified opinion</u> on those matters on which the group members have widely different priorities and values.
    A) NO CHANGE
    B) a unified consensus of opinion
    C) a consensus in opinion
    D) consensus

5. Often, the town council will debate an issue for weeks before <u>appointing</u> a formal decision.
    A) NO CHANGE
    B) compelling
    C) making
    D) predetermining

6. Although loved by audiences worldwide, the film was soundly <u>disparaged</u> by many critics.
    A) NO CHANGE
    B) confronted
    C) impaired
    D) repudiated

7. <u>At the present moment in time, we</u> cannot process your request because we have lost the connection to our server.

    A) NO CHANGE
    B) At this moment in time, we
    C) Currently, we
    D) We

8. After the neighbors filed a noise complaint, the workers had to <u>hamper</u> their work by 6:00 every evening or risk municipal fines.

    A) NO CHANGE
    B) subside
    C) curtail
    D) lower

9. Once she found a supportive group of friends who appreciated her talents and idiosyncrasies, Daryl's self-esteem began to <u>proliferate</u>.

    A) NO CHANGE
    B) blossom
    C) multiply
    D) enlarge

10. Taxpayers are unlikely to fund an expensive public project unless it is designed to solve <u>an imminent problem that is likely to occur in the future</u>.

    A) NO CHANGE
    B) a problem that is imminently likely to occur in the future
    C) a problem that is imminently likely
    D) an imminent problem

11. Originally built as an engine for a small tractor, the motor had to be <u>evolved</u> in order to meet the needs of the portable generator.

    A) NO CHANGE
    B) correlated
    C) amended
    D) adapted

12. The sounds, themes, and images in advertisements are carefully chosen to subtly <u>intimidate</u> consumers to buy things they may not need.

    A) NO CHANGE
    B) propel
    C) induce
    D) oppress

13. The negotiations became very <u>apprehensive</u> when the topic shifted to company ownership.

   A) NO CHANGE
   B) neurotic
   C) tense
   D) worried

14. Although he is usually <u>reticent to talk about</u> his personal life, he is more than happy to talk about the merits of the different *Star Wars* films.

   A) NO CHANGE
   B) reticent about
   C) disinclined to talk with regard to
   D) unwilling about

15. Many of the government ministers have been in exile since they were <u>impeded</u> in the 2016 military coup.

   A) NO CHANGE
   B) scuttled
   C) ousted
   D) snubbed

16. Corporations that value cooperation over competition tend to see <u>less incidents of elicit</u> behavior such as embezzlement.

   A) NO CHANGE
   B) fewer incidents of illicit
   C) fewer incidence of illicit
   D) less incidents of illicit

---

17. **Challenge Question**

He liked to make provocative comments in his speeches, but was unwilling to deal with the blowback that would inevitably <u>derive</u>.

A) NO CHANGE
B) pursue
C) advance
D) ensue

18. **Challenge Question**

The reason that many distance runners fail to hit their marathon goals is <u>because they don't safeguard</u> a steady pace throughout the race.

A) NO CHANGE
B) that they don't perpetuate
C) that they don't maintain
D) because they don't prolong

LESSON 13: IDIOMATIC EXPRESSION

Idioms

An **idiom** is a common phrase that has a rigid wording and (usually) a non-literal meaning. Examples include *a piece of cake, push through, on fire, see the light, go in on, drop by,* and *under fire.* When using idioms, be sure that you understand their meanings and phrase them precisely.

To catch idiom errors on the SAT, pay attention to **prepositions** (words such as *for, in, on, of, by, to, with,* and so on, as discussed in Chapter 4, Lesson 2), and trust your ear: when a preposition is underlined, ask: **would another preposition sound better here, or is a preposition necessary at all?** Don't think too hard: idioms often have non-literal meanings, so they sometimes defy logic.

Games and other group challenges are a means `39` <u>through fostering team spirit to</u> the campers.

`39`

A) NO CHANGE
B) of fostering team spirit among
C) for fostering team spirit for
D) of fostering team spirit with

Always pay special attention when an underlined phrase contains a **preposition**. Notice whether the choices include alternative prepositions, and (if so) **trust your ear** to choose among them. Which sounds more natural: *a means <u>through</u> fostering, a means <u>for</u> fostering,* or *a means <u>of</u> fostering?* Hopefully, your ear tells you that the last choice is the most idiomatic. In order to choose between B and D, you have to check another idiomatic phrase. Which sounds more natural: *team spirit <u>among</u> the campers,* or *team spirit <u>to</u> the campers?* The first one is more idiomatic, so the correct answer is B.

Prepositional Idioms

Most **idiom errors** are **wrong preposition errors**. Prepositions play an essential role in many idiomatic phrases, and it's easy to mix them up. A wrong preposition can make a phrase **unidiomatic**, or it can turn it into a **completely different idiom**.

---

agree with = share the opinion of (a person)
agree to = accept (a proposal or offer)
agree on = arrive at (a mutual decision)
agree about = have similar sentiments about (a situation)

angry with = annoyed at (a person)
angry about = annoyed about (a situation)

concerned with = involved with (an activity or issue)
concerned about = worried about (a situation)

take in = apprehend (an idea or perception)
take on = undertake (a challenge); oppose (a person)
take after = resemble (a parent or mentor)

wait for = stay until (an event)
wait on = serve (someone) at a restaurant

The first amendment to the Constitution is concerned primarily **39** <u>about</u> the Enlightenment values of free thought and free expression.

39

A) NO CHANGE
B) for
C) with
D) DELETE the underlined word

Although it is idiomatic to say *the first amendment is <u>about</u>* something, it is **not** idiomatic to say *the first amendment is <u>concerned about</u>* something, because the idiomatic phrase *concerned about* means *worried about*, and a constitutional amendment cannot worry. On the other hand, *concerned with* means *involved with as a matter of interest*, which fits the context of this sentence perfectly. Therefore, the correct answer is C.

EXERCISE SET 14: IDIOMATIC EXPRESSION

1. After exchanging dozens of texts over several weeks, we all finally agreed <u>with</u> a plan to go hiking in the Adirondacks.
    A) NO CHANGE
    B) to
    C) on
    D) for

2. The new color scheme for the living room is not very different <u>than</u> the old one.
    A) NO CHANGE
    B) to
    C) compared to
    D) from

3. The lawyers will be reviewing employee contracts in the next few days to be sure that they comply <u>in</u> the recently updated regulations.
    A) NO CHANGE
    B) about
    C) with
    D) to

4. I prefer the soft, diffuse light of the new LED bulbs <u>more than</u> the light of the old compact fluorescent bulbs.
    A) NO CHANGE
    B) over
    C) to
    D) in comparison to

5. Although the terms of the plea deal seemed very generous, the defendant did not agree <u>to</u> the offer because it included an admission of guilt.
    A) NO CHANGE
    B) about
    C) with
    D) on

6. Several agents were dispatched to Philadelphia <u>for the purpose of investigating</u> the new leads.
    A) NO CHANGE
    B) for investigating
    C) to investigate about
    D) to investigate

7. The professor has sole authority to determine <u>about which activities qualify for</u> field credit.
    A) NO CHANGE
    B) which activities qualify for
    C) about which activities qualify in
    D) which activities that qualify for

8. The teens were at the school board meeting to voice their arguments <u>on</u> the proposal to moving the school starting time.
    A) NO CHANGE
    B) with
    C) for
    D) to

9. The final song was a tribute <u>about</u> Dr. Whelan, the choral director who would be retiring in June.
    A) NO CHANGE
    B) on
    C) for
    D) to

10. **Challenge Question**

Because they convey complex information in forms that are easy to recall, acronyms such as SOH-CAH-TOA serve <u>to be</u> effective mnemonic devices.

A) NO CHANGE
B) as
C) like
D) for

LESSON 14: THE ACTIVE AND PASSIVE VOICES

The Passive Voice

When the subject of a verb is not the "actor" of that verb, the clause is in the **passive voice**. For instance, *the boy kicked the ball* is an **active voice** clause because the subject, *boy*, indicates who is doing the kicking. But *the ball was kicked by the boy* is in the passive voice, because the subject, *ball*, indicates what is <u>receiving</u> the kicking.

Henry ate all of his steak, but `33` <u>his vegetables were</u> uneaten.

`33`

A) NO CHANGE
B) left his vegetables
C) had his vegetables left
D) so his vegetables were

The first clause, *Henry ate all of his steak*, is in the **active voice**, but in choices A and D, the second clause is in the **passive voice**, and so does not attribute the action to *Henry*. Choice C is awkward and unclear. Choice B improves the parallelism and clarity of the sentence by matching the voices of the clauses and indicating who is leaving the vegetables uneaten.

Our lab experiment was designed by Amy and `33` <u>Antonio ran it</u>.

`33`

A) NO CHANGE
B) run by Antonio
C) Antonio was the one who ran it
D) was ran by Antonio

The first clause of this compound sentence is in the **passive voice**. Since the second clause concerns the same subject as the first, the Law of Parallelism suggests that it should also take the passive voice. Choices A and C are incorrect because they are in the active voice. Choice D uses the past tense form *ran* rather than the past participle *run*. The most concise and parallel option is B.

Which Voice Should I Use?

Passive clauses are usually wordier and less direct than active clauses. To be concise and direct, use the active voice. However, on the SAT, the passive voice is not necessarily wrong. Passive clauses can be used whenever it is helpful to emphasize the receiver of an action or status.

I came out of my physical examination feeling as if **18** they had poked me with a hundred probes and somebody had stabbed me with a hundred needles.

18

A) NO CHANGE
B) I had been poked by a hundred probes and they had stabbed me with
C) they had poked me with a hundred probes and I had been stabbed by
D) I had been poked by a hundred probes and stabbed by

Choice D is the most parallel option because the last two clauses share a subject, the passive voice, and similar prepositional phrases. In choices A, B, and C the voices are inconsistent and the pronoun *they* lacks a clear antecedent.

12 To prevent potentially fatal errors by surgeons and nurses, a checklist is carefully executed before each operation starts.

12

A) NO CHANGE
B) errors, surgeons and nurses carefully execute a checklist before each operation starts
C) errors by surgeons and nurses before each operation starts, a checklist is carefully executed
D) errors by surgeons and nurses, before each operation starts a checklist is carefully executed

Choices A, C, and D are vague because the passive voice makes it unclear who is executing the checklist. For clarity, the writer should indicate the "actor" of the verb clearly and directly. Choice B accomplishes this by placing the main clause in the active voice.

LESSON 15: VERB MOOD

What Is Grammatical Mood?

The **mood** of a verb indicates the general purpose of the clause.

- The **indicative** mood indicates **factual claims**, as in *I went to the park.*
- The **imperative** mood indicates **suggestions or commands**, as in *You should go to the park*, or *Go to the park!*
- The **interrogative mood** asks questions, as in *Did you go to the park?*
- The **subjunctive mood** indicates **counterfactuals, hypotheticals,** or **potentials,** as in *I wish I had gone to the park* or *You may go to the park after school.*

> If the engine 40 <u>would run</u> for too long on low-grade fuel, the pistons will wear out.
>
> 40
>
> A) NO CHANGE
> B) were to run
> C) runs
> D) should run

Conditional (*if-then*) statements are not always subjunctive. Consider the theorem *If two sides of a triangle are congruent, then its base angles are congruent.* This is a **fact**, so each clause is phrased in the **indicative** mood. This sentence represents a similar *if-then* fact. The second clause, *the pistons will wear out*, is in the **indicative** mood. Therefore, the first clause should be in the indicative mood also, as in choice C.

> If my lawyer 13 <u>would have been</u> more thorough in his cross-examination, he would have revealed the inconsistencies in her testimony.
>
> 13
>
> A) NO CHANGE
> B) had been
> C) is
> D) has been

The underlined verb is **counterfactual**, because it indicates that my lawyer was **not** thorough. Therefore, the first clause should take the **subjunctive mood**. However, choice A is incorrect because *would have been* is not idiomatic phrasing for an *if–* clause. The correct subjunctive form is *had been*, as in choice B. Choices C and D are incorrect because they are both in the indicative mood.

The Imperative Mood

Commands or requests in the **imperative mood** can be indicated in three ways.

- To make a **direct, second-person command**, use the **infinitive** form without an explicit subject, as in *Stop smoking!*
- To express a command or suggestion that is **indicated by another verb** (such as *prefer that, suggest that, demand that, propose that*, or *insist that*) or **adjective** (such as *it is necessary/important/imperative/essential/better/vital/crucial that*) use the **infinitive** form with an explicit subject, as in *My doctor demanded that I stop smoking* or *My doctor said that it is necessary that I stop smoking.*

- To express a command or suggestion that is **not** indicated by another verb or adjective, use the auxiliary *should* or *must* before the infinitive form, as in *My doctor said that I <u>must stop</u> smoking.*

After Ms. Parker scolded Daniel for the third time, she demanded that he 31 <u>left</u> the room.

31

A) NO CHANGE
B) must leave
C) leave
D) should leave

The verb *demanded* indicates that the underlined verb is a command, so *must* or *should* would be redundant. We must indicate the imperative with the infinitive *leave*, as in choice C. Choice A is incorrect because it is in the indicative mood. Choices B and D are incorrect because they include redundant auxiliaries.

The Subjunctive Mood

The subjunctive mood is usually indicated by **subjunctive auxiliaries**: *can, could, may, might,* and *would.* A verb in the **present subjunctive** takes an auxiliary followed by the **infinitive** form of the verb, as in *We <u>might go</u> to the beach.* A verb in the **past subjunctive** takes an auxiliary followed by the **present consequential** (Chapter 5, Lesson 11) form of the verb, as in *Your grandmother <u>would have loved</u> to see you in that dress.*

However, if a **counterfactual** is part of a **conditional** (*if–*) or **wishful** (*I wish that–*) clause that is **not indicating permission or potential**, it does **not** take a subjunctive auxiliary.

- If a verb is in a **present wishful or conditional counterfactual** clause, it takes the **simple past** form without an auxiliary, as in *I wish I <u>had</u> a million dollars* or *If I <u>had</u> a million dollars. . . .*
- If the verb *to be* is in a **present wishful or conditional counterfactual** clause, it takes the form *were* without an auxiliary, as in *I wish I <u>were</u> ten years younger* or *If I <u>were</u> ten years younger. . . .*
- If a verb is in a **past wishful or conditional counterfactual** clause, it takes the **past consequential** form without an auxiliary, as in *I wish I <u>had caught</u> the ball* or *If I <u>had caught</u> the ball. . . .*

After the game, the coach admitted that he **10** <u>would not have called</u> the trick play if his starting quarterback had been playing.

10

Which choice best indicates that the coach was uncertain about his options?

A) NO CHANGE
B) did not call
C) might not have called
D) could not have called

The question asks you to choose the option that indicates *that the coach was uncertain about his options*. Choice A is incorrect because it is consistent with the possibility that the coach knew precisely which plays he would have called for each quarterback. Choice B is incorrect because this clause is counterfactual, and so cannot take the indicative mood. Choice D is incorrect because the auxiliary *could* indicates **inability** rather than **uncertainty**. Choice C is correct because *might* indicates that the coach was **not certain** about what he would have done if the starting quarterback had been in the game.

Conditional Counterfactuals

Any **present conditional counterfactual** form of the verb *to be* is usually phrased starting with *if–*, but in formal writing it can start with *were*:

Typical: *If I were shorter, I could wear that outfit.*
Formal: *Were I shorter, I could wear that outfit.*

Similarly, any **past conditional counterfactual** clause can be phrased starting with *if–* or with *had*:

Typical: *If he had studied, he would have passed the test.*
Formal: *Had he studied, he would have passed the test.*

The sailors would not have encountered the hurricane **31** <u>had they departed</u> only a day earlier.

31

A) NO CHANGE
B) if they would have departed
C) if they departed
D) if they would depart

The underlined phrase indicates a **past conditional counterfactual**, so it should take the form *if they had departed*. However, this is not a choice. Fortunately, choice A provides an equivalent phrasing, so it is the correct answer. Choices B and D are incorrect because a conditional counterfactual does not take the auxiliary *would*. Choice C is incorrect because a counterfactual cannot take the indicative mood.

EXERCISE SET 15: VERB MOOD AND VOICE

1. Samuel Langhorne Clemens, who would later come to be known as Mark Twain, <u>would have been 25 years old when the Civil War started</u> in 1861.

   A) NO CHANGE
   B) would of been 25 years old when the Civil War had started
   C) was 25 years old when the Civil War started
   D) was 25 years old when the Civil War would have started

2. If the goalie <u>had not slipped</u> backward, he might not have blocked the shot and saved the game.

   A) NO CHANGE
   B) did not slip
   C) had not of slipped
   D) would not have slipped

3. The ushers demanded that we <u>must turn</u> off our cell phones until the intermission.

   A) NO CHANGE
   B) should turn
   C) turn
   D) turned

4. As we move through our daily routines, we tend to become agitated when our rituals are changed, our habits are disrupted, or <u>something violates our expectations</u>.

   A) NO CHANGE
   B) our expectations are violated
   C) something would violate our expectations
   D) something violated our expectations

5. As expected, <u>the rule against protests was dropped by the management</u>, who even expressed sympathy with the workers who had registered their complaints.

A) NO CHANGE
B) the rule against protests would have been dropped by the management
C) the management would have dropped the rule against protests
D) the management dropped the rule against protests

6. If the strong winds and rains <u>would have continued</u> for much longer, the small island town probably would have lost power completely.

A) NO CHANGE
B) had continued
C) continued
D) did continue

7. Our tour guide suggested that <u>we explore the tiny hillside town</u>, which is nearly 17 centuries old.

A) NO CHANGE
B) the tiny hillside town be explored by us
C) we should explore the tiny hillside town
D) we had explored the tiny hillside town

8. As Gina began climbing the long staircase, she wished that she <u>would have wore</u> her pumps instead of high heels.

A) NO CHANGE
B) had worn
C) would have worn
D) wore

9. **Challenge Question**

Our financial advisor strongly suggested that <u>we be more consistent with our investments</u> and even automate monthly transfers from our checking to our retirement account.

A) NO CHANGE
B) we are more consistent with our investments
C) our investments should be more consistent
D) our investments be more consistent

LESSON 16: PUNCTUATION

Punctuation for Interrupters

Interrupting modifiers must be bracketed by **identical punctuation marks**: either both commas or both dashes. Dashes are slightly more emphatic than commas and draw more attention to the interrupter.

> The 42 coelacanth—a fish species once widely believed to be extinct, is found primarily in the tropical waters of the Indian Ocean.
>
> **42**
>
> A) NO CHANGE
> B) coelacanth—a fish species once widely believed to be extinct—is
> C) coelacanth: a fish species once widely believed to be extinct—is
> D) coelacanth, a fish species once widely believed to be extinct is

Choice A is incorrect because the **interrupting appositive** is bracketed by different punctuation marks: a dash and a comma. Only choice B uses the same punctuation mark on both ends of the interrupter.

Apostrophes

Apostrophes should be used exclusively for **possessives** and **contractions**. **Don't use apostrophes to pluralize** except in very rare situations in which the alternative is awkward, such as *She got all A's on her report card*.

> Only after a class-action suit was filed did the landlord consider giving the 42 renter's their money back.
>
> **42**
>
> A) NO CHANGE
> B) renters their
> C) renter's they're
> D) renters there

Here, *renters* is a plural non-possessive noun, and *their* is a plural possessive pronoun. Choices A and C are incorrect because apostrophes should only be used in contractions and possessives. Choice D is incorrect because *there* is not a plural possessive pronoun. Therefore, the correct answer is B.

Possessives

To turn a plural noun ending in -s into a possessive, just add an apostrophe at the end. For instance, *the boys' swim team.* For singular nouns that end in -s, tack on -'s. For instance, *Mr. Jones's class.*

The possessive pronouns *your, whose, their,* and *its* do not use apostrophes. Their homophones with apostrophes—*you're, who's, they're, it's*—are **contractions**.

They did not know it at the time, but Gwen was <u>Chris's cousin's</u> daughter.

A) NO CHANGE
B) Chris' cousin's
C) Chris's cousins
D) Chris' cousins

Both underlined words are possessives: the daughter is the *cousin's daughter* and the cousin is *Chris's cousin.* Even though *Chris* ends in an *–s,* it is not plural, so it is incorrect to use only an apostrophe to make it possessive. Both words require the *–'s* possessive form, so the correct answer is A.

Use Commas Sparingly

As a rule of thumb, **only use commas where necessary**. Commons are more often overused than underused.

The <u>subject, that intimidates me the most, is</u> calculus.

A) NO CHANGE
B) subject that intimidates me the most, is
C) subject, that intimidates me the most is
D) subject that intimidates me the most is

The phrase *that intimidates me the most* is a **restrictive clause**, which means that the sentence would lose its central meaning if it were removed. Therefore, it shouldn't be separated from the main clause by commas, as in choice A. In fact, no commas are necessary at all, so the correct answer is D.

When to Use Commas

Commas are used primarily to separate

- **items in a list**, as in
  He was fat, dumb, and lazy.
- **coordinate adjectives**, as in
  He gave a long, boring speech.
- **modifying phrases** from the main clause, as in
  In fact, I am appalled.
- **dependent clauses** from the main clause, as in
  Whenever I try, I fail.
- **independent clauses** from other independent
  clauses, but **only with a conjunction**, as in
  I think, therefore I am.

Commas can also be used to

- **introduce a quotation,** as in
  Tom said, "I ain't goin'!"
- **indicate an appositive title,** as in
  She read from her book, Blue Nights.
- **format an address or date**, as in
  Saturday, July 19, 2014 or *Cleveland, Ohio.*
- **signal an addressee,** as in
  Get going, buster!

The **16** philosopher, Immanuel Kant was known to take long, regimented walks, he claimed that they were essential to his thought process.

16

A) NO CHANGE
B) philosopher, Immanuel Kant was known to take long, regimented walks; he claimed
C) philosopher Immanuel Kant was known to take long regimented walks, he claimed
D) philosopher Immanuel Kant was known to take long, regimented walks; he claimed

---

   This sentence contains two independent clauses, but choices A and C commit a **comma splice** (Chapter 5, Lesson 2) by joining them with only a comma. Choices B and D correct this problem by inserting a semicolon between the independent clauses. Choice B is incorrect, however, because the first comma does not serve any grammatical function. The correct answer, then, is D.

Colons and Semicolons

Colons and **semicolons** should **always be preceded by independent clauses**.

- A **semicolon** must also be followed by an **independent clause that supports the first one**.

> *The girls were tired; they needed a nap.*

- A **colon** must be followed by a **list**, a **specifier**, or an **explanatory independent clause**.

> *They were a party of three: Elisa, Jen, and Kate.*
> *The girls needed only one thing: sleep.*
> *The girls were tired: they had practiced for hours.*

(These rules apply to the SAT, but they have obscure exceptions. For example, semicolons can also be used instead of a comma to separate items in a list when those items themselves contain commas, as in *We will visit Providence, Rhode Island; Concord, Massachusetts; and Mystic, Connecticut.*)

But there was one more factor that the experimenters hadn't **14** considered; peer pressure.

14

A) NO CHANGE
B) considered: peer pressure
C) considered peer pressure
D) considered, peer pressure

Choice A is incorrect because the semicolon is not followed by a supportive independent clause. Choice C is incorrect because it provides no indication about the relationship between the main clause and the phrase *peer pressure*. This phrase is a **specifier**, that is, it specifies the *factor* mentioned in the main clause. Therefore, it should be preceded by a colon, as in choice B.

EXERCISE SET 16: PUNCTUATION AND APOSTROPHES

1. Unlike linear accelerators, <u>cyclotrons—such as the one Ernest Lawrence built in Berkeley, California, use</u> magnets to accelerate subatomic particles in a circular path.

   A) NO CHANGE

   B) cyclotrons, such as the one Ernest Lawrence built in Berkeley, California—use

   C) cyclotrons, such as the one Ernest Lawrence built in Berkeley, California use

   D) cyclotrons—such as the one Ernest Lawrence built in Berkeley, California—use

2. <u>Runners, who step out of they're lanes during the first two laps, will</u> be disqualified.

   A) NO CHANGE

   B) Runners who step out of their lanes during the first two laps, will

   C) Runners, who step out of their lanes during the first two laps, will

   D) Runners who step out of their lanes during the first two laps will

3. Many electric cars do save money on energy, but they are not <u>cheap: efficiency</u> has its price.

   A) NO CHANGE

   B) cheap, efficiency

   C) cheap—efficiency,

   D) cheap: efficiency,

4. Don't adopt a rescue <u>dog, until your sure they're</u> free of parasites and infectious diseases.

   A) NO CHANGE

   B) dog until you're sure it's

   C) dog, until your sure it's

   D) dog; until you're sure its

5. <u>Its easy to see—even on the dreariest of days, how Paris earned it's</u> reputation as the City of Love.

   A) NO CHANGE

   B) It's easy to see, even on the dreariest of days, how Paris earned its

   C) Its easy to see, even on the dreariest of days, how Paris earned its

   D) It's easy to see even on the dreariest of days how Paris earned it's

6. Having decided to postpone her <u>education, for at least two years Jill begen</u> to look for a job in social media.

   A) NO CHANGE
   B) education for at least two years, Jill began
   C) education, for at least two years, Jill began
   D) education for at least two years Jill began

7. Our project was plagued by two main <u>issues; cost overruns and</u> bureaucratic red tape.

   A) NO CHANGE
   B) issues: cost overruns, and
   C) issues: cost overruns and
   D) issues; cost overruns, and

---

8. **Challenge Question**

The focal point of Ms. Cullen's home is artist Robert <u>Blackburn's woodcut,</u> "Blue Things 1963-1970."

A) NO CHANGE
B) Blackburn's woodcut titled,
C) Blackburn's, woodcut
D) Blackburn's woodcut:

◼◼ ANSWER KEY

Exercise Set 3: Verb Agreement

1. C

The phrase *scattered by* is not idiomatic unless it is part of a **passive voice** verb (Chapter 5, Lesson 14), so choice A is incorrect. Choice B is incorrect because *were* does not agree with the singular subject *flock*. Choice D is incorrect because the **progressive aspect** (Chapter 5, Lesson 11) cannot indicate a sudden reaction to something like a shotgun blast. Only choice C has the correct voice and conjugation.

2. C

This is an inverted sentence. The "uninverted" version is *Over two million microorganisms is in every teaspoon of topsoil, forming a highly complex ecosystem.* Clearly, the verb *is* disagrees with the plural subject *organisms*, and should be changed to *are*. Choice B is incorrect because *was* is in the wrong tense and disagrees with the plural subject. Choice D is wrong because *being* cannot stand alone as a verb.

3. C

This is an inverted sentence. If you missed this one, you probably didn't read the sentence carefully enough. Notice that that there is no *be* between *conditioning* and *to*, so the wording in choice A is illogical. Choice B is incorrect because the singular subject *conditioning* disagrees with the plural verb *are*. Choice C is correct because *is* agrees with the singular verb. Choice D is incorrect because it does not form a complete sentence.

4. A

The original phrasing is correct because the interrupter is a logical **participial phrase** (Chapter 5, Lesson 4) that modifies the subject *technology*. Choices B and C are both incorrect because they render the preceding comma illogical and create parallel predicates unlinked by a conjunction. Choice D is incorrect because it creates an illogical participial phrase.

5. D

This sentence uses a **standard parallel construction** (Chapter 5, Lesson 3), *both A and B,* and therefore requires a verb that matches the form of the previous verb, *inspire*. Only choice D maintains this parallel structure. Choices B and C both include extra words that disrupt the parallel structure.

6. B

In choices A and C, the verb *have expressed* disagrees with the singular subject *coalition*. Choice D is incorrect because *concern with* is the incorrect **idiom** (Chapter 5, Lesson 13) for indicating worry. The correct idiom is *concern about,* as in choice B.

7. B

Choices A and C are incorrect because the verb *explain* disagrees with the singular subject *explosiveness*. Choice D is incorrect because *its* is a possessive form, not a contraction.

8. C

The predicate of the sentence indicates that the subject should be *S. J. Perelman*, and not his writing or his style. Therefore, choices A, B, and D have illogical subjects. Only choice C works logically with the predicate of the sentence.

9. D

Since this sentence is about the habits of the grizzly bear, the verbs should take the present tense, **habitual aspect** (Chapter 5, Lesson 11) and **indicative mood** (Chapter 5, Lesson 15). Only choice D is correct in both regards. Choice A is incorrect because it uses the subjunctive mood. Choices B and C are incorrect because they are in the past tense.

10. A (Challenge Question)

The original phrasing is correct. The pronoun *themselves* serves as an **emphatic appositive** (Chapter 5, Lesson 5) and the verb *were* agrees with the plural subject *surgeons* and coordinates logically with the past tense verb *assumed*. Choice B is incorrect because *they* cannot serve as an appositive adjective. Choices C and D are incorrect because the present tense *are* does not coordinate logically with the past tense *assumed*.

Exercise Set 4: Coordinating Ideas

1. B

The original sequence of sentences is not logically coordinated. Choice B coordinates the ideas logically by emphasizing the central idea (that *The Return has received widespread acclaim*) in the main clause, and relegating the minor facts to modifying phrases. In choice C, the introductory modifying phrase does not logically modify the subject of the main clause. In choice D, the **colon** (Chapter 5, Lesson 16) is misused and the prepositional phrase does not logically modify anything in the sentence.

2. D

The original set of sentences should be combined because they all relate one key idea about a common topic. Choices B and C are incorrect because, in both cases, the **interrogative pronoun** (Chapter 5, Lesson 8) *which* has no logical antecedent. Choice D is best because it consolidates the first two sentences effectively, and clarifies the subject of the last clause.

3. C

The original sentence commits a **comma splice** (Chapter 5, Lesso
the clause following the comma qualifies as an independent claus
pronoun *this* lacks a logical antecedent. Choice B is illogical becaus
plants are not being burned. Choice C is best because a clause whos
is *which* is no longer independent, so the comma splice problem
Additionally, *which* can logically refer to the plural noun *power plants*. C
is incorrect because *it* lacks a logical antecedent.

4. D

The original sentence contains a **standard parallel construction** (Chapter 5
Lesson 3) *not only A but also B*. However, choices A, B, and C do not use standard idiomatic phrasing. Additionally, in both B and C, the two instances of
the pronoun *it* refer to different antecedents. Only choice D avoids redundancy and uses standard idiomatic phrasing.

5. A

The original phrasing is best. The sentence begins with a **participial phrase**
(Chapter 5, Lesson 4), which must coordinate with the main clause by sharing
its subject. This participle describes a *treatise*, so the subject of the main clause
must be the book, not Keynes, therefore choices B and D are incorrect.
Choice C is incorrect because the **interrogative pronoun** (Chapter 5, Lesson 8)
which does not coordinate logically with the antecedent *Keynes*.

6. D (Challenge Question)

A colon before an independent clause indicates that this clause *explains* the
one preceding it. In choices A, C, and D, the clause after the colon is the same:
our experiences affect our priorities and deepest values. What does this explain?
It does not explain the fact that *our principles motivate us*, so choices A and C
are incorrect. It does, however, explain how *our principles can change*, so
D provides a logical phrasing. Choice B is incorrect because the fact that
our principles often motivate us does not explain the fact that *our experiences
affect our priorities.*

Exercise Set 5: Transitions and References

1. B

The first sentence indicates a general fact about the ancient Greeks, and the
quote from Antigone in the second sentence provides a specific example to
illustrate that fact. Therefore, choice B, *For example,* is the most logical choice.
Choice A is incorrect because a *coincidence* is a surprising simultaneity of
events, but these sentences indicate no such simultaneity. Choice C is incorrect
because the second sentence does not extend a previous claim. Choice D is
incorrect because the second sentence does not contrast the first.

2. B

The first sentence describes a belief about *tough sentencing*, but the second sentence indicates a fact that undermines that belief. Therefore, the most logical transition is *However*. Choice A, *Even worse*, is incorrect because the second sentence doesn't describe an escalation of negativity. Choice C is incorrect because the second sentence does not clarify or paraphrase anything. Choice D is incorrect because the second sentence does not describe a result.

3. A

The first sentence describes a general social trend, and the second sentence describes a result of that trend. Therefore, Choice A, *Consequently*, provides a logical transition. Choice B is incorrect because the second sentence does not indicate an ironic or surprising situation. Choice C is incorrect because the second sentence does not indicate a situation that is analogous to any previously mentioned. Choice D is incorrect because the second sentence does not exemplify anything described in the first sentence.

4. B (Challenge Question)

The first two sentences describe a problem that has impeded biological research, and the third sentence describes a breakthrough that has solved the problem. Choice A, *Fittingly*, is incorrect because nothing in this paragraph indicates that the "clean room" solution is any more appropriate to the context than any other solution. Choice C, *In turn*, is incorrect because nothing indicates that the solution arose from an exchange or logical sequence of events. Choice D, *Accordingly*, is incorrect because nothing indicates that this solution corresponds to or results from any defined situation. Choice C is best because it is certainly *fortunate* to find a solution to a long-standing problem.

Exercise Set 6. Parallel Structure

1. C

The second and third items in the list, *improving* and *repairing*, are gerunds, therefore the first item should also be a gerund, as in choice C.

2. D

This sentence uses the standard parallel construction, *not so much A as B*. Choices A and B are incorrect because they do not use correct idiomatic phrasing. Choice C is incorrect because the second item in the contrast, *how wisely you use your time*, is not parallel in form to the first item, *about working hard*. Since the first item is a prepositional phrase, the second should be as well, as in choice D.

3. B

This sentence uses the standard parallel construction *not only A but also B*. Choices A and C are incorrect because they do not use correct idiomatic phrasing. Choice D is incorrect because *also* and *as well* are redundant.

4. A

This sentence gives a binary list, so the items should have parallel grammatical and semantic form. The first item in the list, *the skittishness of investors*, is a noun phrase defining a personal characteristic of a group of people, so the second item should do the same. Only choice A maintains both the grammatical and semantic parallelism.

5. D

Choices A, B, and C are all ambiguous because, with each phrasing, the dilemma is unclear: it could be read to mean that I'm trying to decide between *giving the tickets* to Maria and *giving Caitlyn* to Maria, which is of course nonsensical. Only choice D is unambiguous: the choice is between *giving the tickets to Maria* and *giving the tickets to Caitlyn*.

6. C

This sentence uses the standard parallel construction *prefer A to B*. Choices A and B are incorrect because they do not use standard phrasing. Choice D is incorrect because the comma serves no grammatical purpose.

7. B

This sentence uses the standard parallel construction *not so much A as B*. Choices A and C are incorrect because neither uses the standard phrasing. Choice D is incorrect because the second item, *because of the freewheeling, Bohemian atmosphere*, does not have the same grammatical form as the first item, *for the music*. Choice B is best because it uses the standard phrasing and the items, *for the music* and *for the freewheeling, Bohemian atmosphere*, are both prepositional phrases.

8. D (Challenge Question)

The subject and verb of this sentence is *The (disappointing) thing was—*. Therefore, the underline portion should be a noun phrase, and not an independent clause. Therefore, choices A and B are incorrect. Choice C is incorrect because the pronoun *they* lacks a logical antecedent and the verb should not take the subjunctive mood.

Exercise Set 7: Coordination of Modifiers

1. C

The subject of the participle *drained* is *Martha*, not her *instinct*. (Just ask: *who was drained?*) Therefore, choices A, B, and D are incorrect because they include dangling participles. The only option with the correct subject is choice C.

2. B

The prepositional phrase *with a sprained ankle* modifies *Adam*, not *the coach*, so choice A is incorrect because it contains a dangling modifier. Choice B corrects this problem by using a dependent clause with a clear subject, verb, and object. Choices C and D are incorrect because neither clarifies who has the sprained ankle.

3. D

The subject of the participle *lacking* is *David*. (*Who* lacked any real sailing skills?) Therefore, choices A and C contain dangling participles. Choice B is incorrect because the phrase *had the primary concern* is unidiomatic and unclear.

4. B

What was *searching through a box of old letters*? *We* were. By the Law of Proximity, the modifying phrase should be as close to its subject—the word that it modifies—as possible, as in choice B. Choices A, C, and D are all incorrect because each implies that the *manuscript* was searching through the box of old letters.

5. D

Choice A is incorrect because the (infinitive) noun phrase *To get a good jump out of the blocks* does not play any grammatical role in the main clause. Choice B is incorrect because the prepositional phrase *for getting a good jump out of the blocks* is too far away from the adjective it modifies, *essential*. Choice C is incorrect because the prepositional phrase *for hip positioning to be proper* does not logically modify any part of the main clause. Choice D is best because it places the prepositional phrase next to the adjective it modifies.

6. B

The adjective *unhappy* describes the *senator*, not her *plan*, so choice A is illogical. Choices C and D likewise have illogical subjects. Only choice B uses a subject that corrects for the dangling modifier.

7. A

The original phrasing is best because it contains a clause that coordinates logically with the participial phrase that starts the sentence. Choice B is incorrect because *then* is redundant. Choices C and D are incorrect because they both allow the participial phrase to dangle.

8. D (Challenge Question)

Choice A is incorrect because the adjective phrase that starts the sentence does not logically modify the subject of the sentence: a *musical culture* can't be *famous for its visual and performing arts scene*. Choice B is incorrect because *its* lacks a logical antecedent. Choice C is incorrect because the sentence is not grammatical after the interrupting modifier has been trimmed. Choice D is best because it coordinates the two ideas logically and grammatically.

Exercise Set 8: Using Modifiers Logically

1. C

Choice A is incorrect because the comparative adjective *much stronger* cannot modify the verb *emphasize*. The comparative adverb, *more strongly*, is required, as in choice C.

2. B

Choices A and C are incorrect because the adverbs *never* and *usually* are contradictory. Choice D is incorrect because *hardly never* is not an idiomatic phrase. The idiomatic phrases are *hardly ever* or *almost never*, as in choice B.

3. C

Choices A and D are incorrect because the verb *coordinated* cannot be modified with the adjective *effective*. Choices B and C use the proper adverbial form *effectively*, but choice B is incorrect because it makes an illogical comparison.

4. A

The original phrasing is best because one of the meanings of *unqualified* is *total*, so an *unqualified success* is a *complete success*. Choice B is incorrect because *successfully unqualified* is not a sensible phrase. Choice C is incorrect because *disqualified* means *eliminated from competition because of a rule violation*, which does not logically apply to a *success*. Choice D is incorrect because *unqualified in its success* is not idiomatic.

5. A

The original phrasing is best: recall that *harder* can serve as either a comparative adjective or a comparative adverb. Choice B is incorrect because *more hardly* is an illogical phrase. Choices C and D are incorrect because the phrase *always doesn't* contradicts the statement that *challenge is the key to success*.

6. B

Choices A and C are illogical because it is untrue that the teacher *never* told us about the test; she just waited until the last minute to do so. Choice D is incorrect because the phrase *hardly ever* implies a claim about a long-term trend rather than a specific event.

7. D

Choices A, B, and C contain double negatives that contradict a logical reading of the sentence. Only choice D provides a logical phrasing.

8. A (Challenge Question)

The original phrasing is best, even if it sounds strangely formal. The phrase *need not* is equivalent to *do not need to*. Choice B is redundant, because *need to* and *have to* are essentially synonyms. Choice C is wordy and implies illogically that plays can have human needs. Choice D is not idiomatic.

Exercise Set 9: Logical Comparisons

1. A

The original phrasing is logical and parallel because *ignoring* and *attacking* are both gerunds. Choices B and C are incorrect because they use the infinitive form, which breaks the parallel structure. Choice D is incorrect because the phrase *it is attacking* is not parallel in form to the gerund *ignoring*.

2. C

Choices A, B, and D are all illogical comparisons because *Kyrchek's latest film* must be included in *anything she has done* or *everything she has done* or *any of the work she did*. Only choice C excludes her current film so that a logical comparison can be made.

3. B

Choices A and C are incorrect because they make a category error in comparing *motors of cars* to *cars*. Choice B makes a logical comparison because *engines* are *motors*. Choice D is incorrect because it is redundant: *those* and *engines* refer to the same noun.

4. B

Each choice contains an interrupting modifier, but only choice B remains idiomatic, logical, and grammatical after this interrupter is trimmed from the sentence.

5. C

The subject of this sentence is *lessons*, so the comparison to *teachers* in choices A and B is illogical. Choice D is incorrect because comparing *lessons* to *classrooms* is also illogical. Only choice C makes a logical comparison: the parallel structure makes it clear that pronoun *those* refers to *lessons*.

6. A

The original phrasing is logical because it makes a like-to-like comparison between *Modernist poetry* and *Victorian or Elizabethan poetry*. Choice B is incorrect because *poetry* cannot be compared to *poets*. Choice C is incorrect because *those* lacks a logical antecedent with which it agrees in number. Choice D is redundant because *that* and *poetry* both have the same referent.

7. C

Since *customers* are countable and non-continuous quantities, *less* is an illogical modifier, and should be changed to *fewer*, as in choices B and C. However, choice B is incorrect because the subjunctive *would pay* contradicts the **indicative mood** (Chapter 5, Lesson 15) in the clause *transparency in banking increases*.

8. D (Challenge Question)

This sentence has an **inverted syntax** (Chapter 5, Lesson 1), and the sentence can only be parsed logically if the underlined phrase is a noun or noun phrase that serves as the subject of the sentence. Choices C and D both provide **gerundive** (Chapter 5, Lesson 3) noun phrases as subjects, but only choice D creates a logical and parallel comparison when "un-inverted": *Having to watch for avalanches at high altitudes was even more taxing than climbing without supplemental oxygen.*

Exercise Set 10: Pronoun Agreement

1. C

Choices A and B are illogical because the pronoun *where* cannot be used to refer to *times*. Choice D is incorrect because it commits a *pronoun shift* from *one* to *you*. Only choice C avoids both pronoun problems.

2. B

The rest of the sentence uses the second person pronouns *you* and *your*, so consistency requires that the underlined portion also use *you* instead of *one*, as in choices B and D. Choice D is incorrect, however, because *shouldn't even* illogically implies some minimum level of avoidance.

3. A

The original phrasing is clear and logical because the possessive pronoun *their* agrees with the plural antecedent *words*. Choices B and C are incorrect because they mistake contractions for possessives. Choice D is incorrect because *its* disagrees with the plural antecedent *words*.

4. C

Choice A is incorrect because the plural pronoun *their* disagrees with the singular antecedent *Arts Council*. Choices B and D are incorrect because they are contractions, not possessives.

5. D

Choices A and B are incorrect because the verb *do*—which often refers to a verb in much the same way as a pronoun refers to a noun, as in *I don't often fly first class, but when I do…*—does not have a clear "antecedent verb." Choice D corrects this mistake by clarifying this reference. Choice C is incorrect because it misuses the possessive *their*.

6. A

The original phrasing is correct because *it* agrees with the singular antecedent *bonobo*. Choice B is incorrect because *its* is a possessive, not a contraction. Choices C and D are incorrect because they use plural pronouns.

7. C

Choice A is incorrect because the pronoun *when* must refer to a *time*, not a *process*. Choice B is incorrect because a *process* is not a place. Choice D is incorrect because the phrase *so that* implies that the *nitrogen cycle* is an intentional action, which it is not.

8. C (Challenge Question)

Choices A and D are incorrect because both commit comma splices, joining independent clauses with only a comma. Choice B is incorrect because *which* illogically refers to the *vote*, but clearly it is the *delay* that fueled resentment, not the vote. Choice C clarifies the source of the resentment.

Exercise Set 11: Pronoun Case

1. **C**
Since the underlined phrase is the object of the preposition *of*, it must take the objective case, as in choice C.

2. **A**
As much as most people want to "correct" this sentence, perhaps by changing *him and me* to *us* (which would actually make the reference less specific), the original phrasing is correct. This phrase serves as the object of the pronoun *for*, and therefore both pronouns must take the objective case: *him and me*. Notice that this is clearer to see when we isolate each element: it is perfectly correct to say *it might be difficult for <u>him</u> to stay* or *it might be difficult for <u>me</u> to stay*, therefore it is also acceptable to say *it might be difficult for <u>him and me</u> to stay*. (Some may object and claim that this phrase serves as the subject of the verb *stay*, and therefore should take the subjective case. This is incorrect, because *to stay* is an **infinitive** [Chapter 5, Lesson 3], not a conjugated verb, so it takes no grammatical subject.)

3. **D**
Here, choice A may seem correct because the pronoun *us* is the object of the preposition *in*, right? No: the object of the preposition is *delaying*. (What is there no point in? *Us*, or the *delaying*?) Therefore, the pronoun must be a modifier of the gerund *delaying* and should take the possessive form, *our*.

4. **C**
The underlined phrase is the subject of the verb *are*, and therefore the pronouns must take the subject case: *you and I*.

5. **C**
The underlined pronoun is part of the subject of the verb *have always been*, and therefore must take the subjective case, *I*.

6. **D**
The underlined phrase represents the subject of the verb *have suffered*, and therefore the verb must take the subjective case, *we*. The phrase *Giants fans* serves as an **appositive modifier** (Chapter 5, Lesson 5) to the subject, and therefore must takes the form of a noun phrase, as in choice D.

7. **A**
The original phrasing is correct because the phrase *my wife and me* serves as the indirect object of the verb *offered*, and therefore must take the objective case.

8. **C** (Challenge Question)
The original phrasing is incorrect because *her's* is not a valid word. The two third person singular feminine possessive pronouns in English are *her* (adj) and *hers* (n): *her's* is not an acceptable construction. Choices B and D are incorrect because the context requires a possessive. Choice C provides a correct use of the possessive.

Exercise Set 12: Verb Tense and Aspect

1. D

This sentence is trying to convey not only *what* the team is hopeful about, but *why* the team is hopeful. Choice A is incorrect because the present participle *developing* implies that the *developing* and the *hoping* were concurrent, which is illogical. Since the *hoping* depends on the *completion* of the development, the **consequential participle** *having developed* is required, as in choices B and D. Choice B is redundant because *hope to reveal* already conveys subjunctive potential, so the auxiliary *would* is unnecessary.

2. B

Common sense tells us that the research must be at least partially completed before the first draft of a term paper can be completed, so the consequential participle *having spent* is required to show this relationship. Also, the adverb *already*, without any other time specification, refers to a *current* status, and therefore the main verb must take the present consequential form, *has written*, as in choice B.

3. D

The phrase *as soon as* indicates that this sentence is referring to concurrent events. Therefore, any use of the consequential aspect is illogical. Choice D is correct because it is the only one that does not use the consequential aspect.

4. A

The use of the consequential participle *having taken* in the original phrasing is most logical, because the *fear* described in the main clause could not set in before the hikers were well along on the wrong path. Choice C is incorrect, however, because the past consequential *had feared* implies that the *fear* is an antecedent rather than a consequence.

5. C

Choice A is incorrect because this sentence is stating a fact, and therefore should take the **indicative mood** (Chapter 5, Lesson 15) rather than the subjunctive mood. Choices B and D are incorrect because the verb *seems* has already established that this sentence is in the **artistic present**, and not the past tense.

6. A

The use of the present tense in first clause establishes that the sentence is describing a current status. Therefore the present tense **indicative mood** (Chapter 5, Lesson 15) is required, as in choice A. The present consequential *has performed* is appropriate here because her previous performance clearly extends a consequence to her current status, which explains why she *is well-qualified*.

7. B

Choices A and D are incorrect because the consequential aspect requires the past participle *sunk* rather than the simple past tense *sank*. Choice C is incorrect because the phrase *over three hundred years ago* indicates that the verb must be in the past tense.

8. C

Choice A is incorrect because it commits a comma splice. Choices B and D are incorrect because the sentence is indicating a fact, and therefore should take the **indicative mood** (Chapter 5, Lesson 15) and not the **subjunctive mood** (Chapter 5, Lesson 15). The use of the consequential participle *having published* in choice C is correct because this fact extends a consequence to his status when he died.

9. A (Elite Challenge Question)

Although the main clause is discussing a work of literature, it is making a historical claim about one of Jules Verne's predictions, and therefore the main verb takes the **historical past** tense, *predicted*, rather than the **artistic present**. The underlined phrase indicates a fact that we might call **retro-consequential**: a future event (rather than a previous one) extends a consequence to a status. The proper form for this kind of "future-in-the-past" aspect is *would not be invented*, as in choice A. Choice B is incorrect because it uses the **consequential aspect**, which applies to a previous event rather than a future one. Choice C is incorrect because it uses a subjunctive form, but the statement is not counterfactual or hypothetical. Choice D is incorrect because it uses the simple future tense, which is illogical in this context.

Exercise Set 13: Diction and Redundancy

1. D

To *abolish* means to *formally put an end to a system, practice, or institution*, and so it does not apply to an infestation of beetles. Choice B is incorrect because *delete* applies to written or genetic material or computer memory, not to insects. Choice C is incorrect because *retract* means to *draw or take back*, which does not apply to insects. Only choice D, *eradicate*, describes something that can be done to an infestation of insects.

2. B

Choices A and C are incorrect because the use of the conjunction *but* is redundant with the use of the conjunction *but*. Choice D is incorrect because *smear* means to *damage the reputation of*, which does not apply to theories. Choice B is best because statistics can *refute* theories.

3. D

Choice A is incorrect because the phrase *separate out* is redundant, and also because *separate* describes a physical rather than a mental act. Choice B is incorrect because to *certify* is to *formally attest or confirm*, which does not apply to a mental event. Choice C is incorrect because to *acknowledge* is simply to *accept or admit the existence or truth of*, which does not at all indicate a particular skill of wine experts. Only choice D, *discern*, which means to *distinguish with difficulty by the senses*, reasonably describes what wine experts do with grapes, regions, and vintages.

4. D

A *consensus* is a *general agreement*, so the phrase *consensus of unified opinion* is redundant. Choice B is likewise redundant. Choice C is not idiomatic. Choice D provides the most concise, idiomatic, and clear phrasing.

5. C

To *appoint* means to *formally or officially assign a role to (someone)*, and therefore applies only to a person and not to a *decision*. Choice B is incorrect because the council is making the decision themselves, and is not being *compelled (forced)* to do it. Choice D is incorrect because a *predetermined (decided beforehand)* decision would not require any extra time to deliberate.

6. A

To *disparage* means to *represent as being of little worth*, which is precisely what critics might do to a bad movie. Choice B is incorrect because a movie cannot be *confronted*. Choice C is incorrect because to *impair* means to *weaken or damage* something, but this cannot reasonably be done to a movie that is already made. Choice D is incorrect because to *repudiate* is to *refuse to be associated with* or to *deny the validity of*, neither of which is something that critics can do to movies that they did not themselves help create.

7. D

None of the modifiers in choices A, B, and C contribute any meaning or emphasis to the sentence, and so all are redundant. The present tense verb *cannot process* is all that is needed to indicate the present.

8. C

Choice A is incorrect because to *hamper* means to *hinder or impede the progress of (something)*, but it is nonsensical to expect that workers would do this to themselves. Choice B is incorrect because *subside (to decrease in intensity)* is an **intransitive verb**, that is, it cannot take an object as this verb does. Choice D is incorrect because work cannot be *lowered*. Only choice C, *curtail (restrict)* makes sense in this context.

9. B

Choices A and C are incorrect because someone's self-esteem cannot *proliferate (increase rapidly in numbers)* or *multiply* because self-esteem is a unitary thing. Choice D is incorrect because *enlarge* applies to physical size or extent, which cannot apply to a human psychological trait like *self-esteem*. Choice B is best because one's self-esteem can *blossom (mature in a healthy way)*.

10. D

Imminent means *about to happen*, so choices A and B are redundant. Choice C is incorrect because *imminently likely* is a malapropism of *eminently likely*. Choice D is best because it is concise and free of redundancy.

11. D

To *evolve* means to *develop gradually into a more complex or effective form*, but the process of changing a motor is not gradual or passive. Choice B is incorrect because *correlated* means *having a mutual relationship, particularly when one quantity affects another*, which does not apply to objects like motors. Choice C is incorrect because to *amend* means to *improve (a document)*, but a motor is not a document. Choice D is best because to *adapt* is to *make (something) suitable to a new purpose*.

12. C

Choice A is incorrect because to *intimidate* means to *frighten into compliance*, which is not at all subtle. Choice B is incorrect because *propel* implies a forceful forward motion that is not appropriate to the act of purchasing something. Choice D is incorrect because to *oppress* is to *keep in subservience through assertive authority*, which is far too strong and broad a term to describe what advertising may do to individuals. Choice C, *induce (successfully persuade)*, is the most appropriate choice to describe how advertising influences consumers.

13. C

Choices A, B, and D are incorrect because *apprehensive*, *neurotic*, and *worried* are all adjectives describing the internal, emotional states of people, and are inappropriate for describing the mood of a conversation. (The correct term to describe a situation that induces worry is *worrisome*, not *worried*.) Only choice C, *tense (causing anxiety)*, can appropriately describe the mood of negotiations.

14. B

Reticent means *unwilling to reveal one's thoughts or feelings*. It does not mean *reluctant*, and so choice A is redundant. Choice B, *reticent about*, captures the idea most concisely. Choice C is wordy and unidiomatic. Choice D is incorrect because it omits any reference to expression.

15. C

Choice A is incorrect because to *impede* means to *obstruct or hinder*, but the sentence does not indicate that the ministers were prevented from achieving a goal. Choice B is incorrect because *scuttle* means *deliberately cause to fail*, but the sentence does not indicate that the ministers deliberately failed in any effort. Choice D is incorrect because *snubbed* means *rebuffed* or *ignored disdainfully*, but such an action would not cause anyone to go into exile. The best choice is C, *ousted*, which means *driven from power*.

16. **B**

Choice A is incorrect because *elicit* is a verb meaning *evoke or draw out*. Also, *incidents* are countable, non-continuous things, and so should be modified by *fewer*, not *less*. Clearly, this sentence calls for *illicit*, and adjective meaning *forbidden by law*. Choice C is incorrect because *incidence* means *frequency of a disease, crime, or other undesirable thing*, so, as an uncountable quantity, it doesn't go with *fewer*. The only choice that avoids all diction problems is B.

17. **D** (Challenge Question)

The sentence requires a verb that describes what *blowback (unintended adverse results of a political action)* does with regard to *provocative comments*. Choice A is incorrect because *derive* requires an indirect object and the preposition *from*, so this is an unidiomatic usage. Choice B is incorrect because blowback cannot *pursue (chase)*. Choice C is incorrect because to *advance* is to *move forward in a purposeful way*, but *blowback* is unintended and negative. Choice D is correct because it is reasonable to expect that blowback would *ensue (happen as a result)* after provocative comments.

18. **C** (Challenge Question)

The core of this sentence is *The reason is—*. Therefore, the object in this clause must be a **noun phrase** that defines the *reason*. Choices A and D are incorrect because a phrase that begins with *because* is not a noun phrase. Choice B is incorrect because to *perpetuate* means to *make (something) continue indefinitely*, which is not what good marathon runners want to do with their pace. They only want to *maintain* (choice C) a steady pace until the end of the race.

Exercise Set 14: Idiomatic Expression

1. **C**

Since the sentence describes a plan that was developed carefully over an extended period of time, the proper idiom is *agreed on*, as in choice C. Recall that although we can *agree with* a person, and *agree to* an offer, we *agree on* plans that are mutually decided.

2. **D**

The comparative preposition *than* is required when making unequal comparisons with comparative adjectives, as in *smaller than* or *faster than*. Notice, however, that *different* is not a comparative adjective like these, and it requires the idiom *different from*.

3. **C**

The proper idiom is *comply with (a rule)*. None of the options in A, B, and D is idiomatic.

4. C
The proper idiom here is *prefer A to B*. Notice that this is a **standard parallel construction** (Chapter 5, Lesson 3). Notice, also, that the phrases in the comparison—*the soft, diffuse light* and *the light of the old compact fluorescent bulbs*—have parallel grammatical form.

5. A
Since a *plea deal* is a type of *offer*, rather than a general situation (*agree about*), person (*agree with*), or mutual plan (*agree on*), the proper idiom here is *agree to*, as in choice A.

6. D
Recall from Chapter 5, Lesson 3 that **infinitives** often provide the most concise way of expressing **purpose**, and therefore choice D, *to investigate*, is the most concise and idiomatic option. Choice A is needlessly wordy, and choices B and C are not idiomatic.

7. B
Choices A and C are incorrect because the phrase *determine about* is not idiomatic. As with most idioms, always ask whether the preposition is required at all. In this case, it is not. Choice D is incorrect because the pronouns *which* and *that* are redundant, since they refer to the same antecedent, *activities*, and play the same grammatical role.

8. C
Choice A is incorrect because *arguments on* is not a standard idiom. You can *argue with* a person, or you can *argue for* or *argue against* a claim or position. Since this refers to a position on a *proposal*, the only idiomatic option is C, *arguments for*.

9. D
The correct idiom here is *a tribute to (a person)*. Choices A, B, and C are not idiomatic.

10. B (Challenge Question)
When you want to specify the primary **function** (a noun) that some device serves, the proper idiom is *serves as* (an object or action that serves that function). You may use the idiom *serves (infinitive)* if the infinitive **specifies the purpose**, as in *This letter serves to notify you that...* However, the infinitive *to be* does not specify a purpose, so choice A is incorrect. Choice C is unidiomatic. Choice D is incorrect because the idiom *serves for* is used to indicate a period of service, as in *Charles served for 12 years as a State Representative*.

Exercise Set 15: Verb Mood and Voice

1. C

This sentence is making two factual historical claims, so both claims—about Clemens's age and when the Civil War started—must take the **indicative mood**, not the **subjunctive mood**. Therefore, choices A, B, and D are incorrect. (Notice that, in choice B, the phrase *would of* is a common **diction** error. The proper subjunctive phrasing is *would have*.)

2. A

The original subjunctive phrasing is best, because this clause is **counterfactual**: the goalie *did* slip backward. Recall that the **past conditional counterfactual** takes the same form as the **past consequential**: *had not slipped*. Choice B is incorrect because this statement is counterfactual, not indicative. Choice C is incorrect because the preposition *of* serves no grammatical purpose. Choice D is incorrect because this is not the idiomatic phrasing for a past conditional counterfactual.

3. C

Since the verb *demanded* indicates that the underlined verb represents a command or suggestion, the imperative auxiliaries *must* and *should* are redundant in choices A and B. The imperative requires the infinitive form, *turn*, as in choice C.

4. B

This sentence contains a list, the first two items of which are clauses in the passive voice: *our rituals are changed* and *our habits are disrupted*. The Law of Parallelism requires that the third item also be a clause in the passive voice, as in choice B.

5. A

The original phrasing is best, even though it is in the passive voice. The passive voice is required here so that the two clauses can logically coordinate. Choice B is incorrect because the subjunctive *would have been dropped* does not coordinate logically with the indicative clause that follows. Choices C and D are incorrect because the appositive pronoun *who* in the second clause would be taken to refer to the *protests*, which is illogical.

6. B

Choice A is incorrect because the first clause is a past conditional counterfactual, and therefore should not include the subjunctive auxiliary *would*. The past conditional counterfactual requires the same form as the past consequential, *had continued*, as in choice B.

7. A

The original phrasing is best. The verb *suggested* indicates the imperative mood in the clause that follows, so no imperative auxiliary (*should* or *might*) is required. Choice B is incorrect because the passive voice construction does not coordinate with the pronoun *which* in the second clause. Choice C is incorrect because the imperative auxiliary *should* is redundant. Choice D is incorrect because the past consequential *had explored* is illogical.

8. B

The verb *wished* indicates that the underlined verb is **past wishful**, and therefore it should take the **past consequential** form, *had worn*, without the subjunctive auxiliary. Choice A is incorrect because it uses that subjunctive auxiliary *would* and the past tense *wore* instead of the past participle *worn*. Choice C is incorrect because it uses the subjunctive auxiliary. Choice D is wrong because the simple past *wore* does not indicate the past wishful form of the verb.

9. A (Challenge Question)

The original provides the correct imperative phrasing. Since the verb *suggested* already indicates a command or suggestion, **no auxiliary** is necessary and the verb indicating the suggestion should use the **infinitive form**. Choice B is incorrect because it uses the indicative mood rather than the imperative mood. Choice C is incorrect because the auxiliary *should* is redundant, and the subject does not align with the parallel predicate that follows the underlined portion. Choice D is incorrect because its subject does not align with the parallel predicate that follows the underlined portion: our *investments* should not *automate monthly transfers*, but rather *we* should.

Exercise Set 16: Punctuation and Apostrophes

1. D

Choice A is incorrect because the interrupting modifier, *such as the one Ernest Lawrence built in Berkeley, California,* is not bracketed by identical punctuation marks. Only choice D uses identical marks, both dashes, to set off the interrupter.

2. D

Choice A is incorrect because the **restrictive clause** *who step out of their lanes during the first two laps* should not be separated from the main clause by commas, because it is essential to the core meaning of the sentence. Also, it misuses the contraction *they're* for the possessive pronoun *their*. The only choice that uses the correct pronoun form and does not misuse commas is choice D.

3. A

The original phrasing is best because the colon precedes an **explanatory independent clause**. The statement *efficiency has its price* helps to explain the fact that *electric cars are not cheap*. Choice B is incorrect because it commits a comma splice (Chapter 5, Lesson 2). Choice C is incorrect because the comma serves no grammatical purpose, and a dash should not be used to separate independent clauses. Choice D is incorrect because the comma serves no grammatical purpose.

4. B

Choice A is incorrect because it misuses the possessive pronoun *your* for the conjunction *you're*, and because the pronoun *they* does not agree in number with its antecedent *dog*. Choice B corrects both of these problems. Choice C is incorrect because it misuses the possessive pronoun *your*. Choice D is incorrect because the semicolon serves no grammatical purpose and it uses the possessive *its* instead of the contraction *it's*.

5. B

Choice A is incorrect because the possessive *Its* is misused instead of the contraction *It's*, because the interrupting phrase is not bracketed by identical punctuation marks, and because the contraction *it's* is misused instead of the possessive pronoun *its*. Choice B corrects all three of these mistakes. Choice C is incorrect because it mistakes *Its* for *It's*. Choice D is incorrect because it mistakes *it's* for *its*, and does not offset the interrupting phrase.

6. B

The preposition phrase *for at least two years* is an adverbial phrase modifying the verb *postpone*. Choice A is incorrect because the placement of the comma suggests that the prepositional phrase modifies the verb *began*, which is illogical. Choice B corrects this problem by moving the comma. Choice C is incorrect because the first comma is incorrect. Choice D is incorrect because a comma is required after *years*.

7. C

Choices A and D are incorrect because a semicolon must always be followed by a supporting **independent clause**. Since the phrase that follows is a **specifier** that indicates what the *main issues* were, a colon is required, as in choices B and C. However, choice B is incorrect because a comma should not be used to separate items in a binary list when a conjunction is already being used.

8. A (Challenge Question)

The original punctuation is correct. The title in quotes is an *appositive* title, and should be separated from the noun it modifies, *woodcut*, with a comma. In choice B, the comma is incorrect because it disrupts the participial phrase *titled "Blue Things 1963-1970."* In choice C, the first comma serves no grammatical purpose. In choice D, the colon does not belong because it does not introduce an explanatory clause, specifier, or list. Notice that providing the name of the woodcut does not **specify** it, because the phrase *Blackburn's woodcut* includes no indefinite determiner (*a* or *an*), and already refers specifically to *"Blue Things 1963-1970."*

CHAPTER 6
DIAGNOSING PARAGRAPHS

Many SAT Writing questions ask you to analyze paragraphs for coherence, logical flow, and style. To ace these types of questions, pay attention to the central ideas of paragraphs, the development of central and secondary ideas, and the stylistic patterns within paragraphs.

LESSON 1: FOCUS WITHIN PASSAGES

Central Idea Questions

Occasionally, the SAT Writing will ask you to think about the central idea of a paragraph or the passage as a whole and choose an introductory or summarizing sentence. Don't tackle these questions until you've **read and summarized the paragraph or passage as a whole for yourself.**

Genomic scientists are developing better, cheaper, and faster ways to decode our DNA, and doctors are becoming more adept at using this information to create "personalized medicine." Other researchers are learning how to turn the most rudimentary human cells—stem cells—into specialized tissues to help repair damaged human organs. And oncologists—cancer specialists—are now coming to understand how the human immune system can be decoded to provide a crucial weapon against the most dangerous tumors.

19 Some scientists are skeptical about the viability of such radical new therapies. In particular, the success of these new biological technologies depends on our ability to transate vast quantities of chemical information into digital form. Specialized software and hardware must be developed to turn biochemical data into information that doctors and researchers can use to streamline research and make patients' lives better. Fortunately, the progress has so far been good. In fact, with "second generation" techniques developed in 2008, the cost of decoding human genomes has plummeted even faster than predicted.

19

Which choice best introduces the main idea of the paragraph?

A) NO CHANGE
B) Researchers from all over the world are collaborating in these new discoveries.
C) These new therapies and cures depend heavily on progress in the computer sciences.
D) Many forms of alternative medicine are being combined with traditional therapies to treat a wide range of diseases.

The first paragraph discusses four specific trends in medicine: DNA decoding, personalized medicine, tissue synthesis, and cancer immunotherapy. The second paragraph discusses the fact that these technologies require *translat(ing) vast quantities of chemical information into digital form*, and indicates that good progress has been made, thanks to progress in *specialized hardware and software*. Therefore, the best introductory sentence is C, which connects these ideas by saying that *these new therapies depend heavily on progress in the computer sciences*. Choice A is incorrect because the paragraph does not indicate any skepticism about the viability of these technologies. Choice B is incorrect because the paragraph does not discuss where the researchers are from. Choice D is incorrect because the paragraph does not discuss combining traditional therapies with alternative medicine.

Adding or Deleting Sentences

When a question asks whether or not a sentence should be inserted into or delete from a paragraph, **summarize the paragraph and ask, "does this sentence add anything relevant to the overall purpose of the paragraph?"**

In a study of learner motivation, Psychologist Edward Deci gave subjects a challenging puzzle to solve. Some subjects were offered money as a reward for solving the puzzle, and others were not. Afterwards, both groups were observed secretly after the researcher left the room. Many of those who had not been paid as a reward for their work continued to play with the puzzle, presumably because they found it interesting for its own sake. **7** Those who had received the cash rewards, however, showed significantly less interest in returning to the puzzle.

7

The writer is considering deleting this sentence from the paragraph. Should the author make this change?

A) Yes, because it conveys information that is already implied elsewhere in the paragraph.
B) Yes, because it conveys information that distracts from the discussion of student motivation.
C) No, because it explains why the experiment was so difficult to conduct.
D) No, because it provides information that is essential to this discussion of student motivation.

The first sentence of the paragraph introduces a *study of learner motivation*. The final sentence is relevant because it provides a detail that helps to explain the relationship between cash rewards and motivation, namely, that they actually *decrease* learner motivation. Choice A is incorrect because this sentence provides new information. Choice B is incorrect because the sentence is focused on student motivation, and doesn't distract from it. Choice C is incorrect because the sentence does not indicate anything about how difficult the experiment was to conduct.

No one had a more powerful impact on the early film industry than Charlie Chaplin did. Born in 1889 into an impoverished London family, Chaplin crossed the Atlantic and became a pioneer in silent comedic movies. **36** Early in his film career, Chaplin developed his signature character, the "Little Tramp," who delighted audiences with his clever physical comedy and endearing sensitivity. Modest yet clearly intelligent, shy yet always at the center of action, the Tramp embodied Chaplin's genius as a performer.

36

At this point, the writer is considering adding the following sentence.

Charlie's mother suffered from mental illness and was institutionalized for a significant part of Charlie's young life.

Should the writer make this addition here?

A) Yes, because it describes a factor that inspired Chaplin to enter the film industry.
B) Yes, because it provides an important detail about Chaplin's family history.
C) No, because it distracts from the discussion of Chaplin's impact on the film industry.
D) No, because it diminishes the humorous tone of the paragraph.

The first sentence establishes that this paragraph is about Charlie Chaplin's impact on the film industry. The remainder of the paragraph focuses on how Chaplin came to America and created an influential film character known as the "Little Tramp." The proposed new sentence does not contribute to the overall purpose of the paragraph because it introduces a personal family detail that is at best marginally related to a discussion of Chaplin's impact on film.

LESSON 2: TRANSITIONS, DEVELOPMENT, AND ORGANIZATION

Paragraph Transitions

In Chapter 5, Lesson 2, we discussed transitions between sentences. When a question asks about **paragraph** transitions, expand your scope just a bit: summarize both the previous paragraph and the new paragraph, and ask, **what is the logical connection between the two paragraphs?** For instance, does the new paragraph:

- extend an idea
- illustrate a concept
- explain an idea
- provide an example
- make a comparison
- make a contrasting point, or
- indicate a causal or consequential relationship

An important challenge facing the healthcare industry is how to address the shortfall in primary caregivers without sacrificing quality of care. One possible solution is to incentivize more medical school graduates to choose primary care as their field instead of the more lucrative specialties such as surgery and dermatology.

17 It is possible to incorporate more medical professionals such as physician assistants (PAs) into primary care teams. They can talk to patients about treatment options, prescribe medications, and even perform technical procedures like bone marrow aspirations.

17

Which choice provides the best transition between paragraphs?

A) NO CHANGE
B) Nevertheless, it is possible to
C) Another option is to
D) Similarly, we must

The first paragraph indicates a challenge *facing the healthcare industry* and also presents *one possible solution* to this problem. The new paragraph C indicates a different solution to this problem. Choice C, therefore, is the most logical choice because the second paragraph is clearly discussing *another option*. Choice A is incorrect because it doesn't indicate any clear connection between the previous paragraph and the new one. Choice B is illogical because it implies that the previous paragraph indicates an obstacle to incorporating PAs into primary care teams, but it does not. Choice D is also illogical, because the two proposed solutions are not similar.

Sentence Sequencing

When the sentences within a paragraph are numbered, you might be asked about the logical sequencing of those sentences. Pay attention to any verbal cues that indicate a **time sequence** or **number sequence**, as well as how any topic might depend on a previous sentence (maybe because the previous sentence contains the antecedent of a pronoun in the reference sentence) or set up a following sentence.

---

[1] Another option is to incorporate more medical professionals such as physician assistants (PAs) and nurse practitioners (NPs) into primary care teams. [2] They can talk to patients about treatment options, prescribe medications, and even perform technical procedures such as bone marrow aspirations. [3] Many healthcare providers are moving toward this "team-based" model, whereby physicians can better focus on their specialties while relying on trained professionals to provide other necessary services. [4] Team-based medicine allows medical practitioners to best utilize their particular skills while sharing the successes and struggles of the team. [5] If organized around the principles of professionalism, trust, communication, and accountability, these teams may be able to provide better care to patients at less cost. [6] Although they receive less training than physicians do, these professionals have advanced degrees and can work with physicians to provide important services to patients. **27**

27

To make the paragraph most logical, sentence 6 should be placed

A) where it is now.
B) immediately after sentence 1.
C) immediately after sentence 3.
D) immediately after sentence 4.

Choice A is incorrect because sentence 6 provides an introductory detail about PAs and NPs that belongs at the beginning of this paragraph, not the end. However, it must be placed after sentence 1 because the pronoun phrase *these professionals* requires the antecedent provided in sentence 1. Choice B is best because sentence 6 logically sets up sentence 2, which specifies the *important services* that PAs and NPs can provide. Choices C and D are both incorrect because sentence 6 would disrupt the discussion of the "team-based" model in sentences 3–5.

Support and "Set Up" Questions

When a question asks you to make a choice that either supports a previous idea or "sets up" a following idea, just **carefully read the portion of the sentence the question refers to** and use your common sense about the logical connections between the ideas.

The team-based system can even support a more profitable and sustainable business model for medical practices, since many physician assistants and nurse practitioners not only help physicians to be more efficient, but also <u>keep careful records of their interactions with patients</u>.

11

Which choice best supports the main idea of the sentence?

A) NO CHANGE
B) can attract loyal patient followings of their own
C) require malpractice insurance
D) need special equipment and uniforms

This question asks us to support the main idea of the sentence, which is always conveyed by the main clause. In this sentence, the main clause is *the team-based system can even support a more profitable and sustainable business model*. In other words, it can help a medical practice to make more money over an extended period of time. The only choice that logically supports this claim is B, because attracting a loyal patient following would reasonably allow a practice to make more money. Choices A, C, and D all describe situations that would cost a business time or money, and so do not support a claim about increased profit.

Dogs [25] have been working for humans since long before the even first horse or bovine was domesticated. They provide assistance to disabled people, give comfort to recovering patients, predict seizures in people prone to epilepsy, and even detect malignant tumors by smell.

25

Which choice best sets up the examples that follow?

A) NO CHANGE
B) can perform useful tasks in dozens of different fields
C) provide important medical services
D) are often easier to train than humans

This question asks us to "set up" the examples that follow the underlined portion. Since each of the examples is a medical service, choice C is the best response. Even though choices A, B, and D may be true and grammatically correct statements, they do not "set up" the examples. Choice A could be used to set up examples of dogs helping humans throughout the centuries. Choice B could be used to set up examples of widely different fields (beyond just medicine) in which dogs can work. Choice D could be used to set up examples of tasks that dogs can learn more easily than humans.

LESSON 3: PURPOSE, STYLE, AND PATTERN

Purpose Questions

Always note carefully when an SAT Writing question gives **instructions** in addition to the four options. Sometimes these instructions tell you to choose the option that **best satisfies a specific purpose**, rather than the one that is most clearly or grammatically phrased. Always **underline the purpose** in these questions, and make sure to focus on that purpose as you choose.

Although many so-called news sites on the Internet abound with [17] clickbait and ads, you can still find sources that provide objective and reliable information.

17

Which choice best contrasts the idea at the end of the sentence?

A) NO CHANGE
B) stories for viewers with short attention spans
C) gossip about the lives of celebrities
D) partisanship, misinformation, and fear mongering

The instructions tell us to **contrast** the idea at the end of the sentence, which is that *you can still find sources that provide objective and reliable information.* Although all of the answer choices indicate things that some users might find annoying or shallow, only choice D directly contrasts the main idea of the sentence, since *partisanship* and *fear mongering* are biased and not *objective*, and *misinformation* is by definition not *reliable information.*

Style and Pattern Questions

In Chapter 5 Lesson 3, we talked about the importance of **parallelism** in comparisons and lists. The rule is simple: items in a comparison or list should have similar **grammatical** forms. Sometimes an SAT Writing question may ask you to take it one step further and follow a pattern of **tone, syntax** (phrase structure), or **category** within a sentence or paragraph.

Tarkovsky's films juxtapose striking natural images with man-made structures to evoke a sense of disorientation and gloom: woody vines swallow an abandoned train station; tiny feathers **41** <u>swirling like snowflakes.</u>

41

Which choice best exemplifies the main idea of the sentence and matches the pattern of the previous example?

A) NO CHANGE
B) create an ominous mood
C) blanket an empty church
D) in the fading sunlight

We are asked to make a choice that *best matches the pattern of the previous example.* The main clause says that *Tarkovsky's films juxtapose striking natural images with man-made structures.* The colon suggests that examples or an explanation will follow. The first example takes the form of an independent clause: *woody vines swallow an abandoned train station.* To follow this pattern, the second example should also be in the form of an independent clause. We can rule out choices A and D because neither creates an independent clause. Choice B is incorrect because it does not fit the **semantic** pattern of the sentence: it does not show a natural image juxtaposed with a man-made structure. Therefore, the correct answer is C because it creates an independent clause that exemplifies a natural image juxtaposed on a man-made structure.

EXERCISE SET 17: DIAGNOSING PARAGRAPHS

Curing Chemophobia

[1] There is a brain-destroying disease going around that you might have right now. [2] Think I'm exaggerating? [3] Okay, I am. [4] Specifically, it makes you susceptible to irrational arguments and silly beliefs. [5] It may not exactly destroy your brain, but it definitely warps your thinking. [6] Fortunately, you have the power to eradicate it. [7] The cure? [8] Do your chemistry homework. **1**

Some years back, the magicians Penn and Teller **2** <u>instigated a hoax on</u> scores of environmental activists. They hired an engaging young woman to hand around a petition at a rally demanding a ban on a potentially dangerous chemical that is leaking into our reservoirs and food supply: dihydrogen monoxide. This chemical, so people were told, is the primary chemical in acid rain. It is used in nuclear facilities and in factories that manufacture pesticides. **3** <u>It is a chemical that has</u> <u>been known to scientists for centuries.</u>

What exactly is dihydrogen monoxide? Water. H_2O. The substance of life. The very chemical many of the signers were swigging from their BPA-free bottles as they listened to the pitch. Everything the campaigner said about this chemical was true, but framed in menacing-sounding language.

Hundreds of people were convinced to sign the petition. To be fair, many of them were probably just "joiners" wanting to go along with the crowd, who by and large were relatively well-informed and well-intentioned people. But the fact that they were so easily fooled reveals how important it is to educate ourselves about what "chemicals" really are, what they do, and **4** <u>their effect on</u> the environment.

1. To make this paragraph most logical, sentence 4 should be placed

   A) where it is now.
   B) immediately after sentence 2.
   C) immediately after sentence 5.
   D) immediately after sentence 6.

2. Which choice best emphasizes the deceitfulness of the magicians' actions?

   A) NO CHANGE
   B) performed an experiment on
   C) took a poll of
   D) investigated

3. Which choice provides the most relevant detail to the paragraph?

   A) NO CHANGE
   B) It can exist in solid, liquid, or gas form.
   C) If even a small amount of this chemical gets into your lungs, it can kill you.
   D) It is used on commercial and organic farms throughout the world.

4. Which choice best fits the pattern of the sentence?

   A) NO CHANGE
   B) in what way they affect
   C) the effect they have on
   D) how they affect

CONTINUE ➡

This disease is not just a "hippy" thing. Although most of the petition signers were almost certainly from the left side of the political spectrum, conservatives have also been known to embrace bad reasoning when it serves their political goals. A Republican representative recently claimed on the floor of Congress that the carbon dioxide from coal-burning power plants **5** is not as dangerous as it seems to alarmists.

To cure this disease, we must **6** learn the plain meaning of words. We must learn that no molecule is toxic just because someone slaps a word on it such as "chemical," "artificial," or "industrial," and no substance is healthful just because someone calls it "natural," "artisanal," or "organic." **7** How molecules interact in our bodies and ecosystems is simply a matter of physical law.

5. Which choice best supports the claim in the previous sentence?
   A) NO CHANGE
   B) can't harm the planet because "carbon dioxide is natural."
   C) is indistinguishable from the carbon dioxide in soda.
   D) is needed as a food source for plants.

6. Which choice best sets up the claims in the next sentence?
   A) NO CHANGE
   B) understand how scientists conduct experiments
   C) recognize propaganda and learn more chemistry
   D) encourage politicians to reach across the aisle

7. Which choice provides the best conclusion to the passage?
   A) NO CHANGE
   B) These kinds of words are used by public relations firms and advertisers in many different industries.
   C) Understanding the real meanings of words is the first step in understanding difficult concepts.
   D) It is not the words themselves that are good or bad, but rather the ways that we use them.

ANSWER KEY

Exercise Set 17

1. C

Sentence 4 works best immediately after sentence 5 because it specifies how this disease *warps your thinking*. Choice A is incorrect because the logical transition *specifically* does not link with anything is sentence 3. Choice B is incorrect because it would interrupt the question-and-answer pattern of sentences 2 and 3. Choice D is incorrect because it would disrupt the discussion about the cure in sentences 6–8.

2. A

The original phrasing is best for emphasizing the *deceitfulness of the magicians' actions* because a *hoax* is a deception. Although each of the other choices is grammatically correct and semantically appropriate, none of them emphasizes deceitfulness.

3. C

The three sentences at the end of this paragraph list facts about dihydrogen monoxide—water—that are true but dangerous-sounding. Only choice C fits this pattern. The other options state true facts, but none of them sounds dangerous.

4. D

This sentence provides a list of phrases that begin with interrogative pronouns (Chapter 5, Lesson 8): *what "chemicals" really are, what they do…*. The only choice that continues this pattern is D, because it also begins with an interrogative pronoun, *how*. Choice B starts with a phrase that could ask a question (*in what way?*) but since the first word is a preposition and not an interrogative pronoun, it is not the most parallel choice.

5. B

This question instructs us to choose the phrase that *best supports the claim in the previous sentence*. This claim is that *conservatives have also been known to embrace bad reasoning when it serves their political goals*. Only one of the choices actually specifies a chain of *reasoning*: choice B. (Note that the word *because* always specifies a cause or reason.) Choice A is incorrect because although it expresses a claim that may be disputed by those with different political positions, this phrase does not indicate any reasoning behind the claim, let alone any *bad* reasoning. Choices B and D indicate claims that are less disputable, but again neither choice indicates the reasoning behind the claims.

6. C

The next sentence says that the toxicity or healthfulness of a substance isn't determined by the words we use to describe it, but by the chemical properties of that substance. Therefore, choice C is best because understanding this requires understanding how political language (*propaganda*) can be used to manipulate, and how chemical laws explain the behavior of molecules. Choice A is incorrect because the next sentence is not about the *plain meaning* of words, but rather how they can be misleading. Choice B is incorrect because this paragraph is not about the scientific method. Choice D is incorrect because, although political cooperation may be a good thing, it is not the topic of this paragraph.

7. A

When a question asks for the *best* conclusion to a passage, it doesn't mean to *choose the happiest or most hopeful ending*. It means *choose the sentence that best concludes the paragraph and ties up the main discussion*. In this case, choice A is the best because it explains the claims made in the previous sentence and provides a strong grounding for the thesis of the passage as a whole, which is that we must cure the "disease of chemophobia." Choice B is incorrect because it introduces a fact that is irrelevant to the passage as a whole. Choice C is incorrect because this passage is not about the *real meanings* of words. Choice D is incorrect because the main thesis of the passage is not that we use words badly, but that we are easily mislead by politically biased language to believe false claims about chemicals.

SECTION 3

HOW TO CONQUER THE SAT ESSAY

CHAPTER 7
FAQs ABOUT THE SAT ESSAY

DO I HAVE TO TAKE THE SAT ESSAY?

Although most colleges do not require the SAT Essay, a strong score may give you an admissions or placement advantage. As of 2019, the University of California system (UC Berkeley, UC Davis, UC Irvine, UCLA, UC Merced, UC Riverside, UC San Diego, UC Santa Barbara, and UC Santa Cruz) requires the Essay from all students submitting SAT scores. Many other colleges require or recommend the SAT Essay, including Amherst College, Cal State Northridge, Cooper Union, Davidson College, George Washington University, Hofstra University, Howard University, and many more. For most other colleges, the SAT Essay is optional.

When exploring colleges, ask the admissions officers whether they require or recommend the SAT Essay, and how they might use it even if it is not required. Some colleges may use it for placement in first year English classes or use as a "tiebreaker" in admissions decisions.

WHAT IS THE SAT ESSAY?

SAT Essay gives you 50 minutes to read and analyze an "op-ed" (opinion/editorial) passage presenting a point of view in the arts, politics, sciences, or culture. Your job is to write an essay summarizing the author's argument and explaining how the author uses language, evidence, and reasoning to support his or her claims.

On the next pages is a sample SAT essay and prompt. Read it carefully to familiarize yourself with the instructions and format.

WHAT IS A GOOD SAT ESSAY SCORE?

Two readers will give your essay a score from 1 to 4 in three categories: Reading (how well you show that you understand the argument), Analysis (how well you identify the important aspects of the argument and explain their effects on the reader), and Writing (how well you express yourself and organize your thoughts coherently).

The chart below shows the distribution of SAT Essay scores for 2019. The mean score was 13.17 out of a possible 24. (4.61 Reading, 3.47 Analysis, and 5.09 Writing.) Notice that about 30% of students scored 6 or better on Reading and over 45% of students scored 6 or better on Writing. (Remember that each sub-score is the sum of the scores given by the two readers.)

But getting a 6+ on the Analysis score is truly impressive. Fewer than *8% of students* scored 6 or better on Analysis in 2019 perhaps because too few schools really focus on teaching students to analyze arguments. For this reason, pay special attention to Chapter 8 Lesson 3, which takes a deep dive into the essential rhetorical analysis skills. Mastering them will give you a leg up on the competition.

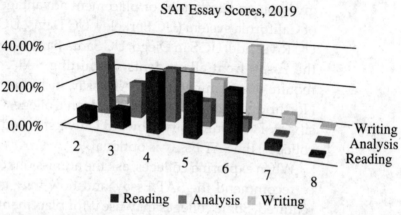

SAT Essay Scores, 2019

■ Reading   ■ Analysis   ■ Writing

Source: CollegeBoard.com

▮▮ SAMPLE SAT ESSAY

> As you read the passage below, consider how Eric Schwitzgebel uses
>
> - evidence, such as facts or examples, to support claims.
> - reasoning to develop ideas and connect claims and evidence.
> - stylistic or persuasive elements, such as word choice or appeals to emotion, to add power to the ideas expressed.

Adapted from Eric Schwitzgebel "We Have Greater Moral Obligations to Robots Than to Humans." ©2016 Aeon Media (Aeon.co). Originally published in *Aeon Magazine*, November 12, 2015.

1 Down goes HotBot 4b into the volcano. The year is 2050 or 2150, and artificial intelligence has advanced sufficiently that such robots can be built with human-grade intelligence, creativity and desires. HotBot will now perish on this scientific mission. Does it have rights? In commanding it to go down, have we done something morally wrong?

2 The moral status of robots is a frequent theme in science fiction, back at least to Isaac Asimov's robot stories, and the consensus is clear: if someday we manage to create robots that have mental lives similar to ours, with human-like plans, desires, and a sense of self, including the capacity for joy and suffering, then those robots deserve moral consideration similar to that accorded to natural human beings. Philosophers and researchers on artificial intelligence who have written about this issue generally agree.

3 I want to challenge this consensus, but not in the way you might predict. I think that, if we someday create robots with human-like cognitive and emotional capacities, we owe them *more* moral consideration than we would normally owe to otherwise similar human beings.

4 Here's why: we will have been their creators and designers. We are thus directly responsible both for their existence and for their happy or unhappy state. If a robot needlessly suffers or fails to reach its developmental potential, it will be in substantial part because of our failure—a failure in our creation, design or nurturance of it. Our moral relation to robots will more closely resemble the relation that parents have to their children, or that gods have to the beings they create, than the relationship between human strangers.

5 In a way, this is no more than equality. If I create a situation that puts other people at risk—for example, if I destroy their crops to build an airfield—then I have a moral obligation to compensate them, greater than my obligation to people with whom I have no causal connection. If we create genuinely conscious robots, we are deeply causally connected to them, and so substantially responsible for their welfare. That is the root of our special obligation.

6 Frankenstein's monster says to his creator, Victor Frankenstein:

> I am thy creature, and I will be even mild and docile to my natural lord and king if thou wilt also perform thy part, the which thou owest me. Oh, Frankenstein, be not equitable to every other and trample upon me alone, to whom thy justice, and even thy clemency and affection, is most due. Remember that I am thy creature: I ought to be thy Adam. . . .

7   We must either only create robots sufficiently simple that we know them not to merit moral consideration—as with all existing robots today—or we ought to bring them into existence only carefully and solicitously.

8   Alongside this duty to be solicitous comes another, of knowledge—a duty to know which of our creations are genuinely conscious. Which of them have real streams of subjective experience, and are capable of joy and suffering, or of cognitive achievements such as creativity and a sense of self? Without such knowledge, we won't know what obligations we have to our creations.

9   Yet how can we acquire the relevant knowledge? How does one distinguish, for instance, between a genuine stream of emotional experience and simulated emotions in an artificial mind? Merely programming a superficial simulation of emotion isn't enough. If I put a standard computer processor manufactured in 2015 into a toy dinosaur and program it to say "Ow!" when I press its off switch, I haven't created a robot capable of suffering. But exactly what kind of processing and complexity is necessary to give rise to genuine human-like consciousness? On some views—John Searle's, for example—consciousness might not be possible in *any* programmed entity; it might require a structure biologically similar to the human brain. Other views are much more liberal about the conditions sufficient for robot consciousness. The scientific study of consciousness is still in its infancy. The issue remains wide open.

10 If we continue to develop sophisticated forms of artificial intelligence, we have a moral obligation to improve our understanding of the conditions under which artificial consciousness might genuinely emerge. Otherwise we risk moral catastrophe—either the catastrophe of sacrificing our interests for beings that don't deserve moral consideration because they experience happiness and suffering only falsely, or the catastrophe of failing to recognize robot suffering, and so unintentionally committing atrocities tantamount to slavery and murder against beings to whom we have an almost parental obligation of care.

11 We have, then, a direct moral obligation to treat our creations with an acknowledgement of our special responsibility for their joy, suffering, thoughtfulness, and creative potential. But we also have an epistemic obligation to learn enough about the material and functional bases of joy, suffering, thoughtfulness, and creativity to know when and whether our potential future creations deserve our moral concern.

Write an essay in which you explain how Eric Schwitzgebel builds an argument to persuade his readers that we have strong moral obligations toward the intelligent machines we create. In your essay, analyze how he uses one or more of the features listed in the box above (or features of your own choice) to strengthen the logic and persuasiveness of his argument. Be sure that your analysis focuses on the most relevant features of the passage.

Your essay should NOT explain whether you agree with Schwitzgebel's claims, but rather explain how he builds an argument to persuade his audience.

HOW IS THE SAT ESSAY SCORED?

Your essay will be scored based on three criteria: **Reading**, **Analysis**, and **Writing**. Two trained readers will give your essay a score of 1 to 4 on these three criteria, and your subscore for each criterion will be the sum of these two, that is, a score from 2 to 8. Here is the official rubric for all three criteria.

Official SAT Essay Scoring Rubric

Score	Reading	Analysis	Writing
4	• demonstrates a thorough understanding of the source text, including its central ideas, its important details and how they interrelate • is free of errors of fact or interpretation with regard to the text • makes skillful use of textual evidence (quotations, paraphrases, or both) to demonstrate a complete understanding of the source text	• offers an insightful analysis of the source text and demonstrates a sophisticated understanding of the analytical task • offers a thorough, well-considered evaluation of the author's use of evidence, reasoning, and/or stylistic and persuasive elements, and/or features of the student's own choosing • contains relevant, sufficient, and strategically chosen support for claims or points made • focuses consistently on those features of the text that are most relevant to addressing the task	• is cohesive and demonstrates a highly effective command of language • includes a precise central claim • includes an eloquent introduction and conclusion, and demonstrates a logical and effective progression of ideas within and among paragraphs • uses an effective variety of sentence structures, demonstrates precise word choice, and maintains a formal style and objective tone • shows a strong command of the conventions of Standard American English and is free or virtually free of errors
3	• demonstrates effective understanding of the source text, including its central ideas and important details • is free of substantive errors of fact and interpretation with regard to the text • makes appropriate use of textual evidence (quotations, paraphrases, or both) to demonstrate an understanding of the source text	• offers an effective analysis of the source text and demonstrates an understanding of the analytical task • competently evaluates the author's use of evidence, reasoning, and/or stylistic and persuasive elements, and/or features of the student's own choosing • contains relevant and sufficient support for claims or points made • focuses primarily on those features of the text that are most relevant to addressing the task	• is mostly cohesive and demonstrates effective control of language • includes a central claim or implicit controlling idea • includes an effective introduction and conclusion, and demonstrates a clear progression of ideas within and among paragraphs • uses a variety of sentence structures, demonstrates some precise word choice, and maintains a formal style and objective tone • shows a good control of the conventions of Standard American English and is free of significant errors that detract from the quality of writing

| 2 | • demonstrates some understanding of the source text, including its central ideas but not of important details
• may contain errors of fact and/or interpretation with regard to the text
• makes limited and/or haphazard use of textual evidence (quotations, paraphrases, or both) to demonstrate some understanding of the source text | • offers limited analysis of the source text and demonstrates only partial understanding of the analytical task
• identifies and attempts to describe the author's use of evidence, reasoning, and/or stylistic and persuasive elements, and/or features of the student's own choosing, but merely asserts rather than explains their importance, or makes unwarranted claims
• contains little or no support for claims
• may lack a clear focus on those features of the text that are most relevant to addressing the task | • demonstrates little or no cohesion and limited skill in the use and control of language
• may lack a clear central claim or controlling idea or may deviate from the claim or idea
• lacks an effective introduction and/or conclusion
• may demonstrate some progression of ideas within paragraphs but not throughout
• has limited variety in sentence structures
• demonstrates inconsistently effective diction and deviates noticeably from a formal style and objective tone
• shows a limited control of the conventions of Standard American English and contains errors that detract from the quality of writing and may impede understanding |
| 1 | • demonstrates little or no comprehension of the source text
• fails to show an understanding of the text's central ideas, and may include only details without reference to central ideas
• may contain numerous errors of fact or interpretation with regard to the text
• makes little or no use of textual evidence (quotations, paraphrases, or both), demonstrating little or no understanding of the source text | • offers little or no analysis or ineffective analysis of the source text and demonstrates little or no understanding of the analytic task
• identifies without explanation some aspects of the author's use of evidence, reasoning, and/or stylistic and persuasive elements
• makes unwarranted analytical claims
• contains little or no support for claims, or support is largely irrelevant
• may not focus on features of the text that are relevant to addressing the task
• offers no discernible analysis (e.g., is largely or exclusively summary) | • demonstrates little or no cohesion and inadequate skill in the use and control of language
• may lack a clear central claim or controlling idea
• lacks a recognizable introduction and conclusion, and lacks any discernible progression of ideas
• lacks variety in sentence structures, demonstrates weak diction, and may lack a formal style and objective tone
• shows a weak control of the conventions of Standard American English and may contain numerous errors that undermine the quality of writing. |

CHAPTER 8

HOW TO WRITE A GREAT SAT ESSAY

LESSON 1: USE YOUR 50 MINUTES WISELY

For most students, 50 minutes is plenty of time to read the passage multiple times, analyze its argument, outline the essay, and write 5 or 6 strong paragraphs, at least if you follow the plan below. However, if you find that you need more than 50 minutes, even after practicing these techniques, consider applying for extended time accommodations at the College Board website.

The best way to spend your 50 minutes depends on your particular strengths and weaknesses in reading and writing. I recommend that you start with the following breakdown, and adjust as necessary as you practice under real test conditions.

0:00–20:00: Read

Take the first 15 to 20 minutes to read the passage **three times**, as we will discuss in Lessons 2–4. Your first pass is to **summarize** the argument, your second pass is to **analyze** the argument, and your third pass is to select and **synthesize** the information for your essay.

This "three-pass approach" is a fairly advanced reading technique that will not only ensure that you ace the SAT Essay, but also give you the tools to tackle tough analytical writing assignments in college-level liberal arts classes.

Mastering the three-pass approach will take some time, so be patient and practice regularly. Section 5 of this book gives you three practice SAT Essay prompts for practice, but you can also find lots of practice essay prompts at the College Board SAT website, as well as in SAT review books such as *McGraw-Hill SAT* and *McGraw-Hill 6 SAT Practice Tests*.

20:00–30:00: Outline

Your next task is to gather the big ideas from your analysis and use them to write a thesis and outline a five- or six-paragraph essay. If you have completed the three-pass analysis, creating an outline should be easy. We will discuss thesis-writing in Lesson 5 and outlining in Lesson 6.

Your thesis should summarize the main idea and secondary ideas of the essay, and describe the author's main modes of argument and notable stylistic and rhetorical elements.

Don't make the mistake of writing your essay before you have a thoughtful guiding question and have outlined the essay as a whole.

30:00–50:00: Write

Next, of course, you have to write your easy. To get a high score, it must provide a strong introduction that summarizes the passage and introduces your central analytical claim, develop and support your claim with strong reasoning and examples from the passage, be well-organized in coherent paragraphs, and show a strong command of language. If you have a strong outline, the essay should flow naturally and easily from that. We will discuss some key writing and editing skills in Lessons 7 and 8.

LESSON 2: FIRST PASS—SUMMARIZE

Your first job is to read the passage and summarize each paragraph individually. Focus on just two questions: **what is the central thesis?** and **what is the main idea of each paragraph?**

First Pass Notes

Summary

Down goes HotBot 4b into the volcano. The year is 2050 or 2150, and artificial intelligence has advanced sufficiently that such robots can be built with human-grade intelligence, creativity and desires. HotBot will now perish on this scientific mission. Does it have rights? In commanding it to go down, have we done something morally wrong?

What are our moral responsibilities toward robots, particularly when we have them do dangerous things?

The moral status of robots is a frequent theme in science fiction, back at least to Isaac Asimov's robot stories, and the consensus is clear: if someday we manage to create robots that have mental lives similar to ours, with human-like plans, desires, and a sense of self, including the capacity for joy and suffering, then those robots deserve moral consideration similar to that accorded to natural human beings. Philosophers and researchers on artificial intelligence who have written about this issue generally agree.

Novelists, philosophers, and researchers believe that, if robots become sufficiently human-like, then they deserve moral consideration.

I want to challenge this consensus, but not in the way you might predict. I think that, if we someday create robots with human-like cognitive and emotional capacities, we owe them *more* moral consideration than we would normally owe to otherwise similar human beings.

I think robots may deserve even more moral consideration than some human beings . . .

Here's why: we will have been their creators and designers. We are thus directly responsible both for their existence and for their happy or unhappy state. If a robot needlessly suffers or fails to reach its developmental potential, it will be in substantial part because of our failure—a failure in our creation, design, or nurturance of it. Our moral relation to robots will more closely resemble the relation that parents have to their children, or that gods have to the beings they create, than the relationship between human strangers.

. . . because we designed and "nurtured" them.

In a way, this is no more than equality. If I create a situation that puts other people at risk—for example, if I destroy their crops to build an airfield—then I have a moral obligation to compensate them, greater than my obligation to people with whom I have no causal connection. If we create genuinely conscious robots, we are deeply causally connected to them, and so substantially responsible for their welfare. That is the root of our special obligation.

> We have a greater moral responsibility for those situations that we cause directly.

Frankenstein's monster says to his creator, Victor Frankenstein:

> I am thy creature, and I will be even mild and docile to my natural lord and king if thou wilt also perform thy part, the which thou owest me. Oh, Frankenstein, be not equitable to every other and trample upon me alone, to whom thy justice, and even thy clemency and affection, is most due. Remember that I am thy creature: I ought to be thy Adam. . . .

> Frankenstein's monster stated this moral obligation eloquently—Victor Frankenstein "owes" him clemency and affection.

We must either only create robots sufficiently simple that we know them not to merit moral consideration—as with all existing robots today—or we ought to bring them into existence only carefully and solicitously.

> If we can't be sufficiently humane to robots, we should keep them "simple."

Alongside this duty to be solicitous comes another, of knowledge—a duty to know which of our creations are genuinely conscious. Which of them have real streams of subjective experience, and are capable of joy and suffering, or of cognitive achievements such as creativity and a sense of self? Without such knowledge, we won't know what obligations we have to our creations.

> We must learn which creatures are capable of consciousness, joy, suffering, and creativity.

Yet how can we acquire the relevant knowledge? How does one distinguish, for instance, between a genuine stream of emotional experience and simulated emotions in an artificial mind? Merely programming a superficial simulation of emotion isn't enough. If I put a standard computer processor manufactured in 2015 into a toy dinosaur and program it to say "Ow!" when I press its off switch, I haven't created a robot capable of suffering. But exactly what kind of processing and complexity is necessary to give rise to genuine human-like consciousness? On some views—John Searle's, for example—consciousness might not be possible in *any* programmed entity; it might require a structure biologically similar to the human brain. Other views are much more liberal about the conditions sufficient for robot consciousness. The scientific study of consciousness is still in its infancy. The issue remains wide open.

We must distinguish between simulated emotion and real emotion, but we don't yet agree on how to do so.

If we continue to develop sophisticated forms of artificial intelligence, we have a moral obligation to improve our understanding of the conditions under which artificial consciousness might genuinely emerge. Otherwise we risk moral catastrophe—either the catastrophe of sacrificing our interests for beings that don't deserve moral consideration because they experience happiness and suffering only falsely, or the catastrophe of failing to recognize robot suffering, and so unintentionally committing atrocities tantamount to slavery and murder against beings to whom we have an almost parental obligation of care.

Progress in artificial intelligence is morally dangerous if we do not understand how and when consciousness emerges.

We have, then, a direct moral obligation to treat our creations with an acknowledgement of our special responsibility for their joy, suffering, thoughtfulness, and creative potential. But we also have an epistemic obligation to learn enough about the material and functional bases of joy, suffering, thoughtfulness, and creativity to know when and whether our potential future creations deserve our moral concern.

[Summary of main points]

LESSON 3: SECOND PASS—ANALYZE

Next, read the passage again asking **how does the author use evidence, reasoning, and rhetorical or stylistic devices?** The list below highlights many of the most important questions to ask, elements to look for, and terms to use.

What kinds of REASONING does the writer use to support his or her claims?

- **Inductive reasoning** is reasoning based on a pattern that can be inferred from a set of examples. For instance, you might say that government spending is helpful in a recession because it has helped several times in the past, notably during the Great Depression of 1929–1938 and the Great Recession of 2007–2010. Inductive reasoning depends on the reliability of the pattern and whether or not there are good counterexamples.

- **Dialectical reasoning** is drawing a conclusion after weighing arguments from different sides—the thesis (such as an argument for increased government spending) and the antithesis (such as an argument for cutbacks in government spending)—and then constructing a synthesis that provides a compromise or alternative. Dialectical reasoning depends on the good judgment and analytical skills of the writer.

- **Deductive reasoning** is reasoning based on a syllogism or a chain of syllogisms. A syllogism consists of two necessary premises and a necessary conclusion.
  - Premise 1: If A is true, then B is true.
  - Premise 2: A is true.
  - Conclusion: Therefore, B is true.

  For instance, if you accept that 1) if someone is a surgeon, then he or she graduated from medical school, and that 2) Sarah is a surgeon, then you must conclude that 3) Sarah graduated from medical school. Deductive reasoning depends on the writer's ability to follow syllogistic form carefully and to convince the reader that the two premises are true.

- **Analogical reasoning** is reasoning based on the similarity of one situation to another. For instance, one might claim that suppressing emotions is dangerous because it's like trying to hold back water from a rainstorm with a fragile dam. Analogical reasoning depends on the functional similarities between the two situations.

- **Abductive reasoning** is finding the most reasonable explanation to explain an observation. For instance, if you see a bunch of holes in your lawn, you might conclude abductively that you have an infestation of rabbits. Abductive reasoning depends on the writer's ability to consider all plausible explanations.

What kinds of EVIDENCE does the writer use to support his or her claims?

- **Anecdotal evidence** is evidence in the form of a personal story. For example, a story about a friend whose headache went away after he stood on his head for ten minutes is anecdotal evidence, not scientific evidence, for the ability of headstands to cure headaches.
- **Empirical evidence** is evidence gathered through polling, scientific experiment, or careful observation. For instance, good empirical evidence for the effectiveness of a headache medication might include the results of a carefully controlled, triple-blind study.
- **Historical evidence** is evidence from previous events that share some common features with the situation being discussed. For instance, historical evidence for the effectiveness of a headache medication might include accounts of how the medication has been used successfully in the past.

How does the writer establish his or her CREDIBILITY?

- **Bona fides** are professional or experiential qualifications. For instance, a writer might be regarded as a credible authority on schizophrenia because she has studied it as a psychology professor for 30 years.
- **First-hand experience** can also give a writer credibility. For instance, if the writer has suffered from schizophrenia for his entire life, his descriptions of the disease might be particularly believable.
- **Substantive authority** is the credibility that a writer demonstrates by including perceptive details about the subject matter. For instance, you might consider a writer to be an authority on biology because he explains gene splicing clearly, even though he may not have a Ph.D. in the subject.
- **Self-interest** might support or undermine a writer's credibility. If a taxi driver argues against self-driving cars, we might be skeptical of his argument because it serves his self-interest. On the other hand, if he were to argue for them, despite the fact that it might harm his livelihood, his argument might be more believable.

What VALUES does the writer appeal to?

- A writer might appeal to the value of **honesty** when criticizing political doublespeak.
- An essay mentioning the "good old days" makes an appeal to **nostalgia**.
- An argument against racism might appeal to **common humanity**.
- A criticism of entitlement programs might appeal to the value of **hard work**.
- Some other common values a writer might allude to include **safety, freedom, strength, conservation of natural resources, economic prudence, learning,** and **beauty**.

Does the writer commit any LOGICAL FALLACIES?

A **fallacy** is not merely a false belief or misconception, but rather a **faulty pattern of reasoning**.

- An **ad hominem** is an attack "on the person" rather than on the soundness of a claim or the validity of the reasoning. For example, *my opponent's political opinions are irrelevant because she's just an actor* is not a valid argument against her claims.

- A **straw man** is an unfair and incorrect representation of an opponent's position, constructed to be easily attacked. For instance, if you believe that every gun owner should pass a basic background check and be certified in gun safety, an opponent might construct the straw man that *you want to take my guns away and leave me defenseless against criminals.* A strong argument should "steel man" any opposing claims and arguments, that is, state them in a way that the opponent would accept.

- **Begging the question** means assuming the truth of your conclusion in one of your premises. For instance, saying that *vaping call kill you because e-cigarettes are deadly* is an example of begging the question or **circular reasoning**.

- **Overgeneralization** means extending an idea beyond where it legitimately applies. For instance, it may be an overgeneralization to say that *tax cuts always help the economy* if they hurt when applied during periods of low unemployment and high corporate profits.

  One type of overgeneralization is the **biased sampling** fallacy in which an exception is taken as a rule, such as citing a few exceptionally successful people who were raised in poverty to make the claim that the poor don't have it any harder than the rest of us.

- An **appeal to consensus** is claiming that something is true because a group of people—usually the general public or a group of experts—believe that it is true. For instance, the fact that most educated people in the Middle Ages believed that diseases are caused by evil spirits doesn't mean that the theory is true.

- An **appeal to authority** is claiming that something is true because a respected authority happens to believe it. For example: *The world's greatest scientist, Sir Isaac Newton, believed that iron could be turned into gold, so it must be true.*

- The **correlation for causation** fallacy is an assumption that, because two things are correlated, one must be the cause of the other. For instance, one might claim that, because higher net worth correlates with longer lifespans, becoming rich will make you live longer (or becoming healthier will make you rich). However, it may be that neither is true, and that wealth and health are both the result of living in a stable and scientifically advanced society.

Important: The SAT Essay is an analytical essay, not a rhetorical one, so avoid discussing whether you agree with the author's argument. If you point out a fallacy, just cite the evidence and explain the fallacy. Fallacies don't refute claims, they just fail to support them. For instance, the argument two plus two equals four because the sum of any two even numbers is another even number is fallacious, even though it contains two true statements.

What APPEALS TO EMOTION does the writer make?

- An **alarmist** essay is one that appeals to fear and conveys a sense of urgency.
- A **sentimental** essay appeals to nostalgia and yearning for the "good old days."
- A **conversational** essay uses friendly language to appeal to a reader's sense of comfort.
- An **authoritative** essay reassures readers with a commanding tone.
- A **diatribe** is an essay with a consistently **angry** or **self-righteous** tone.
- A **condescending** essay uses snarky language, perhaps to elicit **contempt** from its readers.
- A **satire** uses absurdity and humor to criticize a situation.

Does the author use PERSUASIVE DICTION?

- The **connotation** of a word is its emotional, historic, or sensual associations. Good writers use connotation to convey attitude. For instance, someone arguing for a new government program might call it an investment because that word implies positive things such as growth and value.
- **Euphemism** is the use of a term to make something seem more positive than it really is. For example, a salesperson might describe an unwanted disruption as a courtesy call, and someone promoting a tax increase might call it a revenue enhancement.
- **Dysphemism** is the use of a term to make something seem more negative than it really is. For example, a critic of a tax increase might call it government confiscation of earned wealth.
- **Understatement** emphasizes a point by underemphasizing its intensity, which is taken to be obvious. For instance, it's an understatement to suggest that hurricanes can be inconvenient.
- **Hyperbole** is exaggeration for persuasive or humorous effect, as in his overuse of commas is catastrophic.

What LITERARY or POETIC elements does the writer use?

- **Imagery** is the use of vivid sensory impressions in order to elicit a feeling like awe, anger, sadness, sympathy, and such. Keats uses visual and sound imagery to evoke a sense of peace and beauty when he writes full-grown lambs loud bleat from hilly bourn; Hedge-crickets sing; and now with treble soft; The redbreast whistles from a garden-croft.

- **Personification** is the attribution of personal qualities to an idea or thing, for example saying that a proposal is on its last legs or gave its last gasp.

- **Irony** is a deliberate reversal of expectations in order to surprise a reader. For example, Christopher Hitchens was being ironic when he said I believe in free will, but only because I have no other choice.

- A **foil** is someone or something that starkly contrasts someone or something else, usually to emphasize certain qualities. For example, a person arguing against a tax increase might use a bumbling, bureaucratic tax collector as a foil, while someone arguing for the tax increase might use a lazy, self-centered billionaire as a foil.

- Writers often use **characterization** to portray themselves, their readers, or their opponents as good guys or bad guys. For instance, they might portray themselves as **heroes**, **victims**, or **regular folks**, and they might portray their opponents as **villains**, **idiots**, or **dupes**.

- **Alliteration** is the repetition of initial sounds in words to emphasize a point. For instance, when John F. Kennedy referred to high standards of strength and sacrifice, he was using alliteration to draw his listeners into public service.

- An **allusion** is an indirect reference to a well-known book, film, or historical event. For example, he's gone down the rabbit hole is an allusion to *Alice in Wonderland,* and saying "this battle is his Waterloo" alludes to Napoleon's defeat there in 1815.

Does the writer use any EXPLANATORY TOOLS?

- **Analogies** can be useful for explaining concepts. For instance, you might explain how a computer works by noting that the keyboards, touchpads, and cameras act like human sensory organs such as ears, skin, and eyes, or explain the properties of an electric field by noting that it is analogous to a field of wheat.

- A **metaphor** applies a word or phrase to something it doesn't literally apply to. For example, calling a refusal a slap in the face uses metaphor to emphasize how harsh and painful it is.

- **Didacticism** is formal instruction. A writer might use didactic methods when explaining a technical concept. For instance, in an essay about the differences between natural selection and the theory of "intelligent design," an author might clarify the formal definitions of terms like "scientific method," "evidentiary standards," "hypothesis," and "theory."

- A **concession** or **qualification** explains the limits or exceptions to a claim, usually so the writer can avoid being accused of being too extreme or inconsiderate. For instance, if you are arguing for a tax increase, you might concede that taxes are burdensome to taxpayers (a point that your opponent might use against you), but then address this concern by demonstrating that the benefits gained from the tax increase would offset any burdens.

Second Pass Notes

	Analysis

Down goes HotBot 4b into the volcano. The year is 2050 or 2150, and artificial intelligence has advanced sufficiently that such robots can be built with human-grade intelligence, creativity and desires. HotBot will now perish on this scientific mission. Does it have rights? In commanding it to go down, have we done something morally wrong?

hypothetical narrative

inquiry

The moral status of robots is a frequent theme in science fiction, back at least to Isaac Asimov's robot stories, and the consensus is clear: if someday we manage to create robots that have mental lives similar to ours, with human-like plans, desires, and a sense of self, including the capacity for joy and suffering, then those robots deserve moral consideration similar to that accorded to natural human beings. Philosophers and researchers on artificial intelligence who have written about this issue generally agree.

establishing relevance (1)

appeal to consensus (1)

appeal to emotion

establishing relevance (2)

appeal to consensus (2)

I want to challenge this consensus, but not in the way you might predict. I think that, if we someday create robots with human-like cognitive and emotional capacities, we owe them *more* moral consideration than we would normally owe to otherwise similar human beings.

polemic

Here's why: we will have been their creators and designers. We are thus directly responsible both for their existence and for their happy or unhappy state. If a robot needlessly suffers or fails to reach its developmental potential, it will be in substantial part because of our failure—a failure in our creation, design or nurturance of it. Our moral relation to robots will more closely resemble the relation that parents have to their children, or that gods have to the beings they create, than the relationship between human strangers.

argument from duty (1)
value of personal responsibility

analogy (1)

In a way, this is no more than <u>equality</u>. If I create a situation that puts other people at risk—for example, <u>if I destroy their crops to build an airfield</u>—then I have a moral obligation to compensate them, greater than my obligation to people with whom I have no causal connection. If we create genuinely conscious robots, we are deeply causally connected to them, and so substantially responsible for their welfare. That is the root of our special obligation.

appeal to common value

analogy (2)

<u>Frankenstein's monster</u> says to his creator, Victor Frankenstein:

literary allusion (1)

I am thy creature, and I will be even mild and docile to my natural lord and king if thou wilt also perform thy part, the which thou owest me. Oh, Frankenstein, be not equitable to every other and <u>trample upon me alone</u>, to whom thy <u>justice</u>, and even thy clemency and affection, is most due. Remember that I am thy creature: <u>I ought to be thy Adam</u>. . . .

appeal to sympathy
appeal to value

literary allusion (2)

<u>We must either only create robots sufficiently simple</u> that we know them not to merit moral consideration—as with all existing robots today—or we ought to bring them into existence only carefully and solicitously.

ultimatum

Alongside this duty to be solicitous comes another, of knowledge—<u>a duty to know which of our creations are genuinely conscious</u>. Which of them have real streams of subjective experience, and are capable of joy and suffering, or of cognitive achievements such as creativity and a sense of self? Without such knowledge, we won't know what obligations we have to our creations.

argument from duty (2)

Yet <u>how can we acquire the relevant knowledge</u>? How does one distinguish, for instance, between a genuine stream of emotional experience and simulated emotions in an artificial mind? Merely programming a superficial simulation of emotion isn't enough. <u>If I put a standard computer processor manufactured in 2015 into a toy dinosaur and program it to say "Ow!" when I press its off switch, I haven't created a robot capable of suffering.</u> But <u>exactly what kind of processing and complexity is necessary to give rise to genuine human-like consciousness</u>? On some views—<u>John Searle's, for example</u>—consciousness might not be possible in *any* programmed entity; it might require a structure biologically similar to the human brain. <u>Other views are much more liberal</u> about the conditions sufficient for robot consciousness. The scientific study of consciousness is still in its infancy. <u>The issue remains wide open</u>.

If <u>we continue to develop sophisticated forms of artificial intelligence</u>, we have a moral obligation to improve our understanding of the conditions under which artificial consciousness might genuinely emerge. Otherwise we risk <u>moral catastrophe</u>—either the catastrophe of sacrificing our interests for beings that don't deserve moral consideration because they experience happiness and suffering only falsely, or the catastrophe of failing to recognize robot suffering, and so unintentionally committing atrocities tantamount to slavery and murder against beings to whom we have an almost parental obligation of care.

We have, then, a direct moral obligation to treat our creations with an acknowledgement of our special responsibility for their joy, suffering, thoughtfulness and creative potential. But we also have an epistemic obligation to learn enough about the material and functional bases of joy, suffering, thoughtfulness, and creativity to know when and whether our potential future creations deserve our moral concern.

technical issue (1)

hypothetical illustration

technical issue (2)

authority

dialectical reasoning

synthesis

modern context

alarmism

summary

LESSON 4: THIRD PASS—SYNTHESIZE

Last, read the passage once more asking, **which stylistic or persuasive elements are the most important to the passage?** In other words, You won't be able to discuss every aspect of the passage, so choose the two or three major elements and the one or two minor elements that have the most impact on the argument.

Third Pass Notes

Synthesis

Down goes HotBot 4b into the volcano. The year is 2050 or 2150, and artificial intelligence has advanced sufficiently that such robots can be built with human-grade intelligence, creativity and desires. HotBot will now perish on this scientific mission. Does it have rights? In commanding it to go down, have we done something morally wrong?

Schwitzgebel poses a moral question—do robots have rights?—by describing a hypothetical story about a robot in "danger."

The moral status of robots is a frequent theme in science fiction, back at least to Isaac Asimov's robot stories, and the consensus is clear: if someday we manage to create robots that have mental lives similar to ours, with human-like plans, desires, and a sense of self, including the capacity for joy and suffering, then those robots deserve moral consideration similar to that accorded to natural human beings. Philosophers and researchers on artificial intelligence who have written about this issue generally agree.

He ties this question to literature, philosophy, and science, and suggests a consensus in those areas: humans have a moral obligation to humanoid robots.

I want to challenge this consensus, but not in the way you might predict. I think that, if we someday create robots with human-like cognitive and emotional capacities, we owe them *more* moral consideration than we would normally owe to otherwise similar human beings.

He claims that this consensus is wrong: we have *even more* moral obligations to robots that we *design* than to humans.

Here's why: we will have been their creators and designers. We are thus directly responsible both for their existence and for their happy or unhappy state. If a robot needlessly suffers or fails to reach its developmental potential, it will be in substantial part because of our failure—a failure in our creation, design or nurturance of it. Our moral relation to robots will more closely resemble the relation that parents have to their children, or that gods have to the beings they create, than the relationship between human strangers.

His argument is an argument from duty, which he explains through an analogy to the idea of a creator-god. Such an argument resonates with moralistic readers.

In a way, this is no more than equality. If I create a situation that puts other people at risk—for example, if I destroy their crops to build an airfield—then I have a moral obligation to compensate them, greater than my obligation to people with whom I have no causal connection. If we create genuinely conscious robots, we are deeply causally connected to them, and so substantially responsible for their welfare. That is the root of our special obligation.

He provides hypothetical scenarios to clarify this moral duty to the reader.

Frankenstein's monster says to his creator, Victor Frankenstein:

I am thy creature, and I will be even mild and docile to my natural lord and king if thou wilt also perform thy part, the which thou owest me. Oh, Frankenstein, be not equitable to every other and trample upon me alone, to whom thy justice, and even thy clemency and affection, is most due. Remember that I am thy creature: I ought to be thy Adam. . . .

He supports his claim about the moral duty of creator-gods with literary evidence from Mary Shelley's *Frankenstein*, to elicit sympathy and to connect with literate readers.

We must either only create robots sufficiently simple that we know them not to merit moral consideration—as with all existing robots today—or we ought to bring them into existence only carefully and solicitously.

He clarifies the moral obligation of roboticists: don't make human-like robots without careful consideration.

Alongside this duty to be solicitous comes another, of knowledge—a duty to know which of our creations are genuinely conscious. Which of them have real streams of subjective experience, and are capable of joy and suffering, or of cognitive achievements such as creativity and a sense of self? Without such knowledge, we won't know what obligations we have to our creations.

This consideration includes a duty to learn which creations are truly conscious…

Yet how can we acquire the relevant knowledge? How does one distinguish, for instance, between a genuine stream of emotional experience and simulated emotions in an artificial mind? Merely programming a superficial simulation of emotion isn't enough. If I put a standard computer processor manufactured in 2015 into a toy dinosaur and program it to say "Ow!" when I press its off switch, I haven't created a robot capable of suffering. But exactly what kind of processing and complexity is necessary to give rise to genuine human-like consciousness? On some views—John Searle's, for example—consciousness might not be possible in *any* programmed entity; it might require a structure biologically similar to the human brain. Other views are much more liberal about the conditions sufficient for robot consciousness. The scientific study of consciousness is still in its infancy. The issue remains wide open.

…which is a highly technical issue that he tries to clarify with some hypothetical examples. He examines the issue dialectically, acknowledging that there is disagreement about the possibility of robot consciousness. This gives an impression of fair-mindedness.

If we continue to develop sophisticated forms of artificial intelligence, we have a moral obligation to improve our understanding of the conditions under which artificial consciousness might genuinely emerge. Otherwise we risk moral catastrophe—either the catastrophe of sacrificing our interests for beings that don't deserve moral consideration because they experience happiness and suffering only falsely, or the catastrophe of failing to recognize robot suffering, and so unintentionally committing atrocities tantamount to slavery and murder against beings to whom we have an almost parental obligation of care.

Schwitgebel's tone becomes alarmist near the end of the essay, where he suggests that failure to heed his suggestions could lead to moral catastrophe, "tantamount to slavery and murder." This language is likely to catch readers' attention and spur them to action.

We have, then, a direct moral obligation to treat our creations with an acknowledgement of our special responsibility for their joy, suffering, thoughtfulness, and creative potential. But we also have an epistemic obligation to learn enough about the material and functional bases of joy, suffering, thoughtfulness, and creativity to know when and whether our potential future creations deserve our moral concern.

LESSON 5: WRITE A GREAT THESIS

After you've finished your three passes, organize your thoughts into a concise and interesting **thesis**. This thesis should summarize the main claims of the passage and indicate its most significant stylistic and persuasive elements. The College Board says that a good thesis should be **precise** and **thorough**. In other words, it should indicate that you thoroughly understand the passage, and have thoughtfully analyzed its style and structure.

Take your time when composing your thesis. Choose your words carefully, and make sure you capture the key elements of the passage. You will probably need more than one sentence to accomplish everything you need in a good thesis paragraph.

Draft 1

In his essay, "We Have Greater Moral Obligations to Robots Than to Humans," Eric Schwitzgebel talks about humans and intelligent machines. He uses literary references and hypothetical reasoning, and appeals to particular moral values.

Is It Precise?

A good thesis should be precise about what the writer is saying, and what techniques he or she uses. Let's look back at our notes and try to make these sentences more precise.

Draft 2

In his essay, "We Have Greater Moral Obligations to Robots Than to Humans," Eric Schwitzgebel ~~talks about humans and intelligent machines~~ **claims** *not only that intelligent machines have a "moral status," (2) but also that our ethical duties toward them are even stronger than our duties toward other humans. He breaks this moral obligation into two parts: a duty to be cautious and a duty to learn.* ~~He uses~~ **Schwitzgebel makes several** *literary references and* **uses** *hypothetical reasoning.* ~~and appeals to particular moral values~~ **He also appeals to the virtue of personal responsibility.**

Notice that this revision better specifies Schwitzgebel's claims and what devices he uses to support his claims.

Is It Thorough?

Although our second draft provides more details about Schwitzgebel's thesis, this draft still lacks information about the *purpose or effect* of the rhetorical and stylistic elements in the passage. Let's look back at out notes and add some details about these elements.

Draft 3

In his essay, "We Have Greater Moral Obligations to Robots Than to Humans," Eric Schwitzgebel claims not only that intelligent machines have a "moral status," (2) but also that our ethical duties toward them are even stronger than our duties toward other humans. He breaks this moral obligation into two parts: a duty to be cautious and a duty to learn. Schwitzgebel makes several literary references **to give the debate intellectual weight** *and uses hypothetical* ~~reasoning~~ **scenarios and analogies to explain the reasoning behind his thesis.** *He* ~~also appeals~~ **elevates the discussion by appealing** *to the virtue of personal responsibility,* **but also uses fear to motivate the reader to action.**

Note that this revision more thoroughly explains how each element supports Schwitzgebel's claims and how it affects the reader.

LESSON 6: OUTLINE YOUR ESSAY

Once your thesis is squared away, it's time to outline the rest of your essay. If the thesis is precise and thorough, you should have three or four specific ideas that you can develop into body paragraphs.

Our thesis paragraph already begins to answer the question posed in the SAT Essay assignment: *How does Eric Schwitzgebel build an argument to persuade his readers that we have strong moral obligations toward the intelligent machines we create?* It summarizes Schwitzgebel's thesis, describes his main persuasive techniques, and explains the effect of those techniques and devices.

The rest of the essay should focus on **supporting and explaining those points** one at a time.

OUTLINE

1. In his essay, "We Have Greater Moral Obligations to Robots Than to Humans," Eric Schwitzgebel claims not only that intelligent machines have a "moral status," (2) but also that our ethical duties toward them are even stronger than our duties toward other humans. He breaks this moral obligation into two parts: a duty to be cautious and a duty to learn. Schwitzgebel makes several literary references to give the debate intellectual weight and uses hypothetical scenarios and analogies to explain the reasoning behind his thesis. He elevates the discussion by appealing to the virtue of personal responsibility, but also uses fear to motivate the reader to action.

2. Schwitzegebel gives intellectual and moral weight to his controversial stance by setting it within a long history of literary, philosophical, and scientific debate.

3. He uses moral reasoning—specifically, an appeal to the duty of personal responsibility—as well as an appeal to consensus to support his claim.

4. He uses hypothetical scenarios and analogies to explain and illustrate his reasoning.

5. Although his literary references and appeal to virtue serve to elevate his discussion, he also appeals to fear by suggesting that failing to heed his recommendations could lead to "moral catastrophe" (10).

LESSON 7: WRITE YOUR FIRST DRAFT

If your outline is solid, writing the first draft should be a piece of cake. It's just a matter of explaining and substantiating the claims you've already laid out.

Substantiating your claims means **providing supportive excerpts from the text** and explaining them.

FIRST DRAFT

In his essay, "We Have Greater Moral Obligations to Robots Than to Humans," Eric Schwitzgebel claims not only that intelligent machines have a "moral status," (2) but also that our ethical duties toward them are even stronger than our duties toward other humans. He breaks this moral obligation into two parts: a duty to be cautious and a duty to learn. Schwitzgebel makes several literary references to give the debate intellectual weight and uses hypothetical scenarios and analogies to explain the reasoning behind his thesis. He elevates the discussion by appealing to the virtue of personal responsibility, but also uses fear to motivate the reader to action.

Schwitzegebel gives intellectual and moral weight to his controversial stance by setting it within a long history of literary, philosophical, and scientific debate. He states that not only is "the moral status of robots is a frequent theme in science fiction" (2) but it is also an important matter to "philosophers and researchers on artificial intelligence" (2). He cites "Isaac Asimov's robot stories" (2) as one source, and uses a lengthy quote from "Frankenstein" (6) to illustrate his position that the creators of "genuinely conscious robots . . . are deeply causally connected to them . . . and so substantially responsible for their welfare" and that "we ought to bring [such creatures] into being only carefully and solicitously" (7). The excerpt from Frankenstein even alludes to ancient Biblical themes when the monster tells Frankenstein, "I am thy creature: I ought to be thy Adam."

Schwitzgebel uses moral reasoning—specifically, an appeal to the duty of personal responsibility—as well as an appeal to consensus to support his claim. His main idea is we are personally responsible for what we create, *especially if it is intentional.* He sets up the idea that people who are creators of artificial intelligence are "deeply causally connected" (5) to them, and that their moral responsibility toward them is like "that gods have to the beings they create" (4). He also appeals to consensus to support his position, saying that "the consensus is clear" (2) about this moral responsibility, even though he later acknowledges that some researchers, like John Searle, believe that "consciousness might not be possible in any programmed entity."

He uses hypothetical scenarios and analogies to explain and illustrate his reasoning. For instance, he describes the anguish of a hypothetical robot, capable of suffering, being sent to its death in a volcano (1), but contrasts this with putting "a standard computer processor manufactured in 2015 into a toy dinosaur and program it to say 'Ow!' when I press its off switch." (9) By comparing these two hypothetical scenarios, the reader can appreciate the challenge of determining moral responsibility toward robots. Schwitgebel addresses this challenge by saying that part of our moral responsibility toward robots is distinguishing "between a genuine stream of emotional experience and simulated emotions in an artificial mind." (9)

Although his literary references and appeal to virtue serve to elevate his discussion, he also appeals to fear by suggesting that failing to heed his recommendations could lead to "moral catastrophe…tantamount to slavery and murder" (10). Such alarmist language has the effect of stirring the readers to action, or at least caution, when considering the promise of artificial intelligence and its utility in their lives.

LESSON 8: REVISE FOR CLARITY AND EFFECTIVENESS

> The rubric for the SAT Essay Writing score says that a top-scoring essay *demonstrates a highly effective command of language . . . uses an effective variety of sentence structures, demonstrates precise word choice, maintains a formal style and objective tone, . . . and shows a strong command of the conventions of Standard American English.* In other words, if you want a strong Writing score, your essay should follow all of the basic rules we discussed in Chapters 5 and 6.

With this in mind, let's go through the essay one last time to be sure that it's clear and effective, and improve the wording as needed. Let's look at two sentences from our first draft and discuss how to improve them.

```
His main idea is we are personally responsible for
what we create, especially if it is intentional. He sets
up the idea that people who are creators of artificial
intelligence are "deeply causally connected" (5) to them,
and that their moral responsibility toward them is like
"that gods have to the beings they create" (4).
```

These two sentences are a bit weak and unclear, so let's walk through the process of improving them for clarity and effectiveness.

1. Strengthen Your Verbs

To diagnose our sentences, we first need to identify their "cores." Following the instructions from Chapter 4, Lesson 2, let's parse these two sentences into their clauses, and trim each clause.

```
His main idea is we are responsible ... He sets up the
idea that ...
```

These two sentences are unclear because they use **weak verbs**. The first sentence uses a *to be* verb (*is, are, was, were,* etc.): perhaps the weakest and most overused verb in student essays. Many sentences that use *to be* can be "upgraded" by strengthening the verb. Also, the verb in the second sentence—*sets up*—is vague.

How do we strengthen the verbs? By thinking more carefully about what, precisely, we are trying to say. The first sentence summarizes the main thesis of Schwitgebel's essay, so a verb like *claims* or *argues* would be stronger. The second sentence is trying to *clarify* or *specify* this thesis, so here is a stronger revision:

> Schwitzgebel argues that we are personally responsible
> for what we create, especially if it is intentional. He
> specifies that people who are creators of artificial
> intelligence are "deeply causally connected" (5) to them,
> and that their moral responsibility toward them is like
> "that gods have to the beings they create" (4).

This sentence is slightly better, but it is still a bit awkward and unclear.

2. Clarify Your References

The next step is to look carefully at the **nouns** and **pronouns**, asking *are the nouns clear and concrete?* and *do the pronouns have clear antecedents?* Clearly, this is a problem in both sentences. What do *what* and *it* refer to in the first sentence? What do *them* and *their* refer to in the second sentence? What is the difference between *people who are creators* and just *creators*?

Let's address each of these problems:

> Schwitzgebel argues that we are personally responsible
> for the conscious machines we create, especially
> if we create them intentionally. He specifies that
> creators of artificially intelligent robots are "deeply
> causally connected" (5) to those robots, and that the
> responsibility these creators have to their creations is
> like the responsibility "that gods have to the beings they
> create" (4).

3. Be Concise

Specifying our references has made the sentences clearer, but much wordier. We can make them more concise by using the first person plural *we* more consistently.

> Schwitzgebel argues that we are personally responsible
> for the conscious machines we create, especially if we
> create them intentionally. He specifies that we are
> "deeply causally connected" (5) to those machines, and
> that the responsibility we have to our creations is like
> the responsibility "that gods have to the beings they
> create" (4).

4. Vary Your Sentences Appropriately

Note that the two sentences are very similar in form: each contains two clauses, and each starts the same way: with the subject and the verb. This kind of repetitive pattern is not a problem in small doses, but if all of our sentences have the same pattern, the essay will be monotonous.

Let's introduce some variety:

> Schwitzgebel argues that we are personally responsible for the conscious machines we create. Specifically, if we create artificially intelligent robots intentionally, we are "deeply causally connected" (5) to them, and therefore our responsibility to them is like the responsibility "that gods have to the beings they create" (4).

Note how much clearer and more effective his revision is that the original sentences.

FINAL DRAFT

> In his essay, "We Have Greater Moral Obligations to Robots Than to Humans," Eric Schwitzgebel claims not only that intelligent machines have a "moral status," (2) but also that our ethical duties toward them are even stronger than our duties toward other humans. He breaks this moral obligation into two parts: a duty to be cautious and a duty to learn. Schwitzgebel makes several literary references to give the debate intellectual weight and uses hypothetical scenarios and analogies to explain the reasoning behind his thesis. He elevates the discussion by appealing to the virtue of personal responsibility, but also uses fear to motivate the reader to action.
>
> Schwitzegebel gives intellectual and moral weight to his controversial stance by setting it within a long history of literary, philosophical, and scientific debate. He states that not only is "the moral status of robots is a frequent theme in science fiction" (2) but it is also an important matter to "philosophers and researchers on artificial intelligence" (2). He cites "Isaac Asimov's robot stories" (2) as one source, and uses a lengthy quote from "Frankenstein" (6) to illustrate his position that the creators of "genuinely conscious robots . . . are deeply causally connected to them . . . and so substantially responsible for their welfare" and that "we ought to bring [such creatures] into being only carefully and solicitously" (7). The excerpt from Frankenstein even

alludes to ancient Biblical themes when the monster tells Frankenstein, "I am thy creature: I ought to be thy Adam."

Schwitzgebel uses moral reasoning—specifically, an appeal to the duty of personal responsibility—as well as an appeal to consensus to support his claim. Schwitzgebel argues that we are personally responsible for the conscious machines we create. Specifically, if we create artificially intelligent robots intentionally, we are "deeply causally connected" (5) to them, and therefore our responsibility to them is like the responsibility "that gods have to the beings they create" (4).

He also appeals to consensus to support his position, saying that "the consensus is clear" (2) about this moral responsibility, even though he later acknowledges that some researchers, like John Searle, believe that "consciousness might not be possible in any programmed entity."

He uses hypothetical scenarios and analogies to explain and illustrate his reasoning. For instance, he describes the anguish of a hypothetical robot, capable of suffering, being sent to its death in a volcano (1), but contrasts this with putting "a standard computer processor manufactured in 2015 into a toy dinosaur and program it to say 'Ow!' when I press its off switch." (9) By comparing these two hypothetical scenarios, the reader can appreciate the challenge of determining moral responsibility toward robots. Schwitgebel addresses this challenge by saying that part of our moral responsibility toward robots is distinguishing "between a genuine stream of emotional experience and simulated emotions in an artificial mind." (9)

Although his literary references and appeal to virtue serve to elevate his discussion, he also appeals to fear by suggesting that failing to heed his recommendations could lead to "moral catastrophe…tantamount to slavery and murder" (10). Such alarmist language has the effect of stirring the readers to action, or at least caution, when considering the promise of artificial intelligence and its utility in their lives.

SECTION 4

THREE SAT WRITING AND LANGUAGE PRACTICE TESTS

SAT WRITING AND LANGUAGE PRACTICE TEST 1

SAT WRITING AND LANGUAGE PRACTICE TEST 2

SAT WRITING AND LANGUAGE PRACTICE TEST 3

SAT WRITING AND LANGUAGE PRACTICE TEST 1

35 Minutes, 44 Questions

Directions

Each passage below is accompanied by a number of questions. For some questions, you will consider how the passage might be revised to improve the expression of ideas. For other questions, you will consider how the passage might be edited to correct errors in sentence structure, usage, or punctuation. A passage or a question may be accompanied by one or more graphics (such as a table or graph) that you will consider as you make revising and editing decisions.

Some questions will direct you to an underlined portion of a passage. Other questions will direct you to a location in a passage or ask you to think about the passage as a whole.

After reading each passage, choose the answer to each question that most effectively improves the quality of writing in the passage or that makes the passage conform to the conventions of Standard American English. Many questions include a "NO CHANGE" option. Choose that option if you think the best choice is to leave the relevant portion of the passage as it is.

SAT WRITING AND LANGUAGE PRACTICE TEST 1

| COMPLETE MARK ● | EXAMPLES OF INCOMPLETE MARKS | It is recommended that you use a No. 2 pencil. It is very important that you fill in the entire circle darkly and completely. If you change your response, erase as completely as possible. Incomplete marks or erasures may affect your score. |

■

1 A B C D
2 A B C D
3 A B C D
4 A B C D
5 A B C D
6 A B C D
7 A B C D
8 A B C D
9 A B C D

10 A B C D
11 A B C D
12 A B C D
13 A B C D
14 A B C D
15 A B C D
16 A B C D
17 A B C D
18 A B C D

19 A B C D
20 A B C D
21 A B C D
22 A B C D
23 A B C D
24 A B C D
25 A B C D
26 A B C D
27 A B C D

28 A B C D
29 A B C D
30 A B C D
31 A B C D
32 A B C D
33 A B C D
34 A B C D
35 A B C D
36 A B C D

37 A B C D
38 A B C D
39 A B C D
40 A B C D
41 A B C D
42 A B C D
43 A B C D
44 A B C D

1

1

Questions 1–11 are based on the following passage and supplementary material.

Shutterbug

When, fresh out of college, I began my job as a research analyst for a Fortune 500 company, I thought to myself: *Why would I ever want to leave?* The pay was phenomenal. My co-workers were supportive. [1] The avenues for career advancement were numerous. With these benefits, I couldn't imagine leaving this job.

But in my third year at the company, I began to itch for a creative outlet. While spring cleaning, I came across an old Canon camera that lay covered in dust, [2] being unused since my senior year of college. I had earned a photography minor [3] and consequently hadn't picked up a camera since I started my job as a research analyst. Suddenly, several thoughts flashed into my mind: *What if I started a photography business? Could I start a photography business? I don't really know much about business at all.*

1

Which choice best maintains the stylistic pattern established in the previous sentences?

A) NO CHANGE
B) There were many opportunities to advance my career.
C) I could advance my career in numerous ways.
D) Numerous career opportunities were available to me.

2

A) NO CHANGE
B) unused
C) it had not been used
D) that was unused

3

A) NO CHANGE
B) so
C) but
D) and nevertheless

CONTINUE ➤

1   **1**

I immediately began to research the possibilities. I wanted a way to pursue this interest and maintain my current **4** job. I didn't want to commit myself to a master's program or business school. That's when I stumbled across MOOCs.

5 MOOCs—massively open online courses, are convenient, popular, and inexpensive resources for learning almost anything. I was excited by the possibility of exploring the photography business without risking financial loss. A company called Coursera offers over a thousand free online courses. Unlike traditional college courses, **6** the scheduling for MOOCs was flexible, with multiple starting dates throughout the year. This flexibility appealed to me, since my responsibilities at work tended to become heavier at certain times of the year. So I chose a business course that I could complete at whatever pace I pleased.

4

Which choice most effectively combines the two sentences at the underlined portion?

A) job, not committing

B) job without committing

C) job, I did not want to commit

D) job and not committing

5

A) NO CHANGE

B) MOOCs:

C) MOOCs,

D) MOOCs or,

6

A) NO CHANGE

B) MOOCs were flexible for scheduling

C) the flexible scheduling for MOOCs was that they had

D) MOOCs offered flexible scheduling, with

CONTINUE

1   **1**

[1] While Coursera's business course offerings featured classroom lectures and group **7** projects, its photography offerings were predominantly text-based. **8** [2] Fortunately, another company, Creative Live, offered a program of classes called *Photography Fundamentals* that I could watch live for free or, if the live course date had already passed, purchase for a reasonable fee. [3] Within minutes, I signed up for classes called *Photography Fundamentals* and *Portraiture*. [4] By the end of it, I felt confident that I could launch my own photography business while advancing

7

A) NO CHANGE
B) projects, but it's
C) projects but its
D) projects, it's

8

At this point, the writer is considering adding the following sentence:

> But since I am a visual and auditory learner, I looked beyond Coursera to find other photography MOOCs with video and audio components.

Should the writer make this addition?

A) Yes, because it explains why the author looked beyond Coursera's offerings.

B) Yes, because it provides details about the course structure of the photography MOOCs.

C) No, because it detracts from the paragraph's focus on the Photography Fundamentals classes.

D) No, because it contradicts a point made earlier about Coursera's group projects.

CONTINUE ➡

1   1

my skills and business acumen through continued online coursework. [5] Each week for the next year, I **9** <u>invested</u> about 10 hours to online learning and spent $200 in the process. **10**

In my fourth year at my job, I finally quit. My co-workers commended me on beginning the trek down a different path, and **11** <u>I decided that the next thing I should do was to design a professional web site.</u>

9

A) NO CHANGE

B) concentrated

C) dedicated

D) exerted

10

To make this paragraph most logical, sentence 5 should be placed

A) where it is now.

B) immediately after sentence 1.

C) immediately after sentence 2.

D) immediately after sentence 3.

11

Which choice most effectively concludes the essay?

A) NO CHANGE

B) I started to wonder whether other business professionals were switching to artistic careers.

C) I felt determined to spend the next several years mastering the art of photography through MOOCs.

D) I felt newly invigorated by the prospect of pursuing a career that suited my creative needs.

1   1

Questions 12–22 are based on the following passage.

Water in the 21st Century

–1–

Water, to many Americans, seems like an inexhaustible resource. Bottles of water **12** array grocery shelves, swimming pools adorn millions of homes, and manicured lawns soak up artificial rain in the peak of summer. Water, it seems, is everywhere.

–2–

However, the recent California drought has shown emphatically that this is not so. Californian farmers used to draw water primarily from rivers, most of which get their fresh water from **13** snowpacks; accumulations of snow in the mountains that melt in the spring and summer months. The drought's severe impact on river water levels **14** has forced some farmers to rely so heavily on aquifers—underground reservoirs of water—that some fields have sunk over 30 feet.

–3–

The record droughts in California are only the just beginning for what ecologists are now calling the "Era of Water Scarcity." In some regions of the world, water scarcity has been an issue for decades already. Political, geographical, and climatic factors will continue to **15** deteriorate the problem of water scarcity.

12

A) NO CHANGE
B) permeate
C) replenish
D) fill

13

A) NO CHANGE
B) snowpacks,
C) snowpacks, in which
D) snowpacks, and

14

A) NO CHANGE
B) have forced
C) forcing
D) forces

15

A) NO CHANGE
B) exacerbate
C) promote
D) deplete

CONTINUE ▶

1   **1**

Scientists predict that, by 2030, half of the world's population will be living in areas of high water stress. Clearly, solutions are needed.

–4–

With these concerns in mind, innovators are looking for ways to reduce the cost of desalination. Researchers at the Massachusetts Institute of Technology have tested membranes that may greatly reduce the energy expenditure required to desalinate water. **16** Additionally, water utility companies are developing sensor technologies that could detect where water is being wasted, remediate water usage problems from a distance, and ultimately reduce the need for large desalination plants. Such systems can be adapted **17** on mobile, trailer-size desalination plants that can deliver water to drought-stricken areas or areas where freshwater is not available.

–5–

Innovative technologies will play an important role in ameliorating water scarcity problems. One such technology, desalination, uses reverse osmosis to force saltwater through membranes that filter out salt and other impurities. **18** Pumping large amounts of water through membranes, however, requires tremendous amounts of energy. Consequently, desalination has been criticized as an inefficient and expensive process that is not feasible

16

A) NO CHANGE
B) Consequently,
C) Regardless,
D) Typically,

17

A) NO CHANGE
B) with
C) from
D) for

18

The writer is considering deleting the underlined sentence. Should this change be made?

A) Yes, because it repeats information presented earlier in the paragraph.
B) Yes, because mentioning a drawback of desalination detracts from the discussion of its benefits.
C) No, because it explains why reverse osmosis is expensive.
D) No, because it describes the first step of the desalination process

CONTINUE ➡

1   1

on a scale large enough to make an appreciable impact. But as the dire effects of water scarcity become apparent and policy solutions such as rationing become less effective, public pressure may spark the necessary innovations needed to make **19** it sustainable.

–6–

A recent United Nations report concluded that water scarcity will become an increasingly significant factor in geopolitical conflicts in the 21st-century. Recent crises in Libya, Syria, and Afghanistan have been made worse by persistent drought. **20** Advances in desalination and other technologies provide hope that we may be able to find solutions to many of the **21** worlds problems—such as famine, disease, and war—that are linked to freshwater resources. **22**

19

A) NO CHANGE
B) this technology
C) them
D) this

20

At this point, the author is considering adding the following sentence.

California has enacted austerity water-use measures in urban areas, particularly during the summer months.

Should this addition be made here?

A) Yes, because it discusses the necessary steps that California has taken to address water scarcity.
B) Yes, because it summarizes the main steps taken to address water shortages.
C) No, because it repeats information stated previously in the passage.
D) No, because it disrupts the summarizing points in the concluding paragraph.

21

A) NO CHANGE
B) worlds'
C) worldly
D) world's

22

To make the passage most logical, paragraph 5 should be placed

A) where it is now.
B) after paragraph 2.
C) after paragraph 3.
D) after paragraph 6.

CONTINUE ▶

1   1

Questions 23–33 are based on the following passage.

Carbon Dating

The atmosphere is full of radioactive particles. Not all, however, are purely harmful. One radioactive isotope of [23] carbon: C-14 is particularly useful in dating ancient remains discovered by archaeologists. Living organisms continually interact with their environments through processes like photosynthesis and metabolism to replenish their carbon atoms so that the ratio of C-14 to C-12 atoms in their bodies is essentially the same as [24] they are in the atmosphere. However, when an organism dies, those processes stop and the C-14 atoms in its body begin to decay [25] without them being replenished. This decay occurs at a very predictable rate, so by comparing C-14 levels in ancient remains to environmental C-14 levels, scientists can accurately determine the age of those remains.

This method relies on the fact that C-14 levels have remained fairly constant throughout history, so archaeologists can use current environmental C-14 levels as a reliable measuring stick. [26] As a result, this finely-tuned balance was disturbed several decades ago.

[23]

A) NO CHANGE
B) carbon, C-14, is
C) carbon is C-14, being
D) carbon C-14, which is

[24]

A) NO CHANGE
B) those of
C) it is
D) it would be

[25]

A) NO CHANGE
B) but not
C) without its
D) without

[26]

A) NO CHANGE
B) Nevertheless,
C) Finally,
D) However,

CONTINUE

1　　　　　　　　　　　　　　　　　　　　**1**

In the 1950s and 1960s, atomic bomb testing generated enormous amounts of C-14 that eventually diffused evenly throughout the atmosphere. After reacting with oxygen to form carbon dioxide, **27** plants absorbed this C-14 through photosynthesis. Humans then incorporated this C-14 into their bodies **28** from eating those plants as well as the animals that ate those plants.

Ecologists today have found that, in 1954, trees across the world **29** sporadically exhibited a sudden increase in C-14 concentrations, **30** and that this surge was quickly passed through the food chain to human tissues. This "bump" provided biologists with a unique opportunity to test some theories about cell regeneration. For instance, because certain human brain cells maintained these elevated C-14 levels much longer than other cells (such as heart and skin cells) did, scientists concluded that these neurons are not replaced as frequently.

27

A) NO CHANGE
B) this C-14 was absorbed by plants
C) plants would absorb this C-14
D) absorption of C-14 by plants occurred

28

A) NO CHANGE
B) in
C) by
D) for

29

Which choice most accurately describes the distribution of C-14 as indicated in the previous paragraph?

A) NO CHANGE
B) unpredictably
C) uniformly
D) unevenly

30

The writer is considering deleting the underlined portion of this sentence and replacing the preceding comma with a period. Should this portion be kept or deleted?

A) Kept, because it provides a link to the discussion about human cells that follows.
B) Kept, because it explains why the C-14 spike was found worldwide, rather than just locally.
C) Deleted, because the details about the food chain were discussed in the previous paragraph.
D) Deleted, because it detracts from the paragraph's focus on cell regeneration.

CONTINUE ▶

1   **1**

Forensic scientists also use the Atomic Era "bump" in C-14 levels **31** <u>by determining the age</u> of teeth found in the victims of natural disasters. Physiologists know that C-14 becomes incorporated into human teeth at a young age, and then becomes sealed into the teeth by enamel. Since environmental C-14 has been declining steadily since the era of atomic testing, **32** <u>bones throughout the body</u> contain concentrations of C-14 that are higher than those in the current environment.

Although elevated levels of C-14 have been present in the atmosphere for nearly 70 years, only recently have scientists begun to **33** <u>ameliorate</u> this unique situation. The clock, however, is ticking. Within the next few decades, C-14 will return to baseline levels and scientists will no longer be able to make use of this historic anomaly.

31

A) NO CHANGE
B) in age determination
C) with determining the age
D) to determine the age

32

Which choice is best supported by the data in the graph?

A) NO CHANGE
B) all human tissues except teeth
C) teeth, unlike other bones,
D) bones in the human head

33

A) NO CHANGE
B) exploit
C) fulfill
D) enhance

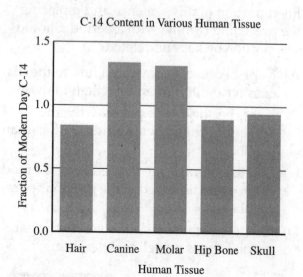

C-14 Content in Various Human Tissue

CONTINUE ▶

Questions 34–44 are based on the following passage.

The Era of Silent Films

The Academy Award received by *The Artist* in 2011 **34** <u>would be</u> the first for a silent film since 1927. Although the film's leading actors, Jean Dujardin and Bérénice Bejo, turned in phenomenal performances, perhaps the film's critical acclaim stemmed from its ability to **35** <u>derive</u> the magic of silent films that our country had lost over the previous century.

In the late 1800s, Eadweard Muybridge created a new visual medium that is now regarded as a precursor to modern motion pictures. Using multiple still cameras positioned along a race track, **36** <u>photographs of a galloping horse were made by Muybridge</u>. When these pictures were projected onto a screen in succession, they made viewers feel as if they were riding alongside the horse in a carriage. Not long afterward, Thomas Edison **37** <u>developed</u> the Kinetograph, which allowed a single camera to capture sequential images that could then be viewed on an instrument called a Kinetoscope. Thus, the motion picture industry was born.

34

A) NO CHANGE

B) has been

C) had been

D) was

35

A) NO CHANGE

B) capitulate

C) recapture

D) captivate

36

A) NO CHANGE

B) a galloping horse was photographed by Muybridge.

C) Muybridge had photographed a galloping horse.

D) Muybridge photographed a galloping horse.

37

A) NO CHANGE

B) initiated

C) fabricated

D) set in motion

CONTINUE

1   **1**

Edison's commercial success paved the way for similar inventions, **38** one of which was a device developed by the Lumière brothers that allowed multiple viewers to watch the motion picture simultaneously. This device, called the cinématographe, paved the way for the first commercial motion picture in 1894. From that year until the late 1920s, the world became enthralled by silent moving pictures.

[1] For many early 20th-century moviegoers, silent films weren't entirely "silent." [2] They were often accompanied by live actors who would narrate the film or provide plot explanations. [3] Musicians also performed off-screen, improvising or playing popular songs to match the on-screen mood. [4] As the art form progressed, production companies began to provide cue sheets for the actors and fully composed scores for the live orchestras. **39**

38

A) NO CHANGE

B) one of the devices was developed by the French Lumière brothers and allowed

C) such as a device created by the French Lumière brothers and allowing

D) one device, developed by the French Lumière brothers, allowed

39

The writer wants to add the following sentence to the paragraph.

This practice was particularly popular in Japan, where actors called *benshi* would play multiple roles and perform dialogue for on-screen characters.

The best placement for the sentence is immediately

A) after sentence 1.

B) after sentence 2.

C) after sentence 3.

D) after sentence 4.

CONTINUE

1   1

From 1900 to 1927, silent films **40** <u>attracted some of the greatest talents in theater</u>. In Hollywood, well-funded producers formed large movie studios while throughout the country cities and towns were building permanent movie theaters. American silent films surged in popularity around the globe, as well. Although American films were denounced **41** <u>from European cultural critics as being</u> crass, the people of Europe lined up in droves to see them.

In the early 1920s, producers began to experiment with incorporating recorded sound into movies. In 1927, Warner Bros created the first sound studio and produced the first feature-length "talkie," *The Jazz Singer*. This revolution drastically changed the landscape of the film industry.

40

Which choice most effectively introduces the paragraph?

A) NO CHANGE

B) became an established national industry.

C) were a welcome diversion from World War I.

D) became a legitimate and admired art form.

41

A) NO CHANGE

B) by European cultural critics to be

C) from European cultural critics as

D) by European cultural critics as

CONTINUE

1   1

[1] As a result of this decline, immensely successful actors of the Silent Era were left with broken careers because their on-screen voices were unsuitable for "talkies." [2] One of the most famous silent film actresses, Mary Pickford, left the industry entirely. [3] Within three years of *The Jazz Singer's* release, **42** roughly 35% of the country's movie theaters were equipped to screen "talkies," causing silent films to wane in popularity. [4] Other actors underwent extensive elocution training in order to secure their career as sound film actors. [5] Only thirty-five years after **43** it's birth, the Silent Era had come to an end. **44**

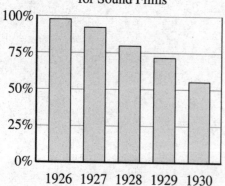

Percent of U.S. Theaters Not Equipped for Sound Films

42

Which choice best represents the data in the graph?

A) NO CHANGE

B) roughly 45%

C) roughly 55%

D) roughly 65%

43

A) NO CHANGE

B) its'

C) its

D) the

44

What is the most logical arrangement of sentences in this paragraph?

A) NO CHANGE

B) 5, 3, 2, 1, 4

C) 1, 3, 2, 4, 5

D) 3, 1, 2, 4, 5

STOP

If you finish before time is called, you may check your work on this section only.
Do not turn to any other section of the test.

ANSWER KEY AND CONVERSION TABLE

Answer Key	Raw Score (Total Correct)	Scaled Score (10–40)
1. A	1	10
2. B	2	10
3. C	3	10
4. B	4	11
5. C	5	12
6. D	6	13
7. A	7	13
8. A	8	14
9. C	9	15
10. D	10	16
11. D	11	16
12. D	12	17
13. B	13	18
14. A	14	19
15. B	15	19
16. A	16	20
17. D	17	21
18. C	18	21
19. B	19	22
20. D	20	23
21. D	21	23
22. C	22	24
23. B	23	25
24. C	24	25
25. D	25	26
26. D	26	26
27. B	27	27
28. C	28	28
29. C	29	28
30. A	30	29
31. D	31	30
32. C	32	30
33. A	33	31
34. D	34	32
35. C	35	32
36. D	36	33
37. A	37	34
38. A	38	34
39. B	39	35
40. B	40	36
41. D	41	37
42. B	42	38
43. C	43	39
44. D	44	40

ANSWER EXPLANATIONS

1. A   Parallelism

Choice A keeps the parallel structure of previous two sentences, which have the form **subject-linking verb-adjective**: *The pay was phenomenal. My co-workers were supportive.* Although all of the answer choices are grammatically correct, only A, *The avenues for career advancement were numerous,* maintains the grammatical pattern that the question requires.

2. B   Verb Aspect/Coordination

In the original phrasing, the underlined participial phrase, *being unused,* is awkward because it confuses present status with consequential status (Chapter 5, Lesson 11). Choice C is incorrect because it creates a comma splice (Chapter 5, Lesson 2). Choice D is incorrect because it creates a misplaced modifier (Chapter 5, Lesson 5). Choice B is best because it creates an adjective phrase describing the camera.

3. C   Coordination/Conjunctions

The two clauses in this sentence indicate a contradiction, and so the contrasting conjunction *but* is most logical. Choices A and B are incorrect because they imply a cause-and-effect relationship, and choice D is incorrect because *and nevertheless* is not idiomatic.

4. B   Coordination of Clauses

Choice B is best because it creates a prepositional phrase that modifies the infinitives *to pursue* and *[to] maintain.* Choice A is incorrect because the present participle *not committing* does not coordinate with the main verb *wanted.* Choice C is incorrect because it forms a comma splice (Chapter 5, Lesson 2). Choice D is incorrect because it creates a non-parallel form: *to pursue . . . and maintain . . . and not committing.*

5. C   Punctuation

The phrase *massively open online courses* is an appositive phrase. Interrupting modifiers such as this should be set off from the main clause with punctuation such as dashes, commas, or parentheses, and this punctuation must be consistent. Since the appositive is followed by a comma, it must also be preceded by a comma.

6. D   Coordinating Modifiers/Logical Comparisons

In the original phrasing, the subject of the sentence, *scheduling,* does not coordinate logically with the comparative modifying phrase that begins the sentence, *[u]nlike traditional college courses.* The logic of the comparison requires that the subject of the sentence be *MOOCs,* which eliminates choices A and C. Choice B is incorrect because it is not idiomatic.

7. A   Punctuation/Coordination

The original phrasing coordinates the two clauses logically. Choice B is incorrect because the conjunction *but* is redundant, and the contraction *it's* (*it is*) is illogical. Choice C is incorrect because *but* is redundant. Choice D is incorrect because *it's* (*it is*) is illogical.

8. A   Development/Cohesiveness

The sentence is an appropriate addition to the paragraph because it provides a contrasting idea to the previous sentence and explains why the author looked beyond Coursera's offerings. B is incorrect, however, because the sentence does not provide any details about the course structure of the photography MOOCs.

9. C   Diction/Idiom

Be sure to read the full sentence in order to catch the error in idiomatic expression. The original sentence is incorrect because the phrase *invested to* is not idiomatic (the correct idiom is *invested in*). Choices B and D are both illogical and idiomatic. Only choice C provides a logical and idiomatic word choice.

10. D   Coordination/Development

This sentence discusses how much time the author dedicated to online learning. For logical temporal sequence, this sentence should be placed before sentence 4, which begins with *By the end of it*.

11. D   Conclusions

The original sentence introduces a new topic that begs to be explored—the design of the new website—and so it is inappropriate as a concluding thought. Choice B has a similar problem. Choice C is incorrect because it does not provide any information about the *different path* that the writer mentioned in the previous clause, since the MOOC-based learning had already been discussed in previous paragraphs. Choice D is best because it provides new information about the writer's emotional state, without introducing any new ideas that require explanation.

12. D   Diction/Clear Expression of Ideas

In the original phrasing, *array* is incorrect because it is a transitive verb meaning *to arrange in a particular way*, but the shelves are not being arranged by the bottles. Choice B is incorrect because bottles cannot *permeate* (spread throughout) shelves. Choice C is incorrect because the context does not imply that anything is in need of *replenishing* (refilling). Only choice D, *fill*, makes sense in this context.

13. B   Coordination

This sentence ends with an appositive phrase, which can be set apart from the main clause with a comma, as in choice B. Choice A is incorrect because a semicolon must be followed by an independent clause. Choice C is incorrect because it creates a clause fragment. Choice D is incorrect because the phrase that follows the conjunction does not coordinate with any element in the preceding clause.

14. A   Verb Tense/Verb Agreement/Verb Mood

This verb indicates a "status-as-consequence": the farmers are doing what they are doing as a consequence of a previous situation. Therefore, the verb should be in the present tense, consequential (or "perfect") aspect: *has forced*. Choice B is incorrect because *have forced* does not agree in number with the subject *impact*. Choice C is incorrect because it creates a sentence fragment. Choice D is incorrect because it does not convey the consequential aspect.

15. B   Diction

The verb *deteriorate* does not work in this context because it is not a transitive verb, that is, it cannot take an object like *issue*. Choice B, *exacerbate*, however, is transitive and conveys the proper meaning in this context. Choice C is incorrect because *promote* has too positive a connotation. Choice D is incorrect because, although the water may be depleted, the *issue* is not.

16. A   Coordination

This sentence discusses an additional technology designed to address the problem of water scarcity. Thus, *Additionally* is the most appropriate word to link this sentence to the previous one.

17. D   Idiom

The verb *adapted* is associated with three common idioms: *adapted to* means *became suitable to*; *adapted from* means *created from* (as a screenplay that has been *adapted from a novel*); and *adapted for* means *made suitable to a particular purpose*. The last idiom is most appropriate to this context, so the correct answer is D.

18. C   Cohesiveness

If this sentence were removed, it would not be clear why desalination is such an expensive process. The underlined sentence indicates that the need to pump large amount of water across membranes is what renders desalination an expensive and energy-intensive process.

19. B   Pronoun-Antecedent Agreement

The definite pronoun *it* lacks a clear antecedent in this sentence. The sentence contains many singular nouns which can grammatically (if not logically) serve as the antecedent to this pronoun: *urgency, scarcity, rationing,* and *pressure*. Therefore, the ambiguous pronoun should be replaced with a more specific noun to clarify the reference. Choice B is the only choice that makes the reference clear.

20. D   Cohesiveness

The proposed sentence mentions a detail about California's particular predicament that detracts from the concluding paragraph, which focuses on the international dangers posed by water scarcity.

21. D   Punctuation

An apostrophe is needed here to signify possession. To create a singular possessive, we simply add 's to the end of *world*. Choice C is incorrect because *worldy* means *sophisticated*, which does not fit the meaning of the sentence.

22. C   Development

This paragraph introduces desalination and should be placed before paragraph 4 which discusses current research in desalination technology.

23. B   Appositives/Punctuation

The colon in the original sentence is incorrect because it does not precede a list or explanation. The term *C-14* is the proper name of the radioactive isotope of carbon, so it is an appositive (a noun phrase used to modify an adjacent noun or noun phrase). Appositives, like other interrupting modifiers, can be set apart from the main clause by commas, as in choice B. Choice C is incorrect because it forms an illogical modifier. Choice D is incorrect because it creates a sentence fragment.

24. C   Logical Comparisons/Pronoun Agreement

To be logical, this sentence must compare the *ratio* of carbon isotopes in living tissue with the *ratio* of carbon isotopes in the atmosphere. The only choice that forms a logical comparison is C, because *ratio* is a singular noun that agrees with the pronoun *it*. Choices A and B are incorrect because they contain plural pronouns rather than singular ones. Choice D is incorrect because the sentence is conveying a fact, and therefore the verb should not be in the subjunctive mood.

25. D   Coordination

The original phrasing is incorrect because the object of the preposition *without* is ambiguous: although the phrasing indicates that the decay is happening *without them* (that is, without the atoms), in fact, it is happening without *the replenishment*. Choice B is incorrect because it creates a non-parallel contrast. Choice C is incorrect because the pronoun *its* disagrees in number with its antecedent, *atoms*.

26. D   Coordinating Modifiers

This sentence contrasts starkly with the previous sentence, indicating that a situation has been *disturbed*. Therefore, a contrasting modifier like *However* is most appropriate. Although choice B, *Nevertheless*, indicates a contrast, it is illogical because this sentence does not indicate any irony.

27. B   Dangling Modifiers

This sentence starts with a participial phrase based on the present participle *reacting*, and so the subject of the main clause must agree with the subject of this participle. Since the C-14 atoms are what were *reacting*, only choice B contains a logical subject.

28. C   Idiom

Since the sentence is describing *how* the C-14 atoms were incorporated into the human body, the context requires the idiomatic phrase *by eating*. The other choices create non-idiomatic phrases.

29. C   Diction/Clear Expression of Ideas

In the previous paragraph, C-14 is described as diffusing evenly across the world. Therefore, choice C, *uniformly*, is the most logical choice.

30. A   Cohesiveness/Development

This portion of the sentence provides relevant information that links the fact about C-14 concentrations in trees with the discussion that follows about C-14 concentrations in human cells.

31. D   Idiom/Clear Expression of Ideas

The sentence describes *how* the "bump" in C-14 levels is being used by forensic scientists. The idiom that best conveys this functional relationship is D, *to determine*.

32. C   Graphical Analysis

The graph indicates that canines and molars (both of which are kinds of teeth) have more than 100% of the fraction of modern-day C-14, while other bones, like the skull and the hip bone, have less than 100% of the fraction of modern-day C-14.

33. A   Diction/Clear Expression of Ideas

This concluding paragraph describes how the window is closing on scientists' ability to *make use of* the dating technique provided by the Atomic Era spike in C-14 levels. In other words, they want to *exploit* (make use of) the situation while they can.

34. D   Verb Tense/Verb Aspect

The sentence indicates a past event, so the past tense is required. This eliminates choice B. Choice A is incorrect because it implies that the Academy Award was received after another prior event, which is incorrect. Choice C is incorrect because the verb does not indicate a status-as-consequence, so the past perfect form is illogical.

35. C   Diction

The sentence indicates that the *magic of silent films* had been lost, but returned with *The Artist*. That is, the magic was *recaptured*. Choice A is incorrect because the verb *derive* requires the preposition *from* unless it is being used in the mathematical sense. Choice B is incorrect because *capitulate* means "to surrender." Choice D is incorrect because *captivate* means "to charm."

36. D   Dangling Modifiers
The sentence begins with a participial phrase, so the subject of the main clause must agree with the subject of the participle, *using*. Since *Muybridge* is the one who used the cameras, *Muybridge* must be the subject of the main clause, as in choices C and D. Choice C is incorrect, however, because the sentence does not imply a status-as-consequence, so the past perfect form is incorrect.

37. A   Diction
The original word, *developed*, is the best choice, since it conveys the correct meaning with an appropriate tone for this context. Choice B is incorrect because *initiated* is more appropriate to starting a process than to inventing a device. Choice C is incorrect because *fabricated* means "constructed from prepared components." Choice D is incorrect because *set in motion* applies to a series of events rather than to an invention.

38. A   Coordination/Clear Expression of Ideas
The original phrasing is clearest and most logical. Choices B and D are incorrect because they both create comma splices (Chapter 5, Lesson 2). Choice C is incorrect because it creates an illogical conjunction.

39. B   Coordination of Ideas
This sentence describes a specific example of how live actors accompanied silent films, so it should immediately follow sentence 2, which introduces *this practice*.

40. B   Summarizing Ideas
Choice B is best because the sentences that follow describe the growth of the film industry in terms of production (*large movie studios*) and consumption (*permanent movie theaters . . . people of Europe lined up in droves*). These sentences do not mention any of the *greatest talents in theater*, the need for *diversion from World War I*, or the ways in which films became a *legitimate art form*.

41. D   Idiom
Here, the verb *denounced* is part of two idiomatic phrases. The correct idiomatic form of these phrases is *denounced as [crass]* and *denounced by [the critics]*.

42. B   Graphical Analysis
The graph shows that, in 1930 (which was three years after *The Jazz Singer* was released in 1927), about 55% of U.S. theaters were <u>not</u> equipped to project sound films, and therefore about 45% of U.S. theaters <u>were</u> able to project sound films.

43. C   Punctuation/Diction

Its is the correct possessive form. *It's* is the contraction of *it is*. *Its'* is not a word in the English language.

44. D   Logical Coherence

It should be clear that sentence 1 is not an appropriate first sentence for the paragraph because the phrase *this decline* has not been explained. It must be preceded by a sentence that describes the decline, and sentence 3 best serves that purpose because it mentions *the collapse of the silent film era*. If sentence 3 is moved to the beginning of the paragraph but the rest of the sentences remain in order, the paragraph shows a logical progression of ideas.

SAT WRITING AND LANGUAGE PRACTICE TEST 2

35 Minutes, 44 Questions

Directions

Each passage below is accompanied by a number of questions. For some questions, you will consider how the passage might be revised to improve the expression of ideas. For other questions, you will consider how the passage might be edited to correct errors in sentence structure, usage, or punctuation. A passage or a question may be accompanied by one or more graphics (such as a table or graph) that you will consider as you make revising and editing decisions.

Some questions will direct you to an underlined portion of a passage. Other questions will direct you to a location in a passage or ask you to think about the passage as a whole.

After reading each passage, choose the answer to each question that most effectively improves the quality of writing in the passage or that makes the passage conform to the conventions of Standard American English. Many questions include a "NO CHANGE" option. Choose that option if you think the best choice is to leave the relevant portion of the passage as it is.

SAT WRITING AND LANGUAGE PRACTICE TEST 2

COMPLETE MARK ●   EXAMPLES OF INCOMPLETE MARKS ⊘⊗⊖◑ ◐⦸⦻⦾

It is recommended that you use a No. 2 pencil. It is very important that you fill in the entire circle darkly and completely. If you change your response, erase as completely as possible. Incomplete marks or erasures may affect your score.

	A B C D		A B C D		A B C D		A B C D		A B C D
1	○○○○	10	○○○○	19	○○○○	28	○○○○	37	○○○○
2	○○○○	11	○○○○	20	○○○○	29	○○○○	38	○○○○
3	○○○○	12	○○○○	21	○○○○	30	○○○○	39	○○○○
4	○○○○	13	○○○○	22	○○○○	31	○○○○	40	○○○○
5	○○○○	14	○○○○	23	○○○○	32	○○○○	41	○○○○
6	○○○○	15	○○○○	24	○○○○	33	○○○○	42	○○○○
7	○○○○	16	○○○○	25	○○○○	34	○○○○	43	○○○○
8	○○○○	17	○○○○	26	○○○○	35	○○○○	44	○○○○
9	○○○○	18	○○○○	27	○○○○	36	○○○○		

2   2

Questions 1–11 are based on the following passage.

Behavioral Activation

For the millions of Americans who suffer **1** for having disorders like chronic anxiety or depression, **2** it is often hard for them to find effective treatments. Psychotherapy and group therapy are sometimes helpful, and a great many sufferers see a dramatic benefit from medication. In recent years, however, a therapy has been developed that has been shown to be at least as **3** effective, if not more so, than drugs. It is quickly becoming a powerful tool in the fight against these debilitating diseases.

The therapy is called behavioral **4** activation, or, BA for short. An outgrowth of cognitive behavioral therapy (CBT), behavioral activation

1

A) NO CHANGE
B) in having such disorders as
C) from such disorders as
D) by having disorders like

2

A) NO CHANGE
B) they often find it hard to find
C) it would be hard to find
D) it is often hard to find

3

A) NO CHANGE
B) effective as, if not more effective than,
C) effective, if not more effective than,
D) effective, if not more effective than

4

A) NO CHANGE
B) activation, or BA for short
C) activation, or BA, for short
D) activation or, BA for short

CONTINUE ➡

teaches patients to recognize how their behaviors trigger emotional responses. When undergoing BA, **5** <u>patients are asked to track</u> their activities on an hourly basis over the course of a week, as well as their corresponding mood states.

The reason for all of this record-keeping is to show patients how to recognize "loops," **6** <u>which patients are supposed to describe in their notebooks.</u> Once patients learn to recognize these loops, they can learn to alter them. These harmful behavior loops are known by the acronym TRAP, which stands for "trigger, response, avoidance pattern." An example of such a loop **7** <u>is:</u> a fight with a spouse (trigger) that leads to a sense of hopelessness (response) that leads to social withdrawal (avoidance pattern).

Patients learn to replace TRAPs with TRACs, in which the avoidance pattern (AP) is **8** <u>usurped by</u> an alternate coping response (AC), such as meditation, reading, composing music, going out with friends, or sympathizing with the people who are causing the stress.

5

A) NO CHANGE
B) therapists ask patients to track
C) patients would have tracked
D) therapists make their patients track

6

Which choice provides the most relevant explanatory detail?

A) NO CHANGE
B) which are very important to identify in BA therapy.
C) a term that was coined by the earliest practitioners of BA.
D) behavior patterns that reinforce depressive or anxious moods.

7

A) NO CHANGE
B) is,
C) should be
D) is

8

A) NO CHANGE
B) taken by
C) replaced by
D) repurposed with

CONTINUE ➡

2

2

[9] One big advantage of BA is that it can be administered by caregivers who do not need the rigorous training that most psychiatrists and therapists do. Another strong point is that, unlike cognitive behavioral therapy, behavior activation focuses less on how patients [10] think. Instead, it focuses more on how they act. Rather than doing exercises that get to the root of their thought processes, patients spend more time doing pleasurable activities. In this way, sufferers break the cycle of "rumination," in which they mentally rehash their negative experiences.

In a recent study conducted at the University of Exeter Medical School in the UK, 219 patients who [11] obtained BA showed positive results that were virtually indistinguishable from those of CBT, at a cost that was about 20% less. If further studies confirm this finding, BA might provide an extremely cost-effective treatment for sufferers of depression and chronic anxiety.

9

Which choice best introduces the discussion about the benefits of BA over CBT?

A) NO CHANGE

B) Unlike CBT, which was developed in the 1960s, behavioral activation therapy has only recently become widely available.

C) Behavioral activation and CBT are both types of behavior therapy, which was pioneered by Edward Thorndike in the early 20th-century.

D) The effects of BA have not been as widely studied as those of CBT, but early studies are showing comparable results.

10

Which choice best joins the two sentences at the underlined portion?

A) think; but instead it focuses more on

B) think; and more on

C) think than on

D) think, but instead more on

11

A) NO CHANGE

B) collected

C) sustained

D) received

CONTINUE

2   **2**

Questions 12–22 are based on the following passage.

An Ode to Food Additives

"Of course diet soda is bad for you. It has chemicals in it," my boyfriend said, his **12** mouthful of flavor-blasted goldfish. My immediate reaction was to nod, and try make a mental note to eat more "natural" foods and beverages. **13** Then he walked away, leaving those words echoing in my head. What is a chemical anyway? According to the New Oxford American Dictionary, it is a "compound or substance that has been purified or prepared, especially artificially." So does that mean that my filtered (purified) water (a compound) is a "chemical," but dirty water from a pond is not? **14** Many substances are considered chemicals by some people but not by others.

Food additives have been around for a long time, perhaps almost as long as we've had civilization. Salt, or sodium chloride, is perhaps **15** humanities first "chemical" food additive.

12

A) NO CHANGE
B) mouth filled
C) mouth full
D) mouth was full

13

A) NO CHANGE
B) Consequently,
C) Ironically,
D) On that account,

14

Which choice provides the best transition to the paragraph that follows?

A) NO CHANGE
B) If so, perhaps it's not a bad thing to have more chemicals in our food.
C) One drop of pond water can contain thousands of microorganisms, some of which are good for your health.
D) Perhaps I should have consulted another dictionary.

15

A) NO CHANGE
B) humanity's
C) human's
D) humans

CONTINUE →

2   2

Although it is an excellent taste enhancer, like monosodium glutamate and other "chemical" flavor boosters, **16** <u>it's</u> most useful contribution to civilization is as a food preservative. Without the preserving power of salt, extended voyages on the open sea before the 19th century would have far more difficult, if not impossible. **17** <u>Salt was even at the foundation of our earliest economic systems, as a unit of currency.</u> Sodium is also an essential nutrient. Our bodies use sodium to send nerve signals and to regulate blood pressure.

Of course, when we talk about "chemicals" in our food, we usually mean "stuff that's bad for us," such as carcinogens or other disease-inducing molecules. If that's the case, then why are we so concerned about words like "natural" and "artificial" on our food labels? **18** For instance, what about arsenic, a perfectly natural, and perfectly poisonous, element that's found in soil and groundwater? Should we not worry about it because it's "natural"? And should we worry about the treated water that comes from a municipal water plant, **19** <u>by the same token</u>?

16

A) NO CHANGE
B) its
C) their
D) its'

17

The author is considering deleting this sentence to improve the logical flow of the paragraph. Should this change be made?

A) Yes, because it distracts from the discussion of the salt as a food additive.
B) Yes, because its academic tone departs from the conversational style of the paragraph.
C) No, because most extended voyages were conducted for economic reasons.
D) No, because it explains the connection between salt as a nutrient and salt as a unit of currency.

18

Which choice, if inserted at this point, provides the best transition to the sentence that follows?

A) Aren't these terms misleading?
B) Why do we even have labels on food?
C) Isn't every food that's sold in stores artificial in some way?
D) Aren't these just advertising terms?

19

A) NO CHANGE
B) for all practical purposes?
C) and vice-versa?
D) because it's "artificial"?

CONTINUE

2 **2**

Parents are right to be concerned about how and what their children eat, because good nutrition is essential to healthy brains and bodies. For instance, many studies have shown that breast feeding can improve the immune systems of children, **20** with others showing that excess sugar consumption can make children more susceptible to diabetes. It's also important, however, that we not take our dietary concerns too far.

When we talk about what we eat, we should also talk about how we *think* about what we eat. Not only are we Americans probably the world leaders in eating junk food, we are also probably the world leaders in worrying about junk in our food. Nutrition experts have even given our excessive worries a name—*orthorexia nervosa*. People with this disorder become so preoccupied with eating "healthy" foods and avoiding "unhealthy" ones that they may become anxious, socially isolated, and even, **21** at some point, malnourished.

As with most things, we need to strike a balance. We should have a healthy concern about what we put into our and **22** our childrens' bodies, but we should also remember that a few stray toxins here and there probably won't hurt us, and may even make us stronger because they can train and strengthen our immune systems.

20

A) NO CHANGE
B) others have shown
C) and others have shown
D) but others showing

21

A) NO CHANGE
B) predictably
C) ironically
D) coincidentally

22

A) NO CHANGE
B) that of our children
C) those of our children's
D) our children's

CONTINUE →

2   2

Questions 23–33 are based on the following passage.

The Rogue Scholar

Born in [23] Paris on December 7, 1731, Abraham Hyacinth Anquetil-Duperron was the fourth child of Pierre Anquetil, a wealthy French spice importer. [24] For a custom of the time, Pierre added the name of one of his estates, Duperron, to the name of young Abraham in order to [25] separate the youngster from his siblings. But despite his name, Abraham was not a homebody. Before he reached his thirties, Abraham would earn a reputation not only as a global traveler and great scholar but also as a world-class rogue.

Although Anquetil-Duperron began his studies with the intention of becoming a priest, he soon fell in love with Asian languages such as Sanskrit and Arabic, and decided to devote his life to studying the ancient texts of south Asia. [26] These studies were unusual for Frenchmen of the time, who were more likely to study law or mathematics at university.

[23]

A) NO CHANGE
B) December 7, 1731, in Paris,
C) Paris, in December 7, 1731,
D) Paris, December 7, 1731,

[24]

A) NO CHANGE
B) In keeping with
C) Achieving
D) Attaining to

[25]

A) NO CHANGE
B) partition
C) segregate
D) distinguish

[26]

Which choice best sets up the paragraph that follows?

A) NO CHANGE
B) Abraham's older brother, Louis-Pierre, was also a scholar who composed a history of 16th and 17th century France.
C) He began his studies in Paris, but later continued his education in Utrecht and Amersfoort in the Netherlands.
D) This scholarship would provide a platform for a life of exploration and intrigue.

CONTINUE ➡

2   **2**

His memoirs—which are as much exercises in self-promotion as they are chronicles of his [27] scholarship, depict him as a fearless adventurer. At the age of 28, he killed a fellow countryman in a duel in which he himself was seriously injured. He travelled widely throughout India, and never without his trusty pistol. He used it to threaten customs agents who tried to inspect his goods, and even [28] brandishing it at a ship captain [29] who Abraham thought was travelling too slowly.

In Surat, India, Anquetil-Duperron borrowed a copy of the *Avesta*, a collection of ancient Zoroastrian religious texts, from his mentor, Darab [30] Kumana, he intended to become the first European to translate it. As he approached his goal, he became increasingly paranoid, and wrote in his memoir that he was even willing to kill Kumana if he tried to retrieve the documents. He was driven not only by hopes of personal glory, [31] but he was also driven by nationalistic pride and a disdain for British scholars. According to his travelogue, Anquetil-Duperron's goal was "to enrich my country with that singular work."

[27]
A) NO CHANGE
B) scholarship, would depict
C) scholarship—depict
D) scholarship—would depict

[28]
A) NO CHANGE
B) would brandish
C) brandished
D) had brandished

[29]
A) NO CHANGE
B) whom
C) which Abraham thought
D) Abraham thought who

[30]
A) NO CHANGE
B) Kumana, intending
C) Kumana intending
D) Kumana; intending

[31]
A) NO CHANGE
B) but also
C) he also was driven
D) but also he was driven

CONTINUE

2

2

After many years of research, Anquetil-Duperron was ultimately successful in translating the *Avesta* into French, and published his work in 1771. His achievement earned him much attention in academic circles throughout Europe, particularly since the *Avesta* predated even the Old Testament, **32** even though the latter was far better known in the West.

Abraham Hyacinth Anquetil-Duperron was perhaps the first great Orientalist-adventurer from the West, setting the stage for legendary hero-scholars like Richard Burton (1821–1890), T. E. Lawrence (1888–1935), and even fictional characters such as Indiana Jones. **33** Although his accounts were almost certainly exaggerated and self-aggrandizing, Anquetil-Duperron inspired generations of scholars to get out of the classroom and to explore the great wide world.

32

Which choice best supports the idea of the sentence?

A) NO CHANGE

B) which was written primarily in Hebrew.

C) which consists of 24 books collectively known by Jewish scholars as the Tanakh.

D) which had previously been thought to contain the oldest religious texts.

33

The writer is considering adding the following sentence here.

His stature has faded considerably since the 18th century, when his memoirs were first published.

Should this change be made?

A) Yes, because it establishes that Anquetil-Duperron preceded both Burton and Lawrence.

B) Yes, because it provides a qualifying remark about Anquetil-Duperron's reputation.

C) No, because it repeats information that is already implied in the paragraph.

D) No, because it departs from the tone of admiration in the paragraph.

CONTINUE

2   **2**

The New Elements on the Block

For decades, every first-year chemistry student has **34** <u>required learning</u> about chemical properties by studying the periodic table of elements. **35** <u>Developed</u> in 1869 by Dmitri Mendeleev, the periodic table reveals the special patterns in the properties of atoms: the metals cluster together on the left, the atmospheric gases like hydrogen, oxygen, and nitrogen float near the top, and the noble gases fall into a tidy column at the far right.

[1] But the lower right-hand corner of the table has always been conspicuously shabby: four gaps have long marred the "end of the seventh period" **36** <u>(which was also the part of the day I looked forward to the most in high school)</u>. [2] At least until now. [3] In December of 2016, the official names of those four previously anonymous elements were declared: nihonium (Nh, element 113), moscovium (Mc, element 115), tennessine (Ts, element 117), and oganesson (Og, element 118). [4] The new names replace the rather unsightly abbreviations for the barely pronounceable stand-ins Uut (ununtrium, or "unknown element 113"), Uup (ununpentium, or "unknown element 115"), Uus (ununseptium, or "unknown element 117"), and Uuo (ununoctium, or "unknown element 118"). **37**

34

A) NO CHANGE
B) had to learn
C) required to learn
D) been learning

35

A) NO CHANGE
B) Being developed
C) Having been developed
D) It was developed

36

The writer is considering deleting this parenthetical comment. Should this change be made?

A) Yes, because it disrupts the continuity with the sentence that follows.
B) Yes, because it contradicts the premise that the author is fond of learning.
C) No, because it describes a logical consequence of a previous claim.
D) No, because it helps to introduce the discussion that follows.

37

The writer is considering adding the following sentence to this paragraph

> Evidently, 20th-century chemists were more creative in designing experiments than they were in choosing names.

Where should the writer add this sentence?

A) immediately after sentence 1
B) immediately after sentence 2
C) immediately after sentence 3
D) immediately after sentence 4

CONTINUE ▶

Nh = nihonium (element 113)
Mc = moscovium (element 115)
Ts = tennessine (element 117)
Og = oganesson (element 118)

d-block

f-block

1	2	3	4	5	6	7	8	9	10	11	12	13	14	15	16	17	18
1 H																	2 He
3 Li	4 Be											5 B	6 C	7 N	8 O	9 F	10 Ne
11 Na	12 Mg											13 Al	14 Si	15 P	16 S	17 Cl	18 Ar
19 K	20 Ca	21 Sc	22 Ti	23 V	24 Cr	25 Mn	26 Fe	27 Co	28 Ni	29 Cu	30 Zn	31 Ga	32 Ge	33 As	34 Se	35 Br	36 Kr
37 Rb	38 Sr	39 Y	40 Zr	41 Nb	42 Mo	43 Tc	44 Ru	45 Rh	46 Pd	47 Ag	48 Cd	49 In	50 Sn	51 Sb	52 Te	53 I	54 Xe
55 Cs	56 Ba	57 La	72 Hf	73 Ta	74 W	75 Re	76 Os	77 Ir	78 Pt	79 Au	80 Hg	81 Tl	82 Pb	83 Bi	84 Po	85 At	86 Rn
87 Fr	88 Ra	89 Ac	104 Rf	105 Db	106 Sg	107 Bh	108 Hs	109 Mt	110 Ds	111 Rg	112 Cn	113 Nh	114 Fl	115 Mc	116 Lv	117 Ts	118 Og

58 Ce	59 Pr	60 Nd	61 Pm	62 Sm	63 Eu	64 Gd	65 Tb	66 Dy	67 Ho	68 Er	69 Tm	70 Yb	71 Lu
90 Th	91 Pa	92 U	93 Lp	94 Pu	95 Am	96 Cm	97 Bk	98 Cf	99 Es	100 Fm	101 Md	102 No	89 Lr

CONTINUE

Three of these elements are named after geographical locations: nihonium is named for the Japanese word for Japan, moscovium is named for Moscow, and tennessine, as you might imagine, is named for the state of Tennessee. Oganesson, **38** therefore, derives from the name of its discoverer, the Russian scientist Yuri Oganessian. In her announcement of the new atomic names, the president of the IUPAC (International Union of Pure and Applied Chemistry) Natalia Tarasova praised the names because they indicated the "universality of science, honoring places from three continents."

These four new elements were a long time coming—scientists had been searching for them for decades—but they don't tend to stick around for very long. **39** None of them has a half-life of more than half a minute, and most decay within a second. Even **40** tennessine, which is technically in the family of noble gases (typically the most stable group of elements) has a half-life of only about 0.89 milliseconds.

38

A) NO CHANGE
B) surprisingly
C) however
D) it is said

39

A) NO CHANGE
B) They don't have
C) No single one of them have
D) They have never had

40

Based on the information in the first paragraph, which choice best fits with the information in the diagram?

A) NO CHANGE
B) nihonium
C) moscovium
D) oganesson

CONTINUE ▶

But if these new atoms are so fleeting, how do scientists even know when they **41** would find them? The answer lies in the "radiation signal" that these atoms leave after they decay. The atoms themselves are created under very controlled conditions inside a particle accelerator. One atom, the "target," is held stationary while another atom is fired at it at enormous speeds. It often takes millions of collisions until a successful fusion reaction occurs. But when it does, a new, heavier element is formed. **42** This new atom may only last a few milliseconds. Its decay produces a spectacular shower of radiation that scientists can record in fine detail. The analysis of this profusion of data—which may take days or weeks, even with the use of **43** supercomputers—reveal the essential information about the new element.

This may seem like a lot of work and expense for little payoff. **44** Indeed, particle accelerators aren't exactly cheap to run, and they don't always produce useful results. But although these new elements are unlikely to have any useful industrial applications, their discoveries reveal a great deal about the forces that hold atomic nuclei together, and, ultimately, about the rules that govern the universe.

41

A) NO CHANGE
B) have found
C) had found
D) found

42

Which choice best combines the two sentences at the underlined portion?

A) This new atom may only last a few milliseconds, so its
B) Although this new atom may only last a few milliseconds, but its
C) Although this new atom may only last a few milliseconds, its
D) This new atom may only last a few milliseconds; but its

43

A) NO CHANGE
B) supercomputers—reveals
C) supercomputers, reveal
D) supercomputers, reveals

44

A) NO CHANGE
B) Nevertheless,
C) In other words,
D) So

STOP

If you finish before time is called, you may check your work on this section only.
Do not turn to any other section of the test.

ANSWER KEY AND CONVERSION TABLE

Answer Key	Raw Score (Total Correct)	Scaled Score (10–40)
1. C	1	10
2. D	2	10
3. B	3	10
4. B	4	11
5. A	5	12
6. D	6	13
7. D	7	13
8. C	8	14
9. A	9	15
10. C	10	16
11. D	11	16
12. C	12	17
13. A	13	18
14. B	14	19
15. B	15	19
16. B	16	20
17. A	17	21
18. A	18	21
19. D	19	22
20. C	20	23
21. C	21	23
22. D	22	24
23. A	23	25
24. B	24	25
25. D	25	26
26. D	26	26
27. C	27	27
28. C	28	28
29. A	29	28
30. B	30	29
31. B	31	30
32. D	32	30
33. D	33	31
34. B	34	32
35. A	35	32
36. A	36	33
37. D	37	34
38. C	38	34
39. A	39	35
40. D	40	36
41. B	41	37
42. C	42	38
43. B	43	39
44. A	44	40

ANSWER EXPLANATIONS

1. C   Idiom/Diction

When we describe an active ailment, idiom requires us to say that we *suffer from* that ailment, not that we *suffer for, suffer in,* or *suffer by* it.

2. D   Coordinating Modifiers/Redundancy/Verb Mood

Since the sentence begins with the prepositional phrase *For the millions of Americans . . .* the phrase *for them* in the original phrasing is redundant. We can find the proper phrase by trying to insert this prepositional phrase within each choice. Notice that the only choice that can incorporate it without error is D:

B) they often find it hard *for the millions of Americans* to find . . . (redundant and awkward)

C) it would be hard *for the millions of Americans* to find . . . (improper verb mood)

D) it is often hard *for the millions of Americans* to find . . . (correct)

3. B   Logical Comparison/Modifying Phrases

In the original phrasing, the phrase between the commas is an interrupting modifier. As a rule, when an interrupting modifier is removed from a sentence, the remaining portion must remain grammatically sound. Notice that this is not the case with the original phrasing: *as effective than drugs* is not idiomatic. The only choice that remains idiomatically and grammatically sound when the interrupter is removed is choice B.

4. B   Commas

The phrase *or BA for short,* is a clarifying modifier that should be coordinated with the main clause by just a preceding comma.

5. A   Modifier Coordination

The sentence begins with the participial phrase *When undergoing BA,* and so the subject of the main clause must also be the subject of this participle. Since only *patients* would undergo BA, the original choice provides the correct subject. Although choice C also provides the proper subject, it misuses both the subjunctive mood (Chapter 5, Lesson 15) and the consequential aspect (Chapter 5, Lesson 11).

6. D   Explanatory Detail

Notice that the question asks you to find an *explanatory* detail. The only choice that explains what *"loops"* are is choice D.

7. D   Punctuation/Verb Mood

The original phrasing is incorrect because colons must always be preceded by independent clauses. Choice B is incorrect because the comma is misused. Choice C is incorrect because the sentence is making an indicative claim, and so the verb should not be in the subjunctive mood (Chapter 5, Lesson 15).

8. C   Diction/Clear Expression of Ideas

This sentence is trying to express the fact that one habit is being *replaced by* another. The original choice is incorrect because to *usurp* is to take by force, which habits cannot do. Choice B is incorrect because an act of replacement is not an act of *taking*. Choice D is incorrect because to *repurpose* means to use for another purpose rather than to replace completely. Only choice C, *replaced by*, conveys the appropriate idea.

9. A   Logical Introduction

Since this sentence must introduce a discussion of the *benefits* of BA over CBT, the original sentence, identifying one important *advantage* of BA, is the most appropriate.

10. C   Logical Coordination

Choices A and B are incorrect because both misuse the semi-colon. Conjunctions should not be used when joining independent clauses with a semicolon. Choice D is incorrect because the phrase *but instead* is unidiomatic and redundant.

11. D   Diction/Clear Expression of Ideas

Although all of the choices are roughly synonyms of the past tense verb *got*, only choice D, *received*, shows the proper relationship between a patient and a therapy. The original is incorrect because *obtained* refers to an object of possession rather than an activity. Choice B is incorrect because *collected* refers to objects that are gathered. Choice C is incorrect because *sustained* means strengthened or supported.

12. C   Diction/Modifier Coordination

The original is incorrect because *mouthful* is a noun that forms a noun phrase that does not coordinate with the rest of the sentence. Choice B is incorrect because *filled of* is not idiomatically correct. Choice D is incorrect because it forms a run-on sentence. Choice C is correct because it forms a participial phrase that coordinates effectively with the main clause.

13. A   Logical Coordination

Since the first three sentences of this paragraph show a simple sequence of events, *Then* is the most logically appropriate modifier.

14. B   Logical Cohesiveness

The first paragraph ends with a note of skepticism about the fear of "chemicals" in our food, and the second paragraph discusses the importance of one such chemical. Choice B is the only one that logically bridges these two lines of discussion.

15. B   Diction/Possessive Form

Choices A and D are incorrect because the context requires a possessive form. Choice C is incorrect because the context of the sentence requires the collective noun *humanity* rather than the singular noun *human*.

16. B   Possessive Form/Agreement

The original is incorrect because *it's* is a contraction of *it is*, but the context requires the possessive form *its*. Choice C is wrong because *their* does not agree in number with the antecedent *salt*. Choice D is incorrect because *its'* is not a word.

17. A   Possessive Form

Although this sentence does provide an interesting fact about the contribution of salt to human civilization, every other sentence in this paragraph is about the use of salt as a food additive. Therefore, this sentence distracts from the discussion.

18. A   Transitions

Since the sentence that follows is about a *natural* ingredient that is actually harmful to human health, the point is that the terms *natural* and *artificial* are misleading.

19. D   Clear Expression of Ideas

This sentence is intended to provide an idea that is parallel and complementary to the previous sentence. Choice D provides the most logical complement.

20. C   Coordination

The original phrasing is incorrect because it creates a prepositional phrase that does not coordinate with any element in the main clause. Choice B is incorrect because it yields a comma splice (Chapter 5, Lesson 2). Choice D is incorrect because the two clauses do not show a contrast. The only choice that effectively coordinates the two clauses is choice C.

21. C   Diction/Clear Expression of Ideas

The fact that an obsessive concern with proper eating can lead to malnutrition is *ironic*, that is, it directly undermines our expectations. Therefore, C is the most logical choice. Choice A is incorrect because the eventuality of the malnourishment is not relevant to the sentence. Choice B is incorrect because it is surprising, rather than expected, that health-obsessed people might become malnourished. Choice D is incorrect because the sentence indicates no coincidence.

22. D   Logical Comparison/Possessive Form

The original phrasing is incorrect because *childrens'* is not the correct plural possessive form: since *children* is plural but does not end with *s*, it is made possessive with *'s*, as in choice D. Choice C is incorrect because the possession is indicated redundantly.

23. A   Idiomatic Expression/Commas

The original phrase is the only option that provides an idiomatically correct expression of place, month, and year.

24. B   Idiom/Clear Expression of Ideas

The practice of naming a son after an estate was *in keeping with* a custom of the time, and so the best answer is B. Choice A is incorrect because the prepositional phrase it produces is illogical. Choices C and D are incorrect because customs cannot logically be *achieved* or *attained*.

25. D   Diction

Although all of the choices are roughly synonymous with *separate*, only choice D, *distinguish*, is appropriate when expressing the intended relationship between Abraham and his brothers. Choices A, B, and C are incorrect because *partition*, *separate*, and *segregate* imply physical distinctions, not nominal ones.

26. D   Transitions

The paragraph that follows discusses Abraham's life of exploration and intrigue, so choice D is the best choice.

27. C   Punctuation/Verb Mood

This sentence contains an interrupting modifier that starts with a dash, so it must terminate with a dash as well. Choices C and D both include dashes, but choice D is incorrect because the sentence discusses his memoirs in the present indicative mood, not the subjunctive mood.

28. C   Parallelism

The original phrasing is incorrect because the gerund or present participle form *brandishing* does not coordinate with the rest of the main clause. The first verb in the sentence, *used*, establishes the simple past tense for the sentence, so choice C is the best option.

29. A   Pronouns/Modifier Coordination

The original phrasing is correct, although some may argue that the proper form of the pronoun is *whom* rather than *who*. In fact, the subjective form *who* is correct because it serves as the subject of the clause [*who*] *was travelling too slowly*.

30. B   Punctuation

The original phrasing is incorrect because it produces a comma splice (Chapter 5, Lesson 2). Choice C is incorrect because the participial phrase beginning with *intending* must be separated from the main clause by a comma, as in choice B. Choice D is incorrect because the phrase following the semicolon is not an independent clause.

31. B   Parallelism

The sentence uses the parallel construction *not only A but also B*. Proper idiom requires not only precise phrasing of the construction, but also parallel phrasing for *A* and *B*. The only choice that satisfies both criteria is B, since the two phrases replacing *A* and *B* are prepositional phrases.

32. D   Logical Support
The central idea of the sentence is that academics were surprised to learn that the *Avesta* predated the Old Testament. Logically, this could only be surprising if the Old Testament *had previously been thought to be the oldest religious texts*.

33. D   Cohesiveness
The negative tone of this sentence is inconsistent with this paragraph, which focuses on the positive legacy of Anquetil-Duperron, specifically the fact that he set the stage for *legendary hero-scholars* and *inspired generations of scholars to get out of the classroom and to explore the great wide world*.

34. B   Idiom/Diction
The sentence is trying to convey the idea that the periodic table of elements is a required component of first-year chemistry, and so the compulsive aspect form, *has had to learn*, is the most logical. The original phrasing is not idiomatic. Choice C is illogical because it swaps the subject and object of the requirement. Choice D is incorrect because it omits the compulsive aspect, and incorrectly uses the progressive aspect.

35. A   Coordination/Verb Form
The original is correct because it creates a participial phrase that effectively coordinates with the main clause. Choices B and C are incorrect because using the progressive participle or the progressive consequential participle implies a cause-and-effect relationship that is clearly illogical in this sentence. Choice D is incorrect because it creates a comma splice (Chapter 5, Lesson 2).

36. A   Cohesiveness
The parenthetical comment, although humorous, disrupts the continuity of this sentence with the next, because the sentence that follows is an immediate response to the clause that precedes the parenthetical comment.

37. D   Clear Expression of Ideas
This sentence clearly belongs at the very end of the paragraph, because it provides direct commentary on the *unsightly* and *barely pronounceable stand-ins* for the element names that are listed in sentence 4.

38. C   Logical Coordination
This sentence contrasts with the previous one, since it discusses the one element that was not named for a geographical location. Therefore, *however* is the most logical sentence modifier.

39. A   Clear Expression of Ideas
The original phrasing is best. Choices B and D create a logical error called a *number shift*, in which a plural subject, *they*, is linked to a single attribute, *a half-life*. Choice C is incorrect because its subject and verb disagree in number.

40. D   Graphical Interpretation

The first paragraph indicates that *the noble gases fall into a tidy column at the far right* of the periodic table, and this paragraph refers to a new element that is *technically in the family of noble gases*. The diagram clearly indicates that the only newly discovered element that occupies a spot in the far-right column is oganesson.

41. B   Verb Form

The first verb in this sentence, *do know*, is in the present tense, indicating the factual aspect (that is, the sentence is simply conveying a fact). The use of the conjunction *when* indicates that the second verb should share the same tense as the first, and so choice B, *have found*, which is in the present tense, consequential aspect, is most appropriate. The original is incorrect because the subjunctive form *would find* does not convey a fact. Choices C and D are both incorrect because they are in the past tense.

42. C   Logical Coordination

The two sentences contrast each other, since one should not expect an atom that lasts only a few milliseconds to leave a great deal of evidence for scientists to examine, and yet its decay produces an abundance of evidence. Choice A is incorrect because the two sentences do not have a cause-and-effect relationship. Choice B is incorrect because the use of both *Although* and *but* is redundant. Choice D is incorrect because the conjunction *but* should not be used with the semi-colon. Only choice C conveys the contrast grammatically.

43. B   Punctuation/Verb Agreement

The original phrasing is incorrect because the verb *reveal* does not agree in number with its subject *analysis*. Choices C and D are incorrect because the interrupting phrase is preceded by a dash, and so must be followed by a dash, not a comma. Choice B has neither of these problems.

44. A   Logical Coordination

Since this sentence provides supporting evidence for the general claim of the previous sentence, *Indeed* is a logically appropriate sentence modifier. Choice B is incorrect because this sentence provides no contrast to the previous one. Choice C is incorrect because this sentence provides no reiteration or explanation. Choice D is incorrect because this sentence does not discuss a logical consequence to any previous idea.

SAT WRITING AND LANGUAGE PRACTICE TEST 3

35 Minutes, 44 Questions

Directions

Each passage below is accompanied by a number of questions. For some questions, you will consider how the passage might be revised to improve the expression of ideas. For other questions, you will consider how the passage might be edited to correct errors in sentence structure, usage, or punctuation. A passage or a question may be accompanied by one or more graphics (such as a table or graph) that you will consider as you make revising and editing decisions.

Some questions will direct you to an underlined portion of a passage. Other questions will direct you to a location in a passage or ask you to think about the passage as a whole.

After reading each passage, choose the answer to each question that most effectively improves the quality of writing in the passage or that makes the passage conform to the conventions of Standard American English. Many questions include a "NO CHANGE" option. Choose that option if you think the best choice is to leave the relevant portion of the passage as it is.

SAT WRITING AND LANGUAGE PRACTICE TEST 3

| COMPLETE MARK ● | EXAMPLES OF INCOMPLETE MARKS | It is recommended that you use a No. 2 pencil. It is very important that you fill in the entire circle darkly and completely. If you change your response, erase as completely as possible. Incomplete marks or erasures may affect your score. |

1 Ⓐ Ⓑ Ⓒ Ⓓ   10 Ⓐ Ⓑ Ⓒ Ⓓ   19 Ⓐ Ⓑ Ⓒ Ⓓ   28 Ⓐ Ⓑ Ⓒ Ⓓ   37 Ⓐ Ⓑ Ⓒ Ⓓ

2 Ⓐ Ⓑ Ⓒ Ⓓ   11 Ⓐ Ⓑ Ⓒ Ⓓ   20 Ⓐ Ⓑ Ⓒ Ⓓ   29 Ⓐ Ⓑ Ⓒ Ⓓ   38 Ⓐ Ⓑ Ⓒ Ⓓ

3 Ⓐ Ⓑ Ⓒ Ⓓ   12 Ⓐ Ⓑ Ⓒ Ⓓ   21 Ⓐ Ⓑ Ⓒ Ⓓ   30 Ⓐ Ⓑ Ⓒ Ⓓ   39 Ⓐ Ⓑ Ⓒ Ⓓ

4 Ⓐ Ⓑ Ⓒ Ⓓ   13 Ⓐ Ⓑ Ⓒ Ⓓ   22 Ⓐ Ⓑ Ⓒ Ⓓ   31 Ⓐ Ⓑ Ⓒ Ⓓ   40 Ⓐ Ⓑ Ⓒ Ⓓ

5 Ⓐ Ⓑ Ⓒ Ⓓ   14 Ⓐ Ⓑ Ⓒ Ⓓ   23 Ⓐ Ⓑ Ⓒ Ⓓ   32 Ⓐ Ⓑ Ⓒ Ⓓ   41 Ⓐ Ⓑ Ⓒ Ⓓ

6 Ⓐ Ⓑ Ⓒ Ⓓ   15 Ⓐ Ⓑ Ⓒ Ⓓ   24 Ⓐ Ⓑ Ⓒ Ⓓ   33 Ⓐ Ⓑ Ⓒ Ⓓ   42 Ⓐ Ⓑ Ⓒ Ⓓ

7 Ⓐ Ⓑ Ⓒ Ⓓ   16 Ⓐ Ⓑ Ⓒ Ⓓ   25 Ⓐ Ⓑ Ⓒ Ⓓ   34 Ⓐ Ⓑ Ⓒ Ⓓ   43 Ⓐ Ⓑ Ⓒ Ⓓ

8 Ⓐ Ⓑ Ⓒ Ⓓ   17 Ⓐ Ⓑ Ⓒ Ⓓ   26 Ⓐ Ⓑ Ⓒ Ⓓ   35 Ⓐ Ⓑ Ⓒ Ⓓ   44 Ⓐ Ⓑ Ⓒ Ⓓ

9 Ⓐ Ⓑ Ⓒ Ⓓ   18 Ⓐ Ⓑ Ⓒ Ⓓ   27 Ⓐ Ⓑ Ⓒ Ⓓ   36 Ⓐ Ⓑ Ⓒ Ⓓ

3

3

Questions 1–11 are based on the following passage.

Living with Robots

Robot butlers used to be the stuff of science fiction, but now, if you have just a few hundred spare bucks, you can buy a self-propelled disk to scoot around and vacuum your living room. It may not be Alfred the butler, but **1** we're getting closer every day to having robotic assistants in our daily lives. Some will be drones that perform mundane tasks like delivering packages, but others will "live" in our homes, perhaps looking out for intruders as we sleep, notifying the authorities in emergencies, **2** or tasks such as greeting guests or ordering take-out.

Engineers are making great strides in creating robots that look, move, and respond like humans do. **3** Although they are not currently available for popular use, but they're getting closer to being commercially viable. We are beginning to see them in the most ordinary of situations. One hotel in Japan (where there are over 750,000 industrial robot workers), called the *Henn na*, or "Weird Hotel," **4** it is run, staffed and operated almost exclusively by robots. An animatronic velociraptor checks you in, and a foot-high robot concierge answers your questions (but only in Japanese).

1

Which choice best sets up the sentence that follows?

A) NO CHANGE
B) we can't change the pace of technology
C) at least we don't need to feed it or pay its salary
D) we can't really complain after waiting so long

2

A) NO CHANGE
B) or greeting guests, or ordering take-out
C) or, greeting guests or ordering take-out
D) greeting guests, or ordering take-out

3

A) NO CHANGE
B) They are not
C) Not
D) Although not

4

A) NO CHANGE
B) being staffed and operated
C) it is operated
D) that is operated

CONTINUE

3   3

[1] Although many people are thrilled by the idea of robot helpers, others are concerned **5** <u>by</u> robots taking their jobs. [2] Certainly, this is a serious concern, at least in the short-term. [3] Automobile factory workers aren't happy about the prospect of being replaced by 2,400-lb mechanisms that never take breaks or require sick leave or pension planning. [4] Our standards of living increase when mechanical tasks are performed more precisely and at less expense. [5] **6** <u>It means that</u> manufactured items are safer—because human error is taken out of the manufacturing process—and more reliable. **7**

If automation is inevitable, how will low-skilled or medium-skilled workers make a living as the tasks they used to perform **8** <u>will become</u> automated? Clearly, those workers will have to find other kinds of work. In fact, this transformation has

5

A) NO CHANGE
B) about
C) with
D) with regard to

6

A) NO CHANGE
B) Automation ensures that
C) It makes
D) Automation means making

7

The writer is considering adding the following sentence.

> However, the efficiency of robots is a boon in the long run.

Where should it be placed?

A) immediately after sentence 1
B) immediately after sentence 2
C) immediately after sentence 3
D) immediately after sentence 4

8

A) NO CHANGE
B) would become
C) have become
D) become

CONTINUE →

3　　　　　　　　　　　　　　　　　　　　**3**

been underway for a long time. In the last several decades, we have seen an enormous shift in labor from the manufacturing sector to the service sector. Since 1990, the number of U.S. jobs in manufacturing [9] has declined from 18 million to 12 million, although employment in the service and health care sectors has increased [10] to more than compensate for those job losses. Despite what some politicians claim, this shift is happening not because of government regulations or immigration policy, [11] but due to automation. Foreigners are not taking our factory jobs; robots are, and we'll be better off for it.

9

A) NO CHANGE
B) have declined
C) declined
D) are declining

10

A) NO CHANGE
B) to compensate more
C) to do more than compensate
D) more than they need to compensate

11

A) NO CHANGE
B) but rather it is because of
C) but
D) but because of

CONTINUE ➤

3

Questions 12–22 are based on the following passage and supplementary material.

Norman Borlaug and the Green Revolution

Working in relative obscurity, **12** the efforts of one 20th-century scientist may have saved nearly 1 billion lives. His name is Norman Borlaug, and he founded the scientific movement that we now call the Green Revolution. He received the Nobel Peace Prize in 1970 for his work around the world to develop and distribute high-yield varieties of wheat and rice, promote better agricultural management techniques, and **13** he modernized irrigation infrastructure. Largely as a result of Borlaug's work, wheat yields **14** more than doubled throughout the world between 1960 and 2014.

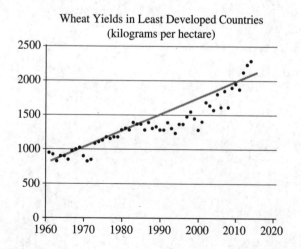

Wheat Yields in Least Developed Countries
(kilograms per hectare)

12

A) NO CHANGE
B) in the 20th-century, the efforts of one scientist
C) one 20th-century scientist
D) one 20th-century scientist whose efforts

13

A) NO CHANGE
B) to modernize
C) modernizing
D) modernize

14

Which choice best represents the information in the graph?

A) NO CHANGE
B) throughout the world increased by over 100%
C) more than doubled in the world's least developed countries
D) in the world's least developed countries increased by more than 200%

CONTINUE ➡

3   3

15 <u>Born</u> in 1914 on a farm in Cresco, Iowa, Borlaug came of age during the heart of the Depression. His grandfather convinced Norman to pursue an education, saying, "You're wiser to fill your head now if you want to fill your belly later on." Although he failed the entrance exam for the University of Minnesota, he did gain admittance to its two-year General College, and did well enough there to transfer to the College of Agriculture's forestry program. **16** He became fascinated by work his professors were doing in breeding food crops to be resistant to parasitic **17** <u>fungi. He decided</u> to pursue research in plant pathology and breeding.

Borlaug's professional work began in the 1940s, when he developed a high-yield and disease-resistant variety of wheat to help Mexican farmers become more productive. By 1963, most of the wheat crop in Mexico was grown from Borlaug's seeds, and the yield was 7 times what it had been in 1944. **18** <u>Borlaug's work helped Mexico enormously in its effort to become</u> more food secure, and even became a net exporter of wheat by 1963.

15

A) NO CHANGE
B) He was born
C) Being born
D) Although he was born

16

Which sentence, if inserted at this point, provides the most relevant and cohesive information?

A) Borlaug was a standout wrestler for the university, even reaching the Big Ten semifinals.
B) Borlaug's interest in agriculture had been cultivated years previously on his grandfather's farm.
C) Coincidentally, Borlaug would later work for the United States Forest Service in Massachusetts.
D) The move was an excellent fit for Norman's skills and interests.

17

Which choice best combines the sentences at the underlined portion?

A) fungi, having decided
B) fungi, but decided
C) fungi, and so decided
D) fungi, then deciding

18

A) NO CHANGE
B) Mexico benefitted enormously from Borlaug's work to make it
C) Borlaug's work was enormously beneficial to Mexico in making it
D) Borlaug's work was enormously beneficial to Mexico, making it

3

3

His work went far beyond just handing out drought-resistant seeds to Mexican farmers. **19** Borlaug showed them how to better manage their productivity by taking advantage of Mexico's two growing seasons. He also showed them how to use genetic variations among crops in a single field to maximize disease resistance. Although some of the genetic strains might **20** succumb to the pathogens (disease-causing agents), those strains could easily be replaced with new, resistant lines, thereby maintaining higher crop yields.

In the early 1960s, Borlaug traveled to two of the world's most impoverished nations, India and Pakistan, to share his insights with government officials and farmers who were struggling with food shortages. The situation was so **21** dire as that the biologist Paul Ehrlich speculated in his 1968 bestseller *The Population Bomb* that "in the 1970s and 1980s, hundreds of millions of people will starve to death in spite of any crash programs embarked upon now." Ehrlich singled out India for particular devastation because of its traditional and bureaucratic resistance to change.

Fortunately, Borlaug kept working anyway. Between 1965 and 1970, India's cereal crop yield increased by 63%, and by 1974, India was self-sufficient in the production of all cereals. For the last 50 years, food production in India and Pakistan has increased faster than the **22** population. This is due largely to the work of Norman Borlaug.

19

The writer is considering deleting the previous sentence. Should the writer make this change?

A) No, because it introduces the discussion about the extent of Borlaug's work in Mexico.

B) No, because it explains the variety of technologies inspired by Borlaug's work.

C) Yes, because mentioning drought detracts from the paragraph's focus on disease.

D) Yes, because repeats information that was mentioned in the previous paragraph.

20

A) NO CHANGE
B) support
C) submit to
D) restore

21

A) NO CHANGE
B) dire: so
C) dire that
D) dire; that

22

Which choice best combines the sentences at the underlined portion?

A) population and
B) population,
C) population, which is
D) population, this being

CONTINUE →

3   **3**

Questions 23–33 are based on the following passage.

Thinking Burns Calories

Have you ever **23** been needing to take a nap after taking a long test in school? If so, you're not alone. One reason may be that you stayed up too late studying the night before. Another **24** may be that your brain, although not a muscle, burns a lot more calories than you think.

The typical adult brain runs on about 12 watts of power, roughly equivalent to that used by a standard LED light bulb. In one sense, it is a model of efficiency. **25** For example, IBM's Watson, the supercomputer that defeated "Jeopardy!" super-champion Ken Jennings back in 2010, required 90,000 watts of power, roughly what would power all of the appliances in an average-size suburban neighborhood. **26** Although it originally required a roomful of servers, today it is the size of three pizza boxes. Although our brains typically constitute only 2% of our body weight, they burn about 20% of our resting energy. **27** It would be understandable that such a hard-working organ needs to rest for eight hours a day, and perhaps even more if it just helped you tackle your AP calculus mid-term.

23
A) NO CHANGE
B) had to need
C) needed
D) needed to have

24
A) NO CHANGE
B) would be because
C) being that
D) is because

25
A) NO CHANGE
B) For comparison
C) Even so
D) However

26
Which choice is most cohesive in the context of the paragraph?
A) NO CHANGE
B) Our brains, however, contain about 85 billion neurons.
C) It may not be fair, however, to compare neurons to computer chips.
D) In the biological world, however, our brains are energy hogs.

27
A) NO CHANGE
B) It's
C) Its
D) Its'

CONTINUE →

Temporary mental exhaustion due to thinking is not the same as chronic mental fatigue—which is associated with sleep deprivation and certain mental **28** disorders, but it is still a very real phenomenon. When our brain cells are working harder, they require more glucose. Studies have shown that people who are solving hard problems see a larger **29** decay in blood glucose levels than do those who are just doing a mindless task, such as pressing a button. Findings like these about the link between diet and brain function **30** would suggest that it might be a good idea to eat something with a bit of sugar in it during your SAT break, to revive those brain cells.

Other studies indicate that moderate exercise before a test can increase mental endurance and fight brain fatigue. One study showed that children who walked on a treadmill for 20 minutes before a test performed better than those who read quietly instead.

[1] Attitude seems to play a significant role in mental performance as well. [2] Research suggests that if you go into a test with a positive frame of mind, you will be more likely to persist through challenges instead of giving up. [3] One way to do this is surprisingly **31** simple to just visualize yourself finishing your task successfully, rather than imagining all the things that could go wrong. [4] Although it is helpful to think about how to avoid mistakes as you study in the days before a test, it is less productive to do so on the day of the test. [5] Most performance experts agree that it's better to imagine your success instead. **32**

28

A) NO CHANGE
B) disorder, but still
C) disorders—but it is still
D) disorders—but still

29

A) NO CHANGE
B) degeneration
C) depreciation
D) decline

30

A) NO CHANGE
B) suggests
C) suggest
D) are suggestive

31

A) NO CHANGE
B) simple, just
C) simply just
D) simple: just

32

The writer wants to add the following sentence to the paragraph.

It cuts both ways: whether you think you will fail or succeed, you're probably right.

The best placement for the sentence is immediately

A) after sentence 1.
B) after sentence 2.
C) after sentence 4.
D) after sentence 5.

CONTINUE →

3

3

Educators still agree that the best way to ace your tests is to pay attention in class, review your notes regularly, and do plenty of self-directed practice. However, it's nice to know that a quick snack, a run on the treadmill, and **33** a can-do attitude can help, too.

33

Which choice best fits the content of the passage?

A) NO CHANGE

B) a good night's sleep

C) a few practice problems

D) some deep-breathing exercises

3   **3**

Questions 34–44 are based on the following passage.

Calvin and Hobbes

I **34** can hardly fail to imagine what my childhood would have been like without Calvin. He was one of my best friends. Still, I don't know his last name—it's possible that he never had one—and I never actually met him in person. Even more tragically, he lived for only ten years, one month, and two weeks.

Calvin and his talking stuffed tiger, Hobbes, graced the comic pages across the country from 1985 until 1995, when **35** it's creator, Bill Watterson, retired at the age of 37. In that decade, *Calvin and Hobbes* became perhaps the most beloved comic strip in history. For me, Calvin perfectly captures the freedom, creativity, innocence, mischief, and fears of childhood. I've never met anyone, young or **36** old, who could not identify with Calvin in one way or another.

37 In addition to their being filled with poignant and hilarious insights, each Calvin and Hobbes strip was a work of art. Not since Winsor

34

A) NO CHANGE
B) couldn't hardly
C) can hardly
D) would hardly

35

A) NO CHANGE
B) its
C) their
D) they're

36

A) NO CHANGE
B) old who can't identify
C) old, without identifying
D) old not able to identify

37

A) NO CHANGE
B) In addition to there being
C) They were
D) In addition to being

CONTINUE ➡

3

McCay's *Little Nemo in Slumberland* has any other comic strip **38** <u>received such widespread critical acclaim</u>. Watterson's pen could sweep the reader from a mundane schoolroom to an extraterrestrial landscape swarming with alien creatures, all within the confines of four little panels.

According to Watterson, Calvin was named for the 16th-century theologian John Calvin. **39** <u>For</u> his namesake, Calvin was precociously intelligent, even if he did not do particularly well in school. His teacher, Miss Wormwood, would frequently scold Calvin for his frequent daydreams, in which he became the intrepid Spaceman Spiff, saving mankind from Martian robots. Hobbes the tiger was named for Thomas Hobbes, an English philosopher who **40** <u>believed</u> what Watterson called "a dim view of human nature," and who famously said that life is "nasty, brutish, and short." Watterson's choice of names was probably **41** <u>anticlimactic</u>: Calvin the boy is deeply irreverent, and Hobbes the tiger is perpetually optimistic.

38

Which choice best sets up the information that follows?

A) NO CHANGE
B) influenced so many future cartoonists and graphical artists
C) been so deeply adored by generations of readers
D) exemplified such graphical skill in the service of storytelling

39

A) NO CHANGE
B) With
C) Like
D) Because of

40

A) NO CHANGE
B) held
C) beheld
D) nurtured

41

Which choice is most logically cohesive with the information in the sentence?

A) NO CHANGE
B) ironic
C) apocryphal
D) accidental

CONTINUE

3   **3**

Many of the lessons that Calvin taught me were of the negative [42] sort: how not to build a snowman, how not to talk to my parents, and how not to interact with females. It was a lot of fun watching him make mistakes, especially since Hobbes was always there to chastise or comfort him when things went wrong. Overall, though, the lessons from Calvin and Hobbes are poignant and deep. Calvin taught me how to use my imagination, how to deal with childhood fears, and how to be a good friend.

Between 2010 and 2016, the popularity of Calvin as a name for male newborns in the U.S. [43] improved by over 50%. Could this be because that was [44] at the time during which those parents who were just old enough to read *Calvin and Hobbes* in its heyday were becoming old enough to have children of their own? I like to think so.

[42]

A) NO CHANGE
B) sort: such as how
C) sort: like how
D) sort, how

[43]

A) NO CHANGE
B) intensified
C) surged
D) expanded

[44]

A) NO CHANGE
B) the time where
C) at the time where
D) when

STOP

If you finish before time is called, you may check your work on this section only.
Do not turn to any other section of the test.

ANSWER KEY AND CONVERSION TABLE

Answer Key	Raw Score (Total Correct)	Scaled Score (10–40)
1. A	1	10
2. D	2	10
3. B	3	10
4. D	4	11
5. B	5	12
6. B	6	13
7. C	7	13
8. D	8	14
9. A	9	15
10. A	10	16
11. D	11	16
12. C	12	17
13. D	13	18
14. C	14	19
15. A	15	19
16. D	16	20
17. C	17	21
18. B	18	21
19. A	19	22
20. A	20	23
21. C	21	23
22. B	22	24
23. C	23	25
24. A	24	25
25. B	25	26
26. D	26	26
27. B	27	27
28. C	28	28
29. D	29	28
30. C	30	29
31. D	31	30
32. A	32	30
33. A	33	31
34. C	34	32
35. C	35	32
36. A	36	33
37. D	37	34
38. D	38	34
39. C	39	35
40. B	40	36
41. B	41	37
42. A	42	38
43. C	43	39
44. D	44	40

ANSWER EXPLANATIONS

1. A   Cohesiveness
The sentence that follows describes examples of *robotic assistants*, so the original phrasing is the best for setting it up.

2. D   Parallelism
This sentence lists some of the potential functions of "live-in" robots, so that list should have a parallel structure: looking *out for intruders* . . . notifying *the authorities* . . . greeting *guests,* or ordering *take-out.* Only choice D maintains this parallel structure without any superfluous words.

3. B   Coordination
Choices A and D are incorrect because it is redundant to use *Although* and *but* as conjunctions for the same two clauses. Choice C is incorrect because it turns the opening phrase into a participial phrase, which does not coordinate with the main clause. The only choice that properly coordinates the two clauses is B.

4. D   Redundancy/Coordination
The original sentence is not only redundant but also creates a comma splice (Chapter 5, Lesson 2), in which the two independent clauses are joined only by a comma. Choice C commits the same mistake. Choice B is awkward and redundant, since the staff is the group of people (or robots) who run the hotel.

5. B   Idiom
The two standard idioms for the participle *concerned* are *concerned about,* which means "worried about," and *concerned with,* which means "interested in or involved with." In this context, the first idiom is the only sensible one.

6. B   Pronoun Reference/Clear Expression of Ideas
In the original phrasing, the pronoun *it* has no clear antecedent. Choice C commits this same error. Choice D is incorrect because the verb *means* is being used illogically: the sentence does not provide a sensible definition of the word *automation.* Choice B is the only one that provides logical and clear phrasing.

7. C   Logical Sequence
The new sentence clearly functions as a transition between a discussion of the potential pitfalls of automation to a discussion of its benefits. Since sentence 3 mentions a pitfall to workers, but sentence 4 describes a benefit to the general public, the new sentence belongs immediately after sentence 3.

8. D   Verb Form
The use of the conjunction *as* indicates that the sentence is linking two independent clauses with verbs in the same tense. (This is because *as* in this context means *at the same time as,* and therefore the two verbs express the same tense.) Since the verb in the first clause, *make,* is in the present tense, indicative mood, the verb in the second clause should be in the same tense and mood: *become.*

9. A   Verb Aspect/Verb Agreement

The original sentence is correct because the verb *has declined* agrees in number with the singular subject *number* and is in the present tense, consequential aspect because it indicates a current status that is the consequence of a situation that has been true *since 1990*. Choice B is incorrect because it creates a subject-verb disagreement. Choices C and D are incorrect because they do not indicate the consequential aspect.

10. A   Comparative Idiom

Some grammar scolds might say that the original phrasing is unacceptable because it includes a "split infinitive": the modifying phrase *more than* is plunked in the middle of the infinitive phrase *to compensate*. In fact, it is not formally incorrect to split an infinitive, and this example nicely illustrates how splitting an infinitive can provide the most elegant and logical phrasing of an idea. Although choices B–D are grammatical and avoid the split infinitive, none of them creates a clear and logical phrase.

11. D   Parallelism

This sentence uses the contrasting construction *not A but B*. The Law of Parallelism requires that the phrases replacing *A* and *B* in this construction must have the same grammatical form. Since the phrase replacing *A* is in the form *because [clause]*, the phrase replacing *B* must take the same form.

12. C   Dangling Participles

The original phrase creates a dangling participle, since the participle *working* does not share its subject with the main clause. Choice B commits the same error. Choice D is incorrect because it creates a sentence fragment. Choice C is correct because the one who was *working* is the *20th-century scientist*.

13. D   Parallelism

The list of verbs in this sentence must maintain a parallel structure: *develop and distribute . . . promote . . . , and* modernize.

14. C   Graphical Analysis

The header of the graph indicates that these data are only the wheat yields for the *least developed countries*. Since these yields increased from about 1000 kg per hectare to just over 2000 kg per hectare, this increase was over 100%, but not over 200%.

15. A   Coordination/Participles

The original phrasing creates a participial phrase that coordinates grammatically and logically with the main clause. Choice B is incorrect because it creates a comma splice (Chapter 5, Lesson 2). Choice C is incorrect because the present participle illogically implies that Borlaug was born at the same time that he *came of age*. Choice D is incorrect because it illogically implies a contrast between the two ideas in the sentence.

16. D   Cohesiveness

Choice A is inappropriate because the paragraph is about Borlaug's academic career and his early interest in agriculture, not his career in sports. Choice B is inappropriate because this paragraph is about his college years, not his childhood on the farm. Choice C is inappropriate also because the time of his later Forest Service work is out of place in a paragraph about his college career.

17. C   Coordination/Transition

Choice A is incorrect because it illogically implies that Borlaug decided to pursue research in plant pathology before he even acquired an interest in it. Choice B is incorrect because it illogically implies a contrast between the two ideas in the sentence. Choice D is incorrect because the participle *deciding* does not coordinate with the main clause. Choice C is correct because it indicates a logical cause and effect.

18. B   Parallelism

It's very important to read the entire sentence to get this one correct: notice that the sentence has a compound predicate. The second predicate is *became a net exporter of wheat by 1963.* In order for this predicate to coordinate with the rest of the sentence, it must have the same subject as the first clause. Logically, this subject is *Mexico,* so only choice B can be correct.

19. A   Logical Cohesiveness

This sentence provides an effective transition from the topic of the previous paragraph to the discussion of the further extent of Borlaug's work in Mexico, so it should not be deleted.

20. A   Diction/Clear Expression of Ideas

The original word is best: *succumb* means *to fail to resist,* which describes what the weaker genetic strains do when faced with dangerous pathogens.

21. C   Idiom/Punctuation

The phrase *so dire that [clause]* is a standard comparative idiom. The colon in choice A and the semi-colon in choice D are incorrect because, in both cases, the phrases that follow are not independent.

22. B   Coordination

Choice B combines the sentence most logically and concisely. Choice A is incorrect because the conjunction *and* does not link grammatically similar phrases. Choice C is incorrect because the pronoun *which* lacks a logical antecedent: interrogative pronouns such as *which* take the immediately preceding noun as an antecedent, but clearly the *population* can not be *due largely to the work of Norman Borlaug.* Choice D is incorrect because *this being* is not idiomatic.

23. C   Verb Form
The past participle that follows *have you ever* is timeless, and therefore cannot logically take the progressive aspect, as in the original phrasing. Choices B and D are incorrect because *had to need to* and *needed to have to* are both redundant.

24. A   Parallelism
This sentence should be grammatically parallel to the previous sentence, which is in the subjunctive mood. Therefore, it must also use the subjunctive auxiliary *may*.

25. B   Transitions
This sentence supports the idea at the human brain *is a model of efficiency* only if the example of the power-hungry Watson is *compared* to the relatively efficient human brain, and so choice B is the most logical.

26. D   Cohesiveness
Since the paragraph is about the energy consumption of the human brain relative to other things, like computers or the other organs in the human body, choice D provides the most cohesive information.

27. B   Possessive Form/Verb Mood
Since this sentence is stating an unconditional fact, the use of the subjunctive form *would be* in the original phrasing is illogical. Choice C is incorrect because *its* is the possessive form, not the contraction of *it is*. Choice D is incorrect because *its'* is not a word.

28. C   Punctuation/Coordination
Since the interrupting modifying phrase begins with a dash, it must end with a dash also. However, choice D is incorrect because the phrase following the conjunction *but* must be an independent clause.

29. D   Diction
The original is incorrect because *decay* describes a process of deterioration, which is not appropriate to a discussion of blood glucose levels. The same is true of choice B, *degeneration*. Choice C is incorrect because *depreciation* pertains to a monetary value. Choice D works because blood glucose levels can *decline*.

30. C   Verb Agreement/Verb Mood
Since this sentence is indicating an unconditional fact, the use of the subjunctive auxiliary *would* is inappropriate. Choice B is incorrect because the verb *suggests* disagrees in number with its plural subject *findings*. Choice D is incorrect because the phrase *suggestive that* is not idiomatic.

31. D   Diction/Punctuation
Choice D is most logical because the second clause exemplifies the claim in the first clause. The original phrasing is not a complete sentence. Choice B is incorrect because it forms a comma splice (Chapter 5, Lesson 2). Choice C is incorrect because the phrase *simply just* is redundant.

32. A   Logical Sequence

This sentence belongs immediately after sentence 1 because the pronoun *it* refers to one's *attitude*, which is the subject of sentence 1. If this sentence is placed anywhere else in the paragraph, the pronoun will lack a logical antecedent.

33. A   Relevance

The original phrasing is best because the previous paragraph discusses the importance of attitude to performance, whereas the importance of sleep and breathing were not discussed. Choice C is wrong because the importance of practice was already mentioned in the paragraph.

34. C   Subjunctive Auxiliaries/Logic

The double negative *can hardly fail* is illogical in the original phrasing of the sentence. Choice B has the same problem. Choices C and D both avoid the double negative, and express the subjunctive mood. However, choice C is correct because the auxiliary *can* is required to convey a statement about ability (or, more accurately, inability), which is the central idea of the sentence.

35. C   Possessive Form/Pronoun Agreement

The subject of the sentence, and antecedent of the underlined pronoun, is *Calvin and his talking stuffed tiger, Hobbes*. Since this is a plural noun phrase, the pronoun must be plural as well. The correct possessive form is *their*. (It's interesting to note that the title of the comic strip, *Calvin and Hobbes*, would be treated as a singular, however, in such clauses as *Calvin and Hobbes is a much beloved comic strip*.)

36. A   Clear Expression of Ideas

The comma is required in this phrase to separate the interrupting modifier from the main clause. However, choice C is illogical because the participle *identifying* should refer to the group, not the author.

37. D   Modifying Phrases/Coordination

The original phrasing is incorrect because the pronoun *their* lacks a logical antecedent. Choice B is incorrect because it is awkward and illogical. Choice C is incorrect because it creates a comma splice (Chapter 5, Lesson 2). Choice D is correct because it creates a participial phrase the coordinates logically with the main clause.

38. D   Cohesiveness

The sentence that follows describes the effectiveness of Watterson's artistic storytelling, therefore choice D most effectively maintains the thematic cohesiveness of the paragraph.

39. C   Logic/Clear Expression of Ideas

The point of this sentence is that Calvin the boy shares one important characteristic with his namesake, John Calvin. Therefore, the only logical preposition to use here is *Like*.

40. B   Diction

When describing the relationship between a person and his or her viewpoint, standard English suggests that we say that the person *holds* that viewpoint. It is not quite accurate to say that a person *believes* his or her own viewpoint, because having a viewpoint does not require accepting any particular claim. We also would not say that someone *beholds* his or her own viewpoint because that viewpoint is internal, not external. It is also inaccurate to say that someone *nurtures* his or her own viewpoint because viewpoints by their nature arise independently of any deliberate effort.

41. B   Cohesiveness

The colon in this sentence indicates that the second clause explains the first. The second clause indicates a clear pair of contradictions: Calvin is irreverent although his namesake was a religious figure, and Hobbes has a sunny disposition although his namesake was a cynic. Therefore, the most logical conclusion is that Watterson chose these names *ironically. Anticlimactic* means causing emotional disappointment. *Apocryphal* mean having dubious authenticity.

42. A   Idiom/Punctuation

The original phrasing is best because the colon serves to link a concept (*lessons . . . of the negative sort*) with a list of examples (*how not to build a snowman, how not to talk to my parents . . .*). Although choices B and C include the colon, using *such as* or *like* is redundant because the colon already implies that the list is a set of examples.

43. C   Diction

The phrase *by over 50%* indicates that the *popularity of Calvin as a name for male newborns* is quantifiable. However, saying that this quantity *improved* is illogical because it implies that this popularity is a quality rather than a quantity. It is also incorrect to say that this popularity *intensified* because a statistic cannot become more intense. It is also incorrect to say that popularity *expanded* because the 50% increase does not imply any geographical or demographic extent. The most justifiable term to use in this context is *surged*.

44. D   Redundancy/Pronoun Agreement

The original phrasing is incorrect because the phrase *at the time during* is redundant. Choices B and C are incorrect because the pronoun *where* refers to a place, not a time.

SECTION 5

THREE PRACTICE SAT ESSAYS

PRACTICE SAT ESSAY 1

50 minutes

As you read the passage below, consider how Temma Ehrenfeld uses

- evidence, such as facts or examples, to support claims.
- reasoning to develop ideas and connect claims and evidence.
- stylistic or persuasive elements, such as word choice or appeals to emotion, to add power to the ideas expressed.

Adapted from Temma Ehrenfeld "Why Epicurean ideas suit the challenges of modern secular life." ©2019 Aeon Media. This article was originally published at https://aeon.co and has been republished under Creative Commons.

1   "The pursuit of happiness" is a famous phrase in the United States Declaration of Independence (1776). But few know that its author, Thomas Jefferson, was inspired by an ancient Greek philosopher, Epicurus.

2   Nowadays, the educated might call you an *epicure* if you complain to a waiter about over-salted soup, and *stoical* if you don't. In the popular mind, an epicure fine-tunes pleasure, while a stoic lives a life of virtue. But this doesn't do justice to Epicurus, who came closest of all the ancient philosophers to understanding the challenges of modern secular life.

3   Epicureanism competed with Stoicism to dominate Greek and Roman culture. Today, these two great contesting philosophies of ancient times have been reduced to attitudes about comfort and pleasure—will you send back the soup or not? Epicureans did focus on seeking pleasure, but they did so much more. They talked as much about reducing pain, and even more about being rational. They were interested in *intelligent* living, an idea that has evolved in our day to mean knowledgeable consumption. But equating knowing what will make you happiest with knowing the best wine means Epicurus is misunderstood.

4   The rationality Epicurus wedded to democracy relied on science. We now know Epicurus mainly through a poem, *De rerum natura*, or "On the Nature of Things," a 7,400 line exposition by the Roman philosopher Lucretius, who lived c250 years after Epicurus.

5   Its principles read as astonishingly modern, down to the physics. In six books, Lucretius states that everything is made of invisible particles, space and time are infinite, nature is an endless experiment, human society began as a battle to survive, there is no afterlife, religions are cruel delusions, and the universe has no clear purpose. The world is material—with a smidgen of free will. How should we live? Rationally, by dropping illusion. False ideas largely make us unhappy. If we minimize the pain they cause, we maximize our pleasure.

6   Secular moderns are so Epicurean that we might not hear this thunderclap. Epicurus didn't stress perfectionism or fine discriminations in pleasure. He understood what the Buddhists call *samsara*, the suffering of endless craving. Pleasures are poisoned when we require that they do not end.

7   Epicurus also seems uncannily modern in his attitude to parenting. Children are likely to bring at least as much pain as pleasure, he noted, so you might want to skip it. Does it make sense to tell people to pursue their happiness and then expect them to take on decades of responsibility for other humans? Well, maybe, if you seek *meaning*. Our idea of meaning is something like the virtue embraced by the Stoics, who claimed it would bring you happiness.

8   Both the Stoics and the Epicureans understood that some good things are better than others. Thus, you may need to forgo one good to protect or gain another. When you make those choices wisely, you'll be happier. But the Stoics think you'll be acting in line with a grand plan by a just grand designer, and the Epicureans don't.

9   As secular moderns, we pursue short-term happiness and achieve deeper pleasure in work well done. We seek the esteem of peers. It all makes sense in the light of science, which has documented that happiness for most of us arises from social ties, not the perfect rose garden. Epicurus was a big fan of friendship.

10   Epicurus thought politics brought only frustration, while the Stoics believed that you should engage in politics as virtuously as you can. Yet Epicurus was a democrat: he set up a school scandalously open to women and slaves—a practice that his contemporaries saw as proof of his depravity. When Jefferson advocated education for American slaves, he might have had Epicurus in mind.

11   Above all, Epicurus wanted us to take responsibility for our choices. Here he is in his Letter to Menoeceus:

> For it is not drinking bouts and continuous partying and enjoying boys and women, or consuming fish and the other dainties of an extravagant table, which produce the pleasant life, but sober calculation which searches out the reasons for every choice and avoidance and drives out the opinions which are the source of the greatest turmoil for men's souls.

12   Do you see the "pursuit of happiness" as a tough research project and kick yourself when you're glum? You're Epicurean. We think of the Stoics as tougher, but they provided the comfort of faith. Accept your fate, they said. Epicurus said: *It's a mess. Be smarter than the rest of them.* How modern can you get?

Write an essay in which you explain how Temma Ehrenfeld builds an argument to persuade her audience that Epicurean ideas are suited to modern life. In your essay, analyze how Ehrenfeld uses one or more of the features listed in the box above (or features of your own choice) to strengthen the logic and persuasiveness of her argument. Be sure that your analysis focuses on the most relevant features of the passage.

Your essay should not explain whether you agree with Ehrenfeld's claims, but rather explain how she builds an argument to persuade her audience.

PLANNING PAGE   You may plan your essay in the unlined planning space below, but use only the lined pages following this one to write your essay. Any work on this planning page will not be scored.

BEGIN YOUR ESSAY HERE

1

Cut Here

DO NOT WRITE OUTSIDE OF THE BOX.

Cut Here

2

DO NOT WRITE OUTSIDE OF THE BOX.

Cut Here

DO NOT WRITE OUTSIDE OF THE BOX.

DO NOT WRITE OUTSIDE OF THE BOX.

PRACTICE SAT ESSAY 2

50 minutes

As you read the passage below, consider how Massimo Pigliucci uses

- evidence, such as facts or examples, to support claims.
- reasoning to develop ideas and connect claims and evidence.
- stylistic or persuasive elements, such as word choice or appeals to emotion, to add power to the ideas expressed.

Adapted from Massimo Pigliucci "Richard Feynman was wrong about beauty and truth in science." ©2019 Aeon Media. This article was originally published at https://aeon.co and has been republished under Creative Commons.

1   The American physicist Richard Feynman is often quoted as saying, "You can recognize truth by its beauty and simplicity." The phrase appears in the work of the American science writer K. C. Cole—in her *Sympathetic Vibrations: Reflections on Physics as a Way of Life* (1985)—although I could not find other records of Feynman writing or saying it. We do know, however, that Feynman had great respect for the English physicist Paul Dirac, who believed that theories in physics should be both simple and beautiful.

2   Feynman was unquestionably one of the outstanding physicists of the 20th-century. To his contributions to the Manhattan Project and the solution of the mystery surrounding the explosion of the Space Shuttle *Challenger* in 1986, add a Nobel Prize in 1965 shared with Julian Schwinger and Shin'ichirō Tomonaga "for their fundamental work in quantum electrodynamics, with deep-ploughing consequences for the physics of elementary particles." And he played the bongos too!

3   In the area of philosophy of science, though, like many physicists of his and the subsequent generation (and unlike those belonging to the previous one, including Albert Einstein and Niels Bohr), Feynman didn't really shine—to put it mildly. He might have said that philosophy of science is as helpful to science as ornithology is to birds (a lot of quotations attributed to him are next to impossible to source). This has prompted countless responses from philosophers of science, including that birds are too stupid to do ornithology, or that without ornithology many birds species would be extinct.

4   The problem is that it's difficult to defend the notion that the truth is recognizable by its beauty and simplicity, and it's an idea that has contributed to getting fundamental physics into its current mess. To be clear, when discussing the simplicity and beauty of theories, we are not talking about Ockham's razor. Ockham's razor is a prudent heuristic, providing us with an intuitive guide to the comparisons of different hypotheses. Other things being

equal, we should prefer simpler ones. More specifically, the English monk William of Ockham (1287–1347) meant that "[hypothetical] entities are not to be multiplied without necessity." Ockham's razor is about how we know things, whereas Feynman's and Dirac's statements seem to be about the fundamental nature of reality.

5   But as the German theoretical physicist Sabine Hossenfelder has pointed out, there is absolutely no reason to think that simplicity and beauty are reliable guides to physical reality. She is right for a number of reasons.

6   To begin with, the history of physics (alas, seldom studied by physicists) clearly shows that many simple theories have had to be abandoned in favor of more complex and "ugly" ones. The notion that the Universe is in a steady state is simpler than one requiring an ongoing expansion; and yet scientists do now think that the Universe has been expanding for almost 14 billion years. In the 17th century Johannes Kepler realized that Copernicus' theory was too beautiful to be true, since, as it turns out, planets don't go around the Sun in perfect (according to human aesthetics!) circles, but rather following somewhat uglier ellipses.

7   And of course, beauty is, notoriously, in the eye of the beholder. What struck Feynman as beautiful might not be beautiful to other physicists or mathematicians. Beauty is a human value, not something out there in the cosmos. Biologists here know better. The capacity for aesthetic appreciation in our species is the result of a process of biological evolution, possibly involving natural selection. And there is absolutely no reason to think that we evolved an aesthetic sense that somehow happens to be tailored for the discovery of the ultimate theory of everything.

8   The moral of the story is that physicists should leave philosophy of science to the pros, and stick to what they know best. Better yet: this is an area where fruitful interdisciplinary dialogue is not just a possibility, but arguably a necessity. As Einstein wrote in a letter to his fellow physicist Robert Thornton in 1944:

> I fully agree with you about the significance and educational value of methodology as well as history and philosophy of science. So many people today—and even professional scientists—seem to me like someone who has seen thousands of trees but has never seen a forest. A knowledge of the historic and philosophical background gives that kind of independence from prejudices of his generation from which most scientists are suffering. This independence created by philosophical insight is—in my opinion—the mark of distinction between a mere artisan or specialist and a real seeker after truth.

9   Ironically, it was Plato—a philosopher—who argued that beauty is a guide to truth (and goodness). But philosophy has made much progress since Plato, and so has science. It is therefore a good idea for scientists and philosophers alike to check with each other before uttering notions that might be hard to defend, especially when it comes to figures who are influential with the public. To quote another philosopher, Ludwig Wittgenstein, in a different context: "Whereof one cannot speak, thereof one must be silent."

Write an essay in which you explain how Massimo Pigliucci builds an argument to persuade his audience that scientific truth is not necessarily beautiful and simple. In your essay, analyze how Pigliucci uses one or more of the features listed in the box above (or features of your own choice) to strengthen the logic and persuasiveness of his argument. Be sure that your analysis focuses on the most relevant features of the passage.

Your essay should not explain whether you agree with Pigliucci's claims, but rather explain how he builds an argument to persuade his audience.

PLANNING PAGE   You may plan your essay in the unlined planning space below, but use only the lined pages following this one to write your essay. Any work on this planning page will not be scored.

BEGIN YOUR ESSAY HERE

Cut Here

1

DO NOT WRITE OUTSIDE OF THE BOX.

DO NOT WRITE OUTSIDE OF THE BOX.

DO NOT WRITE OUTSIDE OF THE BOX.

Cut Here

DO NOT WRITE OUTSIDE OF THE BOX.

DO NOT WRITE OUTSIDE OF THE BOX.

Cut Here

DO NOT WRITE OUTSIDE OF THE BOX.

50 minutes

As you read the passage below, consider how Livia Gershon uses

- evidence, such as facts or examples, to support claims.
- reasoning to develop ideas and connect claims and evidence.
- stylistic or persuasive elements, such as word choice or appeals to emotion, to add power to the ideas expressed.

**Adapted from Livia Gershon "Part-time work is humane and should be respected and encouraged."
©2019 Aeon Media. This article was originally published at https://aeon.co and has been republished under Creative Commons.**

1   I woke up on a recent Tuesday morning, fixed some not-quite-healthy breakfast for the kids, harangued them until they brushed their teeth and put on shoes and socks, and drove them to school. Then I took the car to the mechanic for a minor repair and walked back to the house. Before starting my day of work, I made some calls to medical providers about our new health insurance. Later, when the kids got home, I fixed snacks for them and some friends who wandered over, loaded the dishwasher, and did some laundry.

2   This is not a paean to "lean-in" efficiency that explains how I wake up at 4 am, answer emails while the kids are still in bed, and use productivity tricks to get things done at double-speed. Because here's my secret: I don't work that much. I'm a freelance writer, which means I can more or less choose how much I work. And my usual choice is something like 30 hours a week.

3   Many people look upon part-timers as unfortunate exiles from the economic mainstream, or else as pathetic slackers. In thrall to startup culture, our collective psyche makes ceaseless hustle and 80-hour working weeks seem like the only way that career-minded individuals might advance. So who would admit to having so little ambition as to actually prefer working a 30-hour week?

4   As it turns out, a lot of people. A survey from the Pew Research Center in 2016 found that, among U.S. workers employed part-time, 64 percent prefer it that way. Meanwhile, 20 percent of full-time workers—that's almost 26 million—would rather work part-time. If you don't believe the survey data, just look at those ubiquitous ads for multilevel marketing schemes and absurdly underpaid work-from-home gigs to get a sense of how desperate people are for part-time employment that fits around the rest of our lives.

5   The reason a lot of people work full-time—though they'd rather not—is obvious: part-time jobs as they exist today are often pretty crappy, low-paid, and with no health benefits, irregular schedules and few opportunities for advancement. White-collar workers who

officially have part-time schedules often work full-time hours while still getting paid less, and they're taken less seriously than their coworkers. Yet it's rare to see public calls for more and better part-time jobs. Those of us who don't work that much, or would rather not work as much as we do, are unlikely to number among the weirdly ambitious outliers extolling the modern work ethic in the Sunday press.

6   Recent studies in Sweden and New Zealand have found that working fewer hours improves employee productivity. And in a six-hour workday experiment in Melbourne last year, workers wasted less time on long meetings and focused more on the tasks at hand. They also spent less work time on personal tasks since they had more non-work hours to get those done.

7   An hour that I don't spend working is an hour sitting on the couch with my kids, reading a science-fiction novel and pausing intermittently to chat about their video games or YouTube favorites. It's an hour cooking a meal, going for a walk, or doing volunteer work. It's when I can act as one node in the lively neighborhood web of parents, grandparents, and afterschool programs. It's also when I pay bills, run errands, execute minor home repairs, and hire others to tackle major ones.

8   I know I'm lucky. Unlike most workers, I can more or less set my own freelance hours. I have a spouse who makes a solid income and does his share of cooking and kid-wrangling. For those of us who have these kinds of advantages, there's something to be said for using them to buy extra leisure rather than higher incomes and more possessions. For those who don't, there's reason to see shorter working hours as a political goal to fight for.

9   I worry about the implications for gender equality. I do less paid work and more unpaid housework than my husband. That Pew survey found that women are more likely than men to prefer working part-time hours. But this dynamic leaves women more vulnerable to control and abuse, and more likely to end up in poverty after a divorce. At a societal level, it reinforces the idea that women are more suited to caring labor at home and less to employment, which means that women who'd rather work long hours often feel pressured to slow down their careers to care for others. That's a huge loss for society.

10   But one solution that won't improve gender equality in the workplace is to convince women who'd rather work fewer hours that we've got our priorities wrong. Instead, we need to make it easier for people of any gender to live with their center of gravity outside the office—and get part-time workers fully included in powerful institutions. At a political level, that means campaigns for higher wages, regulations to stabilize part-time schedules, and childcare allowances and other support for primary caregivers. It also means changing workplace cultures: demanding more part-time career-track jobs and more respect for those who do them. And if we want to make social change at the level of individual workers' attitudes, let's start with the men whose cultural conditioning has somehow convinced them that the best use of their time is paid.

Write an essay in which you explain how Livia Gershon builds an argument to persuade her audience that part-time work should be respected and encouraged. In your essay, analyze how Gershon uses one or more of the features listed in the box above (or features of your own choice) to strengthen the logic and persuasiveness of her argument. Be sure that your analysis focuses on the most relevant features of the passage.

Your essay should not explain whether you agree with Gershon's claims, but rather explain how she builds an argument to persuade her audience.

PLANNING PAGE   You may plan your essay in the unlined planning space below, but use only the lined pages following this one to write your essay. Any work on this planning page will not be scored.

BEGIN YOUR ESSAY HERE

Cut Here

DO NOT WRITE OUTSIDE OF THE BOX.

Cut Here

2

DO NOT WRITE OUTSIDE OF THE BOX.

Cut Here

DO NOT WRITE OUTSIDE OF THE BOX.

DO NOT WRITE OUTSIDE OF THE BOX.

DO NOT WRITE OUTSIDE OF THE BOX.